C000199427

ELSINOR
VERLAG

Jim McCann

6000 Days

Elsinor

This edition 2021
by
Elsinor Verlag (Elsinor Press), Coesfeld, Germany
e-mail: info@elsinor.de
website: www.elsinor.de

Some of the names in this book have been changed for legal reasons.

EEOT · Elsinor English Original Texts, vol. 6

This book appears in the catalogue of the German National Library; details
are available on the Library's website: www.dnb.de.

Cover design & illustrations by Tony Bell
Typesetting: Elsinor Verlag, Coesfeld
Printed in Germany
ISBN 978-3-939483-58-8

CONTENTS

Glossary 6

Prologue 9
I – 1976 12
II – Ar an Pluid 33
III – 1977 H4 50
IV – To H5 56
V – For the Long Haul 78
VI – Summer of '78 96
VII – Winter of '78 112
VIII – 1979 – More Brutality 120
IX – Joe McDonnell 127
X – The 1980 Hunger Strike 135
XI – The 1981 Hunger Strike 146
XII – Out of the Cells 167
XIII – The Big Escape 185
XIV – The Aftermath 215
XV – The Escape Trial 230
XVI – The Honour of Having Served 243

Acknowledgements 258

GLOSSARY

Admin – administration

Ar an Pluid – on the blanket

As Gaeilge – in Irish

Bairt/bairteanna – a parcel/parcels of contraband, concealed internally

Bangling – to insert smuggled contraband up one's back passage

Craic – fun, laughter, latest news

Deoch – drink, alcohol

Dirty protest – a somewhat pejorative term for the no-wash/no slop-out protest which began two years after the blanket protest started

Ealu – the big escape of 25th September, 1983

Fáinne Óir – pin badge awarded for basic fluency in Irish

Fir donna – bad men; name given to the screws who beat prisoners

Fir pluid – blanket men

Fluiche – urine

Gaeilgeoir – Irish language speaker

Hooded Men – group of prisoners who were subjected to torture by the British during the introduction of internment in August 1971

LT – loose talk

Maggie Taggart – codename for a tiny, contraband crystal-set radio used by the prisoners to monitor news; named after a local BBC journalist

Na Fianna Éireann – a junior organisation of the IRA. Also, 'the Fianna' or 'Fians'

NIO – Northern Ireland Office, British government department based at Stormont, Belfast (and London) which administered the North, often for decades, under a British minister in the absence of a devolved government

OC – Officer Commanding (an IRA title)

ODC – Administration and media slang for 'Ordinary Decent Criminal'

On the blanket – prisoners who were stripped of their civilian clothes and refused to wear a prison uniform (which to them symbolised the criminalisation of the fight for Irish freedom), wrapped themselves in blankets

On the boards – an additional punishment, often for minor infractions, when prisoners were sent to a special wing, totally separated from other prisoners

POW – Prisoner Of War (political prisoner)

Raker – a mischievous person, a practical joker

Rang(anna) – class(es)

RAC – Relatives Action Committees

Red Book – introduced after the 1983 escape it was a category designating the most 'dangerous' of the republican prisoners, who were never allowed to settle in one block and were regularly moved around

RTP – slang for Rough Tough Provo

RUC – Royal Ulster Constabulary, an armed force whose members were largely drawn from the unionist community

Sagart – a priest

Scairt/Scairteoiri – to shout/a shouter

Scéal – news, gossip

Screws – jail argot for prison warders

Seachtain Donna – the Bad Week

Sin é – that's it

Skins – cigarette paper

Slagging – informal, bantering

SLR – self-loading rifle, used by the British army until 1994

Slua – a military company or unit of Na Fianna Éireann

Stailc ocrais/stailceoirí ocrais – hunger strike/hunger strikers

Taobh Amuigh – the IRA leadership outside of prison

Teachtaireachti/teachts – communications/comms, written in small script on cigarette papers and wrapped for waterproofing in cling film for smuggling to outside

Wee Buns – easy, straightforward, not difficult

YP/Yippies – young prisoner(s)

To Marian with Love

PROLOGUE

This was not part of the plan. I had been told, emphatically, "Your feet won't even touch the ground!" Along with my IRA comrades I would be transported to freedom. It was too good to be true and, as life had taught me, things don't always go to plan. My comrades didn't want to discuss contingency plans. There was to be no talk of a Plan B. Plan A was going to work – *Sin é*.

Plan A did go well. We had secured H7, taken over the entire block, arrested the prison officers and stripped them of their uniforms, which some of us now wore. We breached the security at the various phases as we silently exited Long Kesh, thirty seven of us hidden in the back of a food lorry. In the well of the passenger seat in the front, hidden, lay Gerry Kelly pointing a gun at the screw driving the lorry. But at the final gate of the prison, the Tally Lodge, the escape had come to an abrupt end.

There I was, standing before the perimeter wall with its huge metal gate inching open, clueless, because with no Plan B I had no idea what lay on the other side. Exposed, vulnerable and almost shitting myself. Worrying that I was well in the sights of the soldier and his rifle perched above in the watchtower. Seconds were passing and decisions had to be made, decisions which I knew would be life-changing. The gate opened, only to reveal a screw's car blocking our path. I was like a rabbit caught in the headlights with no idea of my next move. Scores of my comrades came spilling out from the back of the hijacked food lorry, our supposed transport to freedom. Bobby Storey, leader of the escape, shouted for us to head out the gate: in other words, improvise.

I raced out the gate, alert, alive, adrenaline racing through my limbs. Yes, I had made it beyond the perimeter wall but danger had increased because as an escaped prisoner I was now liable to be shot.

I was immediately confronted with a line of screws, batons in hand and equally pumped-up. Two of my comrades, outnumbered, were standing before them. But fear, instinct – I don't know what – propelled me to charge through. A dozen comrades were coming behind me. We beat a passage and emerged at the other end. A red car appeared, with a screw behind the wheel, but before his eyes a bewildering scene of bedlam. I belted towards the car and grabbed the door handle on the passenger side but it wouldn't open. The driver accelerated, pulling me along. I desperately held on until the last second before the car sped off into the distance.

There was screaming and shouting. Total chaos. Total confusion. Comrades, some in prison officers' uniforms, being pursued by *prisoners*, were running across the fields covered in rolls of barbed wire that stretched out for about two hundred yards from the perimeter wall. I didn't fancy their chances because they could easily be picked off by the Brits in the watchtowers. As if reading my thoughts, the screws were roaring to the soldiers above, "Shoot them! Shoot them!"

I noticed that another screw's car had been commandeered and made a bee line for it. I pushed my way through screws and dived through the driver's open window, past Meader who was behind the steering wheel, and with relief got seated beside him. Three more comrades had jumped in the back. But then a screw suddenly reached in and pulled the keys from the ignition. Meader immediately jumped out, punched him, took back the keys and got back in. Harry Murray appeared, and was banging my window with imploring eyes but I couldn't get the fucking door to open and screws were swarming around the car. Harry took off towards the fields.

The screws were like a bunch of wild animals. They were frothing at the mouth, screaming, lashing at the windows with their batons. Meader was cursing and struggling to get the car to start. Then one of the screws pointed a gun at us but, when he attempted to fire, the gun jammed. The windscreen caved in under the blows and we were showered with glass but at that very instant the car kicked into life. The screw flung the gun at Meader's head but missed.

We were off and we now had to drive the half-mile road around the perimeter wall which was still inside the British army's security zone, in order to get to the final barrier and the gate to freedom.

I looked up to the towers, and was shaking as we approached and passed them. My heart was racing, close to panic as I felt sure we were about to be shot. I shrunk into the seat to make myself as small as possible. Then I remembered the screw's gun and began frantically searching for it. "Where to hell is that gun!" No shots came and it dawned on me that the Brit above the Tally Lodge must have radioed ahead and an ambush was being prepared. No sooner had this thought occurred when I noticed a red car, that one I had tried to seize, racing behind us. I told Meader to put the boot down but he told me to "Fuck up." He was driving at normal speed in the hope that the Brits would assume we were prison officers.

We turned the final bend and there before us was the camp gate. The Brit sentry, alerted to our appearance, dived to shut it. Meader put the pedal to the floor and as we roared full speed towards freedom I was sure this was going to be the end of the world, with us mangled against the gate and riddled to death.

I
1976

Even though I was destined to end up in jail, I still had a strong sense that I shouldn't be there, that it was an injustice and a scandal. I had lived my life, as with my peers, conforming to the rules and norms of society, never causing my parents any concern. Well, maybe some concern, but nothing out of the ordinary. Yes, my involvement in the Republican Movement dramatically changed my life, and theirs, but there was never any sense of wrongdoing. In fact, there was never a doubt in my mind that I wasn't doing the right thing and I had a strong sense of pride that I had taken the right path.

My capture was not easy to accept. Then again what capture is easy to accept. I kept going over and over the circumstances of the shooting, questioning and berating myself – why didn't I do this, why I didn't do that ...

I was driving a hijacked Suzuki motorbike, Martin Livingstone was the pillion passenger and was armed. We were following an RUC man and, from earlier surveillance, we expected him to be alone but he was accompanied by a woman in the passenger seat. We were following him up the Lisburn Road and knew we had to act before we got to Blacks Road junction where there was a checkpoint. Martin opened fire but the shots struck the back of the car which abruptly came to a halt. The RUC man turned around and returned fire. I opened the throttle but the bike was more powerful than I expected, it went up in the air. Martin landed on his feet but the bike brought me down and lay on top of me. We then ran off on foot, me limping, but were chased by other patrols and within minutes were caught just below the M1 flyover. We got a kicking. Martin was kicked in the face and lost his front teeth.

They dragged us off to Dunmurry Barracks and after three days we were charged with attempted murder.

Martin and I were escorted to Crumlin Road Jail ('the Crum') and underwent the usual formalities at reception – being finger-printed, photographed, before having the compulsory bath in front of gloating screws.

We were brought to B Wing. It was not what I had envisaged. I had expected to see friendly faces of comrades and to find some comfort associating with them. Screws strutted about, keys jangling, barking out orders while orderlies scurried about. The environment could only be described as hostile. As I was placed in a cell, the door banged behind me and my morale sank even further as I took in my surroundings. It smelt, was dirty, paint peeled off the walls, and sections of the glass that made up a window in front of the bars were smashed and cracked. The mattresses that lay on top of the two single metal beds, which took up most of the cell, would have been more at home in a council dump.

No sooner had the door banged behind me when it opened again. A screw shouted out what were to become familiar words: "Slop-out!" Of course, I hadn't a clue what he was talking about and he was well aware of this. With a pained, impatient expression he spoke very slowly and, as if he was dealing with a simpleton, explained that I had to take the chamber pot from the corner of the cell, walk down the wing and empty it into the bowl at the ablutions. I was left with the distinct impression that he felt superior because I was ignorant about slopping out whereas he was expert. For my sanity, it was just as well that I didn't know that this was to become a ritual that I would perform every day for over seventeen years (apart from the 'no slop-out' during the blanket protest). I didn't want to touch that pot but I wasn't sure what the consequences would be if I refused or even if, according to the republican POW code, in which I was not yet fully versed, it was the *done* thing to refuse.

Still smarting from my experience in the barracks and wanting a breather, hesitantly I lifted it. It was quite heavy, and as I walked down the wing I found it a bit of a challenge to balance the pot. Walking too fast or unsteadily, slight movements of the arm would cause the pee to swish from side to side. The danger was the swishing could gain momentum and would be difficult to rectify, leading to spillage.

Making it successfully to the ablutions, I lifted the lid off the pot and was hit with the most unmerciful, pungent odour that made me retch. Desperately trying to control myself and avoid vomiting, which I would have done had I something in my stomach, and covering my mouth and nose with my hand, with outstretched arm I quickly emptied the pee into the bowl. Forty years on, I can still say that I have never experienced a viler smell. That pee must have been putrefying for at least a week. I wondered was this their sick way of introducing new intakes or was I just unlucky.

Back in the cell I read the scratches on the walls. "Joe ... 8 years," "Seany ... 10 years." My depression deepened. This was not what I expected would be the life of a POW. How did these men endure these conditions for all those years?

My spirits were lifted when the door opened again and in walked Martin. Thankfully, we were to share the cell. We were a great comfort to each other. As we talked away about our experience in the barracks, our friends and families outside, and comrades in the jail whom we hoped to meet soon, the discomfort of the abject conditions melted away. I put my head down to sleep that night a little easier and stronger than when initially entering the jail.

Some say that when you sleep you are no longer in jail.

Life became that much better the next day. Standing on the metal frame of the bed it was possible to reach up and see out the window between the bars onto C Wing yard. C Wing was where remand prisoners charged after March 1st 1976 were held. Political status had been removed for anyone arrested after that date and subsequently convicted. A Wing held those whose charges predated March 1st and they were treated as political prisoners who would continue with that status in the Cages of Long Kesh after conviction. This gave rise to the anomaly of my having comrades in A Wing treated as political, comrades in C Wing treated as criminal, and yet all were combatants in the IRA, and only a date on a calendar separated them. Had I been captured a few months earlier my life would have been hugely different. That's not a complaint. Change presents opportunity, and through the struggle to reinstate political status we politicised people to our cause not only in Ireland but throughout the world. Yes, it would have been that much easier to have been able to 'run the jail' ourselves, to have worn our own clothes, receive regular visits and parcels, and not to have lost years of remission on the impending protest. But the battle for political status meant that my part in the struggle no longer ended with my capture. It gave me a purpose. I felt proud and honoured to carry on the fight, along with comrades who inspired and supported me, enduring the worst excesses the prison administration could throw at us.

From my window I watched as the remands from C Wing came pouring into the yard. They split up into two groups. One congregated near the C Wing end of the yard, the other near the B Wing end. I was to discover very quickly that the latter were republicans, the former loyalists. With the withdrawal of political status the prison admin farcically, and, ultimately with fatal consequences, attempted to mix republicans and loyalists. In the yard we socialised separately. Walking around the yard in a circle in twos or threes each side maintained its distance from the other. Initially, I found walking around in a circle odd, like going around a hamster wheel.

Martin was an ex-internee, so he knew quite a few of the lads. He shouted out to them and within seconds we had a group below our window exchanging pleasantries. The leader of the group, JT, who was the Officer Commanding (OC) the IRA prisoners, informed us, much to my relief, that we would soon be transferred to C Wing. He asked if we needed anything – papers, biscuits, cigarettes. He was particularly concerned about tobacco. Later, I understood that he would sell his granny for a smoke! He was the first person I came across who rolled his own cigarettes.

Cigarettes, papers and biscuits were passed up to our cell. A couple of lads from our area, Jim O'Callaghan and Marty Lynch, familiar, friendly faces, spoke to us when John Thomas (JT) was finished and continued along the same lines, consoling us, that life would be much better when we were transferred.

Later that day we were moved to C Wing. We went before a governor who in very sombre tone informed us of our rights as remand prisoners, which basically amounted to zilch. Separately, we were taken to a cell that was used as a store and handed a bed pack and plastic mug. For the duration of my incarceration I was to drink from plastic mugs which I hated. At least the Victorians had tin mugs. The screw who escorted me to my new cell wasted no time in telling me that there were no OCs in here, except him. He, he said, was my only OC. I decided it might be best not to put him right about JT. He asked if I knew how to make a bed pack. It didn't seem appropriate to tell him my Mum had always made my bed, so I said I didn't. He proceeded to show me the art of bed-pack making. I say 'art' because he appeared to treat it with the utmost seriousness, as if it was a skill that perhaps took years to perfect. Maybe it did take him years. Chuffed with his demonstration, with his chest puffed out he left with the warning that it must be made in this fashion every morning before unlock for breakfast.

I was to share the cell with Martin and Aidan O'Carroll from Armagh. Three to a cell was the norm as C Wing was overcrowded. At first, the admin tried to mix republicans and loyalists in the same cells but, bizarrely, and tellingly, a Protestant minister complained to the Northern Ireland Office (NIO) that republicans were a bad influence on Protestants (that is, loyalists), consequently the practice was ended.

While still wrestling with the bed pack I heard the sound of approaching feet, the jingle of keys, the clunk of the lock (sounds that would punctuate each and every day), followed by the opening of the door to reveal a screw. He informed me that I had a visit or as he put it, and as I was to become known by screws, "1049 McCann for a visit." I was escorted through a maze of corridors and grilles to the visiting area. The room contained two rows of tables separated by small wooden partitions so that the patrolling screws would have a full view. My Mum and Marian O'Callaghan, a close friend, were already in the visit box, as we called it, awaiting me. They stood up to greet me. My Mum looked weary. My imprisonment clearly was taking its toll. Marian, not wanting to intrude in this emotional moment, stood back as my Mum gave me a heartfelt hug. Releasing my Mum's grip and urging her to sit down I turned to Marian and gave her a hug. My Dad didn't come. It was too much for him. Marian's brother, Brendan, was on remand in A Wing, as he had political status. She regularly visited him and was familiar with the routine. It was fortunate that she was able to take my Mum by the hand and guide her through what must have been a traumatic experience.

I did my best to console my Mum that I was fine, among my friends and comrades. They found it strange that that didn't include

Brendan since we were both in the Crum. I didn't get into the issue of political status with them, but it was soon to become clear and was to frame my Mum's life for many years to come.

I don't know if she was left feeling any better or worse from the visit. I do know she was heartbroken. I tried not to think about it. Worrying about family wasn't going to change anything. My motto has always been, "Just get on with it." A thick skin is necessary to do that.

My cell in C Wing looked out onto St Malachy's College. This made me a little nostalgic. I had attended the college and it didn't seem that long ago that I was on the opposite side, looking into the jail. As a young lad it had intrigued me. I regularly would gaze at the bleak edifice with its ominous barred windows and had a strong sense that I was destined to enter its walls. I had been in *Na Fianna Éireann* ('the *Fianna*') and was totally preoccupied with the conflict. Now, from my cell I could hear the school bells that structured the school day and see pupils responding to those bells, moving to their classrooms. There was me, four years earlier! What a turnaround. I couldn't help wondering if now there was some lad staring up at my window, destined to follow my path.

Wouldn't you know it, there was a heat wave in my first month on remand. From letters and visits it was clear that my friends were having a whale of a time. I was getting all the craic about the Hunting Lodge Bar, the discos, who was dating who, where they were going on holidays. I was hearing about water fights with the girls, one of whom I was crazy about. Could that have been my girl, Marian, enjoying those fights? I couldn't help but feel the timing of my arrest was most unfortunate.

With the heat, we had our own water fights in the yard. This came close to creating a major incident when one of our lads hit a loyalist with a water bomb (a half-full plastic bag knotted like a balloon). I don't know if it was deliberate but it crossed the boundary. The loyalist was furious. Everybody froze. It was up to the loyalists to make a move. One of theirs had been insulted in front of his comrades but if he laid one finger on a republican that would be a challenge to which we would have to respond. The incident exposed the fine balance in this 'them and us' situation which could not be sustained. The prisoner sensed the danger and sounded off just enough to save some face and avert a riot. The inevitable was merely postponed. The two sides could not live cheek by jowl. It was only a matter of time before an incident would occur that would lead to a riot.

We discuss 'criminalisation'

There was no direction as to what to do when sentenced but we were determined not to wear the prison gear, derisively known as the 'monkey suit.' Discussions were held, formal and informal, but there was no agreed strategy because quite simply we did not know what refusing to wear their prison uniform would entail. I do remember during one of the formal IRA meetings we all gathered around JT and were invited to voice our opinions. One of the 'ABC squad' (a Belfast IRA bombing unit intercepted and caught outside the ABC Cinema), either Finbarr McKenna or Jimmy ('Tea Pot') McMullen, suggested we should go on hunger strike. It was a solitary voice and received a muted response. Hunger strike had been a common form of prison protest for republicans, going as far back as 1917 when Thomas Ashe died in prison. In 1972, Billy McKee and other republican prisoners secured political status as a result of their hunger strike on which no one died. It was the status won in 1972 which was now being withdrawn. While the suggestion of a hunger strike was dismissed, during the subsequent protest years it would always be lurking in the background, taunting, as if to say, "You know it has to be. Reject me today but I'll be back tomorrow."[1]

At the beginning of July, what was left of the republican remand prisoners with status were moved to the Cages in Long Kesh, about eight miles from Belfast, to await trial. Subsequently, some of the remand prisoners in C Wing, which included Martin and me, were moved to A Wing but were separated on different landings. The wing

---

[1] In May 1987, after his release, Finbarr was killed on active service whilst attacking a British army/RUC barracks in Belfast. Mourners at his funeral were baton-charged by the RUC and rioting erupted throughout West Belfast.

was a lot bigger and dirtier than C Wing and was infested with cockroaches. Unlike C Wing, which had only one communal canteen, A Wing had a canteen on each of the three landings, which I wasn't happy about because it meant that the only time I would see Martin and some other friends would be in the exercise yard. Martin was placed in a cell on the Threes (the third landing) whereas I was on the Ones.

I shared a cell with Midge Donaghy from the Lower Falls. A year earlier the British Army opened fire for no reason on Midge and Tea Pot, wounding both men. Midge lost a number of fingers in the shooting. His brother, John, had been killed in 1972 along with two other volunteers. I had been in the *Fianna* at the time and skipped school to march in his funeral. It was a day I remember well. I was part of a *slua* (company) of *Fians*, wearing our standard uniform of the day: green berets and green, bomber-type jackets with fur collars. The OC gave the order to fall into ranks. We were about three deep, with about a dozen in each row, standing at ease in military fashion with our backs against a gable wall in a side street in the Lower Falls awaiting the cortege when we heard the whirr of Saracen armoured cars racing towards us. Tension filled the air. Quite a crowd had gathered, as was the norm for republican funerals, and anxious to avoid confrontation and arrests, some of the mourners pleaded with us to disperse or take off the berets and blend into the crowd. Not a chance! The OC rightly told us to stay in our ranks. The Saracens came roaring up and hemmed us in at both ends. We didn't flinch. The Brits did some jeering at us, which we ignored, and made comments about "little IRA men and targets for the future." It was one of my proud moments. I felt good about being a republican and facing them defiantly, head-on. Yes, we were the future and it wouldn't be long before many of us were looking down the barrel of a rifle at *them*. The Brits, surrounding us with their Saracens and SLRs (self-loading rifles), realising they were making us look good, and with the mourners applauding our stance, then withdrew.

Not long after I had been transferred to A Wing, the loyalist prisoners in C Wing had wanted to watch the Twelfth of July parades on the TV. The republicans didn't. Somebody threw a bun at the television and the place erupted, with tables, chairs, and trays flying, blows exchanged and hand-to-hand fighting. The loyalists then withdrew from the canteen and went on lock-up. This worked to our advantage because it meant republicans had the yard and canteen to themselves. For the time being we had achieved de facto segregation on both wings.

But before us towered the threat of criminalisation and what it would mean to our lives. We speculated about it continually.

The screws were anxious to assert themselves and, as if to convince themselves, in disregard to the reality, went on large about there being "No OCs." Their superiors had wound them up to treat us like criminals. I don't know what they anticipated but we certainly weren't going to fall in line. They actually expected us to stand to attention at our cells doors and shout our number and name as they locked us up. Not a chance! Needless to say, they binned that idea very quickly. There was a great deal of pettiness and our parcels were a favourite target. We relied on parcels for everyday consumables such as cigarettes and newspapers and especially for food as the jail cuisine left a lot to be desired. It was common for items to be damaged or to go missing. Mail could be censored to a ridiculous level for no apparent logical reason other than vindictiveness. For example, if a letter said something like "Mary and Jim were at the club last night," their names would be blacked out. Or a reference to a march and numbers attending would be scored through.

Regardless of what the NIO and the prison admin tried to impose we had our own structure. This was led by the OC and his staff which consisted of a Vice OC, an Intelligence Officer (IO) and a Public Relations Officer (PRO). The PRO's role included writing articles and letters to the newspapers about prison conditions and our struggle to be recognised and treated as political prisoners. Naturally, this communication would be smuggled out. The PRO had a team to help him. Due to the increasing numbers of republicans being arrested there were three or four IOs to manage the workload. It was their task to debrief prisoners about their interrogation, read their trial depositions and pass on sensitive information to the OC and then to the IRA outside, *Taobh Amuigh*.

The governors and screws knew we had our own command structures, not that they could do much about it, and unofficially they recognised and dealt with the OC. It was in the interests of all concerned that they did, but they didn't always do so, especially if the bigots (of which there was no shortage) were in the ascendancy.

In contrast to C Wing, there were only a handful of republicans in A Wing, and even fewer loyalists, the most prominent of which was Robin Jackson. Known as 'Jacko', and later 'the Jackal', Jackson was a former British soldier who led a loyalist assassination squad. However, he kept a very low profile on the wing. One of our lads, Peter McGowan, a Derry republican, gave him some abuse about the Miami Showband massacre in which he had been involved but never charged.[2]

We also bantered Peter on a quite separate issue. He would often say, "I don't care what sentence I get as long as my girl waits for me." Few relationships survive jail and the lengthy sentences served inside and *outside*. He was facing a sentence of at least ten years. He worshipped his girlfriend, Olive. We told him there was no chance of that and teased the life out of him with our predictions of how long it would be before the 'Dear John' came. When I met him forty years later, he and Olive were happily married with children and grandchildren!

Lack of numbers, especially of former POWs with plenty of jail experience, meant that in A Wing we proceeded cautiously and relied on instructions from C Wing. However, it wasn't long before this changed as our numbers increased, almost daily, and included republicans imprisoned for the second or third time who knew all about jail struggle. Apart from the initial group who were transferred from C Wing, the first republican prisoners to enter A Wing were from South Armagh. It was a rarity to have South Armagh lads in the Crum because the South Armagh Brigade was one of the most elusive IRA commands. They controlled their area and the Brits, afraid to be on the ground, confined most of their operations to helicopters dropping troops off and picking them up within a short period of

---

[2] In July 1975 the Miami Showband were stopped in their minibus on a dark country road by what they thought was a routine British Army patrol. However, the patrol was made up of soldiers (Ulster Defence Regiment) and loyalist paramilitaries whose plan was to hide a bomb among the instruments, which would explode later as the band crossed the border, killing the musicians who would then be accused of being IRA members transporting explosives. The bomb exploded prematurely and the gunmen opened fire. Three band members were killed, two wounded and two of the bombers also died.

time. But unfortunately for Paddy Quinn, Dan McGuinness and Raymond McCreesh, the Brits had dug themselves into a hidden position and after a gun battle and chase managed to capture them.

When the three lads walked into A Wing yard, we knew immediately from their dress and gait, they were country boys. I would describe their attire as smart casual – trousers, sports jackets and shirts with only the ties missing, which could well have been taken from them at reception. They looked like they were going for a job interview and stuck out from the rest of us, who tended to conform to the teenage dress code of the day – jeans, Harrington or bomber-type jackets, Ben Sherman shirts and Oxford shoes or DMs (Doc Martens). New lads tended to be the centre of attention for about twenty-four hours as the circumstances of their arrest and general news of the outside world were squeezed out of them by prisoners hungry for information and striving to keep in touch with outside. My years in jail confirmed that news, or *scéal* as we called it, was the most sought-after commodity, unless you were a smoker!

Unlike Paddy and Dan, Raymond didn't have much to say. He let his two comrades do the talking and only spoke when spoken to directly and even then he was parsimonious with his words. In conversation I discovered that he went to St Colman's in Newry and had been in the same class as a very good friend of mine. My friend, who visited me regularly, was very surprised to learn that Raymond was in the IRA as he had always kept his politics to himself. Once Raymond got to know us his shyness receded, but never entirely left him. He was also deeply religious, very soft spoken and never ever swore.

He was always up for a laugh and, as his future cell mate Frank Hughes was to discover, loved practical jokes. Ironically, it was Frank who, in South Derry, shot and killed the British soldier who was involved in Raymond's capture in South Armagh two years before, Lance Corporal David Jones of the Parachute Regiment.

My time spent in Crumlin Road Jail was filled with protests. If the IRA shot a screw, in retaliation for what was going on in the H-Blocks or the Armagh Prison (where republican women political prisoners, totalling almost thirty, were on protest), we could be locked up for a week and visits cancelled. If we held a parade in the yard, we were locked up for three days. During these lock-ups the screws brought the food to our cells, which we refused and demanded access to the canteen. This meant there were periods when we lived off our parcels. Those were hungry days. One time all that I and my cell mate Jimmy (B) Burns had to live on was a packet of Mikado biscuits. Jimmy B said he wasn't fond of them, so I scoffed them down in five minutes, just in case he changed his mind. They made me so sick. Over forty years later I still can't look at a Mikado without getting that sickly taste from that day.

Jimmy B was OC at the time. He'd been in prison before and had escaped. Unlike the previous OC he brought a lot of experience to the role. Jimmy's predecessor had been asked, rather than volunteered to become OC. Ninety per cent of us were under twenty-one but he was slightly older. I watched him one day dandering down the wing to the governor's office to inform him about the reasons why we were about to take some action. Under his arm he carried *The Irish News* and his shirt tail was hanging out. I found it difficult to take him serious after that. Call me old fashioned but I believe appearance is important, especially if qualities in other areas are lacking.

Once a week, about eight of us were locked in the back of a police van, handcuffed in pairs, and were driven through the town to the remand courts at Townhall Street. We enjoyed rocking the van back and forth trying to overturn it, not that it ever would. I'm not sure what we would have done had we succeeded but the mindset was that every upset for them was a victory for us. We were placed in the cells below the courtrooms and taken in turn up to the dock to be remanded for another week. Once there, we would shout demands for political status. Of course, we would only manage to get a few words out before being dragged from the dock. On a number of occasions we refused to leave the cells and were dragged into the dock. When we attempted to speak we'd be brought to the floor. A cop would keep you down by pressing his knee into your chest. It was farcical. The judge, the press, the public, could see nothing but could hear the scuffles and shouts for political status. Of course, it gave the cops the opportunity to beat us. Handcuffed to another prisoner, we couldn't really put up a decent fight. But one day I pushed back a cop manhandling me and we ended up trading blows.

The scuffle ended very quickly as more cops piled in and dragged me away, and by extension, before he had the chance to become directly involved, the other prisoner. I was uncuffed and thrown back into a cell on my own. Half an hour later the cops came into the cell and charged me with 'assaulting a police officer.'

Escape was always on the minds of republican prisoners. We talked, plotted and dreamed about it. Jimmy B, who became my cell mate after Midge, was put on a special watch because of his previous escape. We didn't have a lot of intelligence on jail security and, at that stage, there was no IRA escape committee set up. My attention, and one or two others, focussed on the hospital outside the walls where I imagined opportunities would present themselves. There were a number of schemes that I can only describe as hare-brained, aimed at getting out to a hospital. No plan existed for escaping once there! The hurdle was getting there. Naive and desperate probably bests sums up my thinking. Although I did get one thing right, getting to the hospital was a hurdle and one, not surprisingly, that I didn't overcome.

Some bright spark claimed that the yellow complexion of jaundice could be simulated by placing Lemon pips under the eye lids for about twenty minutes. More importantly, jaundice would mean immediate removal to the hospital. I didn't stop to think of the ridiculousness of both assertions and just went with it. Nothing happened!

Failure number two, maintaining consistency, also fell within the ridiculous. I had only recovered from a broken jaw when I was arrested. I still had a wire in place and some expert (obviously not medical) suggested that my jaw could be easily broken again. A broken jaw would be my ticket to the hospital. Jimmy B agreed to break my jaw. I want to believe he took a lot of persuading. Accompanied by a few comrades for moral support we entered the ablutions where the deed would be accomplished. Jimmy took a swing at me but instinctively I stepped back and his fist went swishing past. After a few words of encouragement, I held my head up and asked Jimmy to try again. He needed no encouragement. He swung a second time with a lot more aggression and, as if my body had a mind of its own, my head instinctively drew back. (That was my story). Unfortunately, Jimmy's fist hit the wall with quite a wallop. He screamed, yelled, cursed, suggesting it had been very painful and he came close himself to being taken to A&E! That put paid to schemes about the hospital and talk of escape was a touchy subject between us – until seven years later when we *left* H7 in the back of that food lorry.

In September the High Court reopened after the summer recess and remand prisoners qualifying for political status and whose trials were listed were moved from Long Kesh back into A Wing. So, we now had republicans with and without status all together: those charged before March 1st and those charged with offences committed after that date. The status lads were allowed to receive hankies and markers which they turned into republican artefacts. We weren't, but of course we were able to make use of *theirs*. POWs traditionally drew poems, songs and slogans on hankies and sent them out to family, friends and supporters. Some of the hankies would be balloted to raise money for the Prisoners Dependence Fund (PDF). With the help of one or two artistic prisoners, who were always tortured for their talent, I was able to draw a few hankies and smuggle them out. I was bursting with pride when I did my first hankie and signed off my name at the bottom followed by the letters 'RPOW.' It was like graduating – only better. As a teacher I now have quite a few letters of qualifications after my name, but none come close to giving me the sense of pride that 'Republican POW' brought.

Kieran Nugent begins the blanket protest

On September 14th Kieran Nugent left us, went to court and literally disappeared. I knew Kieran by his nickname 'Header.' What I found odd about him was his only choice of footwear was sandals. Then I learnt that he could not wear shoes because once while being chased by the Brits, he had jumped from several floors in Belfast's Divis Flats and broke his ankles in the fall. When Kieran was fifteen he was shot eight times in a loyalist assassination bid which killed his teenage friend Bernard McErlean. Kieran had also been imprisoned twice before, including being interned in Long Kesh.

He was given a relatively short sentence for a vehicle hijacking – three years – and was the first of us to be taken to the Blocks. He was ordered to put on a uniform, refused, and was beaten by the screws and stripped and thrown into a cell. He wrapped a prison blanket around himself for warmth and began the blanket protest. He was refused any communication and his parents only learnt of his whereabouts after some weeks.[3]

As the months wore on and the Crum continued to fill up, we became more and more organised. Experienced volunteers took on leadership roles and this was given a boost in October when Bobby Sands, Seamus Finucane, Sean Lavery and Joe McDonnell joined us in A Wing after they were captured following a shootout during a bombing raid. Two other volunteers shot during the operation were taken to hospital. Seamus, Sean and Joe were in the Movement in Lenadoon where I had been based. It was great to be with them as we had much in common and they were able to give Martin and me lots of local *scéal*. I knew Seamus and Sean well but not Joe. Joe kept a very low profile on the outside and in order not to attract Brit attention he didn't mix with IRA volunteers. Walking into the yard for the first time he cut a distinguished figure with his long black hair, swarthy skin and long black leather coat. A yard filled with bomber jackets and jean-clad prisoners accentuated the difference. He wouldn't have been amiss on the front cover of a men's fashion magazine. Although we did have a QM, whose role was really supplies, being *Lenadoonians*, Martin and I took personal responsibility and ensured they had enough provisions. Joe's main concern was cigarettes although, like the others, he was also provided with biscuits, fruit and books. I was to discover soon that he, like JT, would go to almost any lengths to ensure he had a smoke.

Bobby Sands made his presence felt the minute he walked in the door. He had leadership qualities written all over him. He was full of ideas, had organisational ability and endless energy and enthusiasm.

---

[3] After his release Kieran worked tirelessly on behalf of the prisoners. Tragically, Kieran died from a heart attack, aged just forty-two.

Change began immediately with his arrival. He organised political lectures and Irish classes. I was very pleased to be part of his Irish classes because I wanted to use my time productively and I had never the opportunity to learn Irish in school. Unfortunately, I missed out on being a beneficiary of the positive changes in the Crum as a few weeks later I was moved to the H-Blocks, of which there were eight in total.

A taste of the Blocks

So many people – particularly young people, from around the North's nationalist working-class districts and deprived rural areas – were being arrested that in order to ease the pressure on the Crum and overcrowding, HI Wings C and D in Long Kesh were turned into remand wings.

And so, many of us were transferred to there. In the same H-Block, A and B Wings housed sentenced prisoners and included blanket men. I recall writing to my cousin shortly after I arrived in the Blocks recommending a Royal Pardon if anyone succeeded in escaping. The security, in comparison to the Crum, was overwhelming. While we called the prison camp Long Kesh, the Maze was actually quite apt a description. There were walls within walls and fences within fences. The Russian matryoshka doll, dolls within dolls, would serve as a close analogy. The British Army manned the sentry boxes on the outer walls, the screws managed the security on the inner walls and fences.

Conditions in the H-Block were actually much better than the Crum. The Blocks were one storey with twenty-five cells in each of the four wings. The cells were smaller than the Crum but they were clean and warm. The windows, while still barred (with concrete slats), were at head level and contained an upper, smaller vent window that could be opened or closed, although there was nothing to look at. Everything was grey – grey walls, fences, gates and bricks. Ironically, the place made me yearn for the Crum. HI was much more oppressive. The PO strutted about the wings with an air of arrogance and I would even suggest hatred. He wore his cap in such a way that the peak almost touched his nose and when he spoke to us his face sometimes contorted as if he was fighting to control aggression as he venomously spat out the words. He demanded a regime where prisoners were to refer to his various staff as 'Mister'; we were to stand by our doors for counts at lock-ups and there were restrictions on movement about the wing. While we obviously refused to conform, it was much more difficult to break down than the Crum. With the smaller wings, our numbers were fewer. There were probably only about a dozen republicans here, the rest being made up of loyalists and non-politicals. The screws ironically referred to the non-politicals as 'ODCs' – Ordinary Decent Criminals. Loyalists and non-politicals did tend to conform to the regime – which made us targets for screw harassment, although being Catholic and republican would have been enough for that on their own. There were good republicans in the wing but they lacked experience and we felt very isolated. I eventually ended up as OC, but I was never comfortable in the role. I dearly wanted back to the Crum where there was comfort and reassurance, having experienced volunteers around giving me direction, where there was an abundance of friends and comrades, and where, despite everything, the craic could be ninety.

Some of the blanket men were across the yard in the wing facing us. At that stage there were only a small number on the protest although by Christmas that was to rise to thirty, housed in the only two Blocks opened at that stage, H1 and H2. The ABC men were on the blanket in H1. An odd time I caught a glimpse of them and would shout across but the screws normally kept them on the far side of the wing to prevent contact. We had a friendly orderly in our wing who smuggled tobacco for us to them. He was also able to give us little bits of information on how they were treated.

The protest was very much on my mind at that stage because the time was fast approaching when I would join it. From all reports the blanket men in H1 were faring okay. While they were locked in their cells twenty four/seven, denied all forms of stimulation, books, newspapers, writing material, a radio, morale appeared to be good. Horror stories however were coming from H2 with reports of systematic beatings. I knew what block I wanted to go to when sentenced!

Christmas Day was really bleak and made worse by the fact that we went on a twenty-four hour fast. Apparently, it was traditional for republican POWs to refuse prison food on that day. I could not understand the reasons behind this but I believe we went on fast that particular Christmas in solidarity with the blanket men. I heard later that we were the only wing that did so, as everybody else ate food from their parcels, but I don't know if that was a wind-up. The lads would say these things just to get a reaction.

At dinner time we walked into the canteen and, trying to be nonchalant, walked past what was a spread of mouth-watering food. The screws taunted us, waving pieces of food, but, contrary to what was burning inside us, we showed no desire to touch it. Good sense did eventually prevail as that was the last Christmas Day republicans refused food.

My role as an OC was short-lived because in late January Martin (my co-accused) and I were moved back to the Crum for trial. It was good to be with old friends again and they were glad to see us, if only to get information about what was going on in the H-Blocks with the blanket men.

No matter who we walked with around the yard the conversation, without fear, began with, "What do you reckon you'll get?" Jackie McMullan had been given the wicked sentence of life imprisonment a few weeks before on a similar charge to ours. It was as if the judges were on commission; the bigger the sentence, the more commission! Speculation about the possibility of eighteen or twenty years or life didn't mean that much to me. I couldn't comprehend that sort of time. My mind wouldn't let me. Furthermore, I was convinced the conflict would only last a few more years, the Brits would withdraw and we would be released. I'll not deny that the prospective sentence didn't play on my mind and that deep down I wished for a judge who would buck the trend and give me five to ten years. Naturally, I didn't put much faith in that happening. To be honest I was more nervous about going on the blanket than any sentence some old bitter unionist judge might hand me down. Concern about the protest wasn't helped by the book I read about the IRA in the forties. In 1941 Sean McCaughey, OC of the Northern Command, was sentenced to life and imprisoned in Portlaoise Prison in the South. He refused to wear the prison uniform and – just as we were to do – went on a blanket protest, spending almost five years naked before going on hunger strike. Five years! That took my breath away. Worse, he then went on thirst strike, and died on the twenty-third day of his protest in May 1946. I tried to console myself that society was more civilised today and that that just wouldn't be repeated.

Little did I know then how prophetic the tragedy of Sean McCaughey would prove to be.

The Trial

Each day of our trial we were escorted, handcuffed as usual, from the jail, through the tunnel which ran underneath the Crumlin Road, to the courthouse and back again when the court finished. I hated that tunnel. It gave me the creeps. I think I must have a touch of claustrophobia because I always felt anxious in it and very relieved when reaching the end. Tunnelling had been the favourite method for escape in Long Kesh. I lost sleep some nights worried that the day would come when I would have to tunnel. I knew there was no way I could help with the digging and even if assumed freedom would be a big enough pull factor to help overcome my fear to crawl its length, would I be allowed? Would visions of Danny's claustrophobic attack in the tunnel in the film *The Great Escape* be prominent in the staff's thinking when it came to the decision, "Should Jaz stay, or should he go?"

We were held in the cells under the court and taken up each day into the dock. There were six of us facing sentencing on the same day: Seanna Walsh, Manuel Collins, Tom McFeely, Brendan McLoughlin and Martin and I. It was good to be in the company of these men, especially at that critical juncture in my life. There was a lot of banter between us. We speculated about the sentences we were about to receive. But the main topic of conversation, which was occupying our minds, was the blanket. Sean McCaughey was still very much on my mind and I had to share it with the rest of the lads. Not that I wanted to torture them. No. I wanted them to dismiss it, as I was trying to do, and agree that society was more civilised today.

I was sorry I mentioned it because I didn't get the response I wanted and they were anything but comforting. In response to my rebuttals to their pessimism, I was asked how long I expected the protest to last. Taking a deep breath, I predicted three months but worst-case scenario maybe pushing to six. I didn't really believe the latter. That was just me trying to act tough or least so I thought.

Seanna (who twenty eight years later would formally announce on behalf of the leadership the end of the IRA campaign) considered my prediction to be hilarious. Amid the derisory laughter I snapped back at him, "What's your prediction?" I really wanted to say, "What's your prediction, then, *big man*!" But I was glad I didn't because when he said, "at least a couple of years", compared to me he really did come across as a *big man* and I as a wimp. However, I didn't put any stock on his prediction and just put it down to bravado on his part, trying to portray himself as an RTP (Rough Tough Provo).

At trial, Martin and I refused to recognise the court and within a couple of days we were sentenced to twenty-five years. Our families were deeply affected by it. I think they tried to console themselves with the belief that we would never have to do the sentence. It didn't do to look too far into the future. To do so may have pushed coping beyond their reach. My parents still had a family to rear, four brothers and two sisters, the youngest six years old, and they had to stay strong for them.

Martin's parents, Archie and Bernadette, had an even bigger cross to bear. During the hunger strike a British soldier killed their fourteen-year-old daughter Julie as she was returning from a local shop. The soldier was never charged with her shooting and the files on the case have been closed by government fiat until 2064. Martin's older brother Pat was sentenced to 'Natural Life' and would serve seventeen years before the court of appeal quashed the conviction, the judges declaring significant unease about the safety of the verdict returned against him.

We were sentenced on Friday 4th February and, since we were no longer remand prisoners, were taken to the Crum's B Wing before being transferred to the H-Blocks. We had it from a good source that transfers did not take place on Friday afternoons or weekends. This gave us a 'stay of execution' and I was delighted and relieved. Given how horrified I was when I first arrived in B Wing it was quite the turnaround now wanting to stay. The austere conditions of jail life must have hardened me, and with the lads in C Wing now passing cigarettes, newspapers and chocolate up to us from the yard, cell conditions didn't seem to matter anymore. Martin and I, in each other's company, would be able to live it up for the next couple of days.

II
AR AN PLUID

I was called for a visit. This was to be my last for quite a while. At that stage I didn't know how long that would be as it depended on how long the protest would last. As a sentenced prisoner in the H-Blocks prison clothes had to be worn for a visit and I wasn't for doing that. As can be imagined the visit wasn't easy. My parents put on a brave face, but I could tell that my mother was just about holding it together. My father, trying to keep all our spirits up, said it would be all over in a couple of years. Meaning the conflict would be over and prisoners would be released. My mother was really upset when I told her I was going on the blanket, meaning there would be no visits. She appealed to me not to, but I could only try to console her by telling her I'd be fine and not to worry. I was glad when the visit was over. I didn't want to be confronted with the suffering I had caused them. Without compromising my principles, I was powerless to do anything. For my sanity I had to put their pain at the back of my mind.

We had just settled down to read the papers and indulge in some of the goodies from C Wing when the door opened and the screw declared, "Get your things together, you're being transferred." I really wanted to put him right and tell him there were no transfers over the weekend. So much for the 'good source'! Is it any wonder I became such a sceptic. My stomach was in knots. I could almost feel what it was like walking to the gallows.

Six of us were handcuffed and placed together in the back of the prison van. Conversation ensued and for me at least helped to relax, but not remove, the tension. There was no sign that the others were uneasy but I'm sure they had to be. Tom McFeely took the lead. He was well into his twenties and we looked upon him as being a man. It is difficult to define when a person becomes a man, marriage and responsibilities are probably part of the criteria, and while age is the main factor, who can put a number on it? The overwhelming majority of republican prisoners were quite young and would have regarded themselves as lads rather than men. A lot of us were still growing up, physically and mentally. I measured 5 foot 8 and a quarter inches entering the jail and 5 foot 11 inches leaving. Tom was a seasoned republican who had served time in, and along with eighteen others escaped from, Portlaoise Prison in the South by blowing a hole in the perimeter wall. He had a steely determination about him that encouraged and emboldened his comrades and made screws tread carefully.

He was full on and you could see the fire in his eyes.

"We're not even going to touch that fucken monkey suit!" he said, forcefully. With unmistakeable passion and conviction, he outlined how we were going to play it. We were going to take 'no shit' from the screws. They could stick their 'gear' where the sun doesn't shine. We were having absolutely nothing to do with it. He really fired us up. My anxiety was replaced with a determination to face whatever was in front of me with confidence.

The van pulled into the reception and we were taken out one at a time and placed in separate cubicles. Once separated I didn't feel as determined and anxiety began to creep back. Whatever was left of my militancy dissipated when I heard scuffling and shouting. The small space between the cubicle door and the frame allowed me a little vision and I could just about see one of my comrades being escorted out. I couldn't make out who it was, but it looked like he was carrying something. While I wasn't positive, I suspected it was the hated 'gear' ('the monkey suit'). I thought to myself, I must be wrong, because Tom was very clear, we don't even touch that gear and we all agreed. I had my face jammed between the door and frame peering rather anxiously in readiness to see what transpired next. Another one of my comrades passed by and once again I only managed a fleeting glance, but it was enough to recognise Seanna and confirm my suspicions – he was carrying the gear! It came to my turn. I was brought before a governor and three screws. I let them know that as a political prisoner I was refusing to wear a prison uniform. Their reaction was not what I had anticipated. In fact, there was no reaction as they appeared indifferent to my defiance and merely plopped the gear into my arms. My defiance didn't stretch to refusing to carry the gear. I had convinced myself there was no point making it an issue and I was aware that others were of the same opinion as they had carried it. It wasn't a principled stand, one worth risking a beating, or so I kept telling myself to ease my conscience. I also wanted to believe that Tom had changed the directive about the gear, that's why the lads carried it and they didn't manage to get word to me. Vindicated was how I felt when the screw opened the back doors of the minibus that was to take us to the Blocks and I saw before me four of the lads sitting quietly with the gear on their laps, but no Tom.

Brushing past the two screws at the seats beside the doors, I took my place beside my comrades. I could feel the tension. The mood was subdued. No one spoke. I had a sense that we were all experiencing the same thought – 'So much for not touching the gear!' – and that our consciences were pricking. Minutes dragged by, but no Tom.

Then breaking into the silence, the back doors dramatically flung open to reveal Tom, eyes blazing and hands empty! He scanned the five of us and I'll never forget the look of disgust on his face. Following him into the minibus, like a servant, was a screw carrying his gear. Embarrassed, shamed, head bowed, I shrank into my seat, not wanting to make eye contact with Tom. That bloody gear burned on my lap and it was as if it had the words written large in block capitals– WIMP!

The day wasn't going to get any better. The minibus drove into H2, not H1. Toss of the coin and I lost again! I was about to find out if the horror stories were true. We were led into the front hall and held between the grilles at the doorway before the Circle. The Circle is the main area that contains the control room, the offices, the Mess and where the screws muster. While it is not a Circle it derives its name from Victorian prisons (such as the Crum) that were constructed as panopticons, with wings radiating from a central hub, known as the Circle, from which all wings could be seen. The grille opened and Tom and Brendan were led into the Circle with the grille banging behind them. The hostility was palpable. The screws were shouting, were almost manic, which was not good for my nerves. I stood with my back to the wall facing the opposite wall, resisting the temptation to look to the left to the melee in the Circle because I wanted to give the screws by my side the impression that I was ever so cool and wasn't fazed by their 'welcome' reception. I didn't particularly want to know what was to happen and, as I had averted my eyes to the left, my view was restricted but I was able to gather that the lads were being made to take their clothes off.

As the grilles opened to admit Martin and me, I took a big breath as I entered the lion's den. The full complement of staff, around twenty or more, appeared to be present, all lined up before us like a lynch mob, baying for blood. Martin was moved to the right, I to the left, with about ten feet separating us. I don't remember whether it was a PO or an SO but he came right into my face and asked me if I was going to conform. He already knew that we had refused to wear the gear in reception but maybe he was hoping I'd be intimidated by their show of strength and submit or possibly he just wanted to flex some muscle and have some fun at our expense. I was intimidated but I wasn't for giving in. Brown bags were placed beside Martin and me. We were told to take off our clothes and put them in the bags. We were to be humiliated in full view of their staff. We could have been brought to the cells and asked to undress but, no, they wanted their sport. I felt numb as I removed my clothing but didn't falter. It was traumatic. Once undressed they kept us standing for a minute or two that seemed like an eternity. I didn't register any emotion and as a deflection fixed my gaze on a spot on the wall. I often wondered if any screw in that line was ashamed.

I was taken to D Wing, Martin to C Wing. With the cell door closing behind me I had hoped that that was the worst over but within minutes it opened again. In walked three screws, one of whom I was soon to learn the lads had christened Rubber Lips.

"What's your name?" he said, knowing damn well who I was as my name, number and sentence were displayed on a card outside the cell.

"McCann," I said, knowing full well that that was not the answer he wanted. He hit me an unmerciful slap on the face that sent me reeling backwards. He squared up to me when I steadied myself, his face in mine and with more menace in his voice, asked me again. I repeated my name and this met with another slap.

"McCann what?" He spoke slowly and with obvious threat as if to suggest I was trying his patience, which was wearing thin and would soon reach the point where he wouldn't be responsible for his actions. Of course, he wanted me to say, "Sir". It wasn't the slapping that was getting to me. Being naked, I felt humiliated, defenceless and vulnerable. After several rounds of slapping, more on the head than the face, with the other two screws joining the action and the verbal insults flying, they left, warning me they'd be back. I was at rock bottom. It was one of the lowest points in my life. I could take the beating; I just wanted a blanket to cover my nakedness.

Pacing the floor and feeling sorry for myself, I could hear the thumps from a cell further down the wing. These sounds of a prisoner being beaten had to be endured for years to come and became a hallmark of the protest.

It didn't take long to discover the horror stories were true – this was hell.

I braced myself for round two when I heard the keys jingling in my cell door. There was no need, it was only to throw in a bed pack. It was such a relief wrapping that blanket around me. My dignity restored, my morale began to pick up.

The cell contained a bed, table, chair, a water gallon, a chamber pot (there being no toilet) and a Bible. There was no other reading material of any description, nothing to stimulate and occupy the mind. The statutory issue of Bibles dates from the Victorian era. The philosophy of the time suggested a prisoner held in solitary confinement will contemplate the error of his ways and influenced by the reading of the Bible will be instilled with Christian morality. The only 'error of my ways' I contemplated was the errors made in getting caught. I thought about that again and again, and each time I did, Martin and I made a clean getaway to fight another day. So, contemplation time was how to be a better IRA operative!

Boring as life could be in solitary, the cell was my friend and security. When the cell door was locked, I was safe, at peace with myself and able to find ways to pass the time. When the door opened, I was on edge, unsure what would transpire, vulnerable and insecure.

The door opened again and I was told, "Slop Out!" I knew the procedure. I grabbed the chamber pot and water gallon and made to walk out of the cell when the screw put his hand out to stop me. He pointed to the blanket wrapped around me and said, "Not with that." I wanted to say, forget about it, I didn't need to slop out, but that would be letting him know that being naked was really affecting me. Not wanting to portray any weakness, and gathering this was going to be the way of life, I took the blanket off and walked up the wing trying hard to act naturally, as if I wasn't naked at all but wearing my jeans and a Ben Sherman shirt. But it was difficult. I did feel degraded and every step was an effort. To add to my embarrassment and humiliation, as I passed the canteen, I noticed there were conforming prisoners in the wing. A couple of them were in the ablutions cleaning, probably timed by the screws to do so, and, as I was to learn, every opportunity would be taken to degrade my comrades and me.

Settling in

The cells are locked up in the Blocks at 8.30 every night, the day-time screws leave and 'the night guard' comes on duty. The night guard consists of about six screws and, apart from hitting the alarm at the end of each wing every hour and supposedly checking cells through the flap on each door (which they rarely did), they tended to stay out of the wings and remain in the Circle. In other words, we could relax and didn't have to be on tenterhooks awaiting an unwelcome visit. Really, after 8.30pm we became alive: it was our time and I suppose by all accounts we were nocturnal.

Shortly after the screws left for the night, I heard a voice down the wing. It was Brendan McLoughlin and he was shouting to Tom McFeely. I can't emphasise just how comforting that was. I no longer felt lonely and isolated. Tom then shouted out to check who was in the wing. I responded, followed by Jake Emmanuel Collins. There were conforming prisoners in the wing but they would have known that Tom was only referring to blanket men, what's more they would have been petrified to speak to us as the screws had them warned off.

There were a number of ways we communicated with each other. We would shout through the gap between the door and frame, shout out the window, or talk at the heating pipes at the wall adjoining the next cell. Two pipes ran through the cells along the bottom of the back wall where the window was. The pipes only allowed for communication with neighbouring cells. At that early stage of the protest, when numbers were few, the screws aimed to isolate us, including spacing us out so that we would have no neighbours. That is why, initially, we had to shout rather than talk out the doors and windows.

There was no response from Seanna Walsh and Martin Livingstone, and we gathered they had to be in another wing. The four of us swapped stories about our induction onto the blanket. Three of us shared a somewhat similar experience with being slapped about, although Brendan's appeared to be more than a slapping. I think he may have said something to them and I always found that in those no-win situations it's best to say nothing. Tom on the other hand wasn't touched and I know he definitely would have said something. They were obviously afraid of him. It was wise to be, but cowardly. Still smarting from the look of disgust he gave me, I was a bit afraid of him myself!

Communicating with the lads lifted my spirits and I'm sure it did the same for them. Tom and Brendan continued to talk but I was a bit worn out so I lay on the bed and just listened. I was content. Having been through the mill that day I felt stronger and absolutely determined to see the protest through. Ironically, that was the way it was going to be. The more pressure the screws exerted, the more it steeled my resolve never to be treated as a criminal.

There were to be times when my comrades and I had to endure extreme brutality, deprivation and abuse and on each of these occasions not only did we prevail, but we felt we were affecting their resolve to break us.

There was an agreement reached that we would wear the prison trousers to go to mass. I believe it was Chaplain Fr Tom Toner who brokered the deal, anxious that we would keep up our faith. Seeing one another at least once a week was important for communications. Mass was thus a valuable opportunity to pass on contraband (tobacco), *teachtaireachtí* (comms) and *scéal*. In H2, two adjacent wings (of the four in a block) would come together to celebrate the Mass in one of the wing's canteen. A and B Wings would have a Mass, and, afterwards, it would be our turn, in C and D. We were told to take a chair from the cell and walk across to C-Wing canteen. It was uplifting to see other comrades – Martin, Seanna and Marty Lynch – but the atmosphere was oppressive. I think the screws hated the fact that we could see each other, consequently they patrolled the canteen to ensure we couldn't communicate. They even tried to prevent any eye contact and tried to space us in rows. I turned around to Marty, gave him the thumbs up and he did the same. I was able to lip read that he wanted to know what sentence I received. I opened and closed my hand, spreading fingers wide so as he could count the fives up to twenty-five. In the middle of this the screw started to bawl at me to turn around and stop gesturing. I felt somewhat on safe ground as the priest was entering and I suspected the screw wouldn't want to reveal his brutality. But he did become a little overexcited and barked out that I was there just for Mass and that if I didn't keep my mouth shut and eyes straight ahead, I'd be removed. Nothing else happened.

Next morning, after banging the flaps and roaring to get up, I heard a screw at the top of the wing shout, "Start getting the Streakers out, to slop out." My door opened, I knew the routine, I grabbed the water gallon and chamber pot, not stopping to wrap the blanket around me as I didn't want to give the screw the chance to tell me to take it off. They only opened our doors one at a time as they didn't want two of us out together – all part of the solitary confinement. Breakfast came next and, as would be the routine at all meal times, I was mortified having to walk into the canteen naked to collect my food and bring it back to the cell. Two orderlies stood behind the hotplate serving the food while other prisoners sat in groups at tables eating. There was silence each time I entered. They didn't stare and, to their credit, I sensed some solidarity. Straining to act natural I had my hands swinging by my side and showed no sign of the humiliation that was burning inside me.

How to get my day in? Yes, I had the Bible but I had to think long term. At that point in my imprisonment long term was six months. I could have read it within a week but then I'd be left with nothing. Thinking of the long haul (which was *still* six months, the limit I could contemplate being *Ar an Pluid*), I decided to confine myself to ten pages a day. I didn't dwell too long on the fact that the maths didn't work out for a long haul because boredom demanded at least ten pages. Indeed, the Bible got the better of me. There were days

I just couldn't help myself and ten pages went to twenty or more. I could only hope when I'd read it from cover to cover, that, like Mr Micawber said, "Something would turn up."

I'd occupy my mind with challenges, as, for example, naming countries in the world and their capitals. I tried to work through the alphabet naming groups or singers and singing their songs. Songs were sung very low as I hadn't a note in my head and the lads were enduring enough. I started with ABBA and singing *Waterloo* (humming the words I didn't know). Moved on to the Beatles, Cat Stevens, Dylan, Eagles, Fleetwood Mac, Gilbert O'Sullivan, Dr Hook and then I got stuck at 'I'. By that stage, several days later, JT arrived to join us on the blanket. He was very knowledgeable, especially regarding sport. There was nothing he didn't know. He was across the wing from me so I was able to shout and ask him about 'I'. Sharp as a razor he fired back, "Isley Brothers!"

If I was going to talk or shout out to someone, during those initial weeks, I would check the wing for screws by looking out the gap in the side of the door. They tried to enforce a strict rule of silence and talking could mean anything from a screw banging the door flap and shouting, "Fuck Up!" to actually entering the cell and handing out a beating. It was the same with the bed rule. We were not allowed to sit or lie on it during the day. There were two screws in particular who were sadistic and I'm convinced not quite right in the head. They would sneak about the wing trying to catch us talking or lying on the bed. One of them we named 'Jack the Maniac'. If he, or one of his sidekicks 'Rubber Lips', were about the wing I made it my business to be extra careful. The Maniac never caught me but he did others and invariably he'd enter the cell and sate his lust for physical violence. He never entered on his own – he wasn't that mad! He didn't actually need a reason, would hit out on a whim and didn't discriminate between conforming and protesting prisoners, although the latter were his preferred target. He would have picked his targets and avoided the likes of McFeely. I wanted to be defiant without leaving myself open to assault. I didn't like the idea of being told to get off the bed and then having to follow through. I didn't have it in me, at that time, to tell them to get lost. Not to put myself in that position, I generally avoided the bed.

Unfortunately, I didn't totally escape the notice of the Maniac.

Cell searches took place on a regular basis and were an excuse for harassment. We were made to stand outside the cell naked while they ran their eye over the place. As I said, the cells were empty, apart from a bed, table, chair, chamber pot, water gallon and the Bible; there was nothing to search. Not that that's what motivated them. Search finished, I walked back into the cell only to be confronted by the Maniac. He mumbled something about the bed pack not conforming to regulation. It didn't take much to set him off. I probably did give him a look of indifference that may well have translated as, "And I give a fuck." But anything that wasn't deferential would have been enough to provoke him. He punched me a few times, but given his reputation and how he had treated others I think I got off lightly. In comparison to the other wings in H2, there were fewer incidents of screw brutality. I think this may have been down to Tom. He was bullish when coming face to face with screws and would challenge their behaviour. Fortunately for my comrades and myself, I suspect his actual presence tempered their behaviour.

Adjudications

Every two weeks we were adjudicated. Meaning we were to appear before a governor charged with refusing to wear prison uniform or do prison work. Beforehand, we had to be declared fit for work, which meant being seen by the doctor who really didn't give a damn what condition we were in. It was just a tick-box exercise which he readily ticked. Never do I recall anyone on the blanket declared unfit for work, despite the fact there were men on crutches (one who'd lost a leg), that we were deprived exercise, were undernourished and held in freezing conditions.

Adjudication meant two naked trips into the Circle and being subjected to the usual sneers and mocking of one's manhood. One trip would have sufficed to see the doctor and then to be brought to the next office for the governor. But this would have halved their fun. I found the adjudication farcical because they tried too hard to make it ceremonial and inject military precision as if it was a court martial. Two screws, one on either side, would march me in to the governor while I dandered. They'd bang their feet and come to attention as if their life depended on it. With their shoulders back and chests puffed out it was as if they were to be decorated for services to the empire rather than charge this skinny, bedraggled, naked prisoner for infraction of prison rules. I couldn't help feeling that they would have loved to have strung me up because I bucked the pomp and ceremony. One of these sentinel's, standing erect, would read out their report.

"Sir! At 0830 hours on February 5th I ordered Inmate 138 McCann to put on his prison uniform and present for prison work. Sir! This he refused to do."

The governor would ask: "How does the prisoner plead?"

I'd say nothing.

He'd declare: "You've been deemed fit by the doctor and I find you guilty of the said charges and award you fourteen days loss of remission, fourteen days loss of all privileges including the wearing of leisure clothing, and three days solitary confinement."

'Award' sounded like he was doing me a favour. The three days solitary confinement was a joke. Every day was solitary. The three days translated into removing the mattress each morning at unlock and returning it at lock-up at 8.30pm until the three days were complete. Some of the lads, who must have had hides of leather, would lie on the bed springs when the mattress was removed. The evidence was clear to be seen because when walking up the wing the diamond pattern of the springs was imprinted on their backs. When the screws saw this 'blasphemy' they'd threaten to remove the bed. As the numbers of blanket men increased and we became more organised and emboldened the screws found control difficult. But that was later. H2 remained a crucible of fear, intimidation and brutality.

A visit to court

The screws came to my cell one morning to inform me I was for court. Apparently, the powers decided that assaulting a cop was not something they could allow to pass, despite the fact the cop was the guilty party. Not only did I not mind, what more could they do to me, but I was actually a little excited, like a schoolboy about to go on a trip. There was a catch. I had to run the gauntlet of the Circle and endure the usual jeers and humiliation. Two loyalists, wearing their own clothes, stood in the Circle awaiting transport to court while I stood naked, for what seemed like an eternity, with a strong sense that I was the focus of everyone and if I wasn't, I soon would be.

Along comes Eddie Wylie. Eddie was a screw who you would hear before you see. He was loud, coarse and I reckon he fancied himself as a bit of a hard man. Eddie and I were to cross paths several times during my imprisonment. He came right into my face, bawling a stream of abuse. The gist being I was a dirty, filthy, lowlife who disgusted him. It was an onslaught peppered with swear words and if I hadn't been at the end of it, I might have been impressed with the large bank of insulting vocabulary he possessed. If there was an entry in the Guinness Book of Records for who could swear and insult the longest, my money would be on Eddie.

A brown bag with my clothes in it was placed beside me and I was told to dress. It was such a great feeling to have clothes on again. My pride and dignity restored, I felt ten inches taller. With confidence I bounced, yes bounced, into the back of the van followed by the two loyalists, Eddie and another screw. They struck up a conversation and I was ignored, which suited. I was getting a day out, a break from the monotony, and I was in my own clothes. Eddie and the loyalists were discussing a prisoner called Robinson who, from what I could gather, wasn't fitting in and was making a nuisance of himself. I was left with the impression this young prisoner was naive and possibly suicidal. Eddie was encouraging the two loyalists to give him "a good slapping". I couldn't decide whether Eddie was just a thug or in his own strange way he did have some concern and a 'slapping' was his solution to bring Robinson to his senses. I was not aware Eddie had ever been involved in any of the beatings in H2 and I was to find that his bark was worse than his bite.

We were taken to the cells below the courts in Belfast's Townhall Street where I had been many times before, although this was the first time in the company of loyalists. They were from Bangor and were members of the paramilitary Red Hand Commandos. While we were political opponents there can be an underlying empathy between prisoners, so we had no difficulty talking to each other. Much of our discussion was about the blanket. They wanted to know was it tough, how I got my day in and did I expect that it would achieve political status. They had a vested interest in us winning because whatever gains were wrought from the protest would extend to them.

Handcuffed, I was escorted by the police through the courts in a route with which I was not familiar. When appearing before the remand court I, and other remands, had been taken from the cells, up a flight of stairs, straight into the dock ensuring we had no contact with the public. On this occasion I was taken through a main corridor which was packed with people that opened up like the red sea to allow the unhindered passage for my entourage, which was quite impressive and consisted of four or five cops. I felt elevated by my celebrity status.

The court doors opened, the place was packed, and I was ushered to seats on the right-hand side, at the top of the court. A case was in progress but there was a lull in the proceedings as a hush fell on the courtroom caused by my entrance. The magistrate was irritated by the interruption. He returned to addressing one of the solicitors. I couldn't quite catch what the case concerned but I believe it was connected to theft. I had the distinct impression that, apart from those directly involved, and I'm not even sure about them, the courtroom lost interest in the case as the focus shifted to me. I could see and feel all these eyes directed at me and I suspect they were wondering, with such a show of security, "What did he do?"

Even the man standing before the judge, who I assumed was the accused, shot me a furtive glance. I was a bit embarrassed by it all but tried to appear nonplussed although I was concerned that maybe some of these people thought I was a criminal, a criminal of the worst kind, possibly a murderer or rapist. I almost had the urge to shout out that I was political and a proud member of the IRA who was carrying on the struggle in prison. When the judge turned to my case it almost seemed like the public sat forward, intrigued and glued to what was to unfold. He said he had examined the case and in view of the fact that I had been sentenced to twenty-five years – and with that I could almost feel the public taking a big collective intake of breath – there was no point in pursuing the assault. I had intended to represent myself but was now robbed of the opportunity to speak out not only about the ill-treatment by the cops but more importantly the brutality of the screws in the Blocks.

The cops whisked me out, heads turning following my direction, as I exited to the corridor. It was buzzing with people and they responded to the cops' warnings to move aside. My heart missed a beat when all of a sudden I spotted my parents coming towards me. The cops told them to move back. It all happened within a matter of seconds and I just about managed to tell them I was fine when I disappeared through another door, out of their sight. I'm not sure if they were convinced. For the first time, seeing the look on their faces, it really brought it home to me how they were suffering. I had no idea how they found out I was to be in court that day. I don't even know if they were actually in the court or waited in the corridor hoping to catch a glimpse of me. Maybe they even hoped for a visit. Needless to say, there was no way the cops would facilitate that. It was nice to see them but it wasn't nice to be exposed to their suffering. My conscience really began to bug me – how long were my parents waiting in the court, did the cops mess them about, were they feeling even worse now having seen me?

Back in the Circle in H2 I went through the same humiliating routine of stripping. There was no Eddie this time, no gauntlet of screws or taunts or abuse. Even had there been I don't think I'd have cared as I was numbed from the experience of seeing my parents.

I cheered up later that night when the topic of conversation out the windows was my trip. Of course, I grossly exaggerated the reaction of the public to my appearance at court, all for a good cause – entertaining the lads.

Some nights later when discussing our general conditions, we unanimously agreed that we would no longer leave our cells naked and if this meant no food, so be it. Having to parade around the block naked was the worst aspect of the protest, even worse than the beatings, hosing and deprivations that were to follow over the years. My comrades and I were up for the fight. We were going to put an end to this daily degradation. It was to be a co-ordinated response from all four wings in H2.

Tom McFeely told the PO that we wanted to be treated in a humane, dignified manner, that the beatings were to stop, and when leaving cells, we insisted on wearing a blanket. It came as no surprise to the screws when opening the cells the following morning to slop out that we refused. I loved it when we were militant. It put the screws on the back foot and our morale soared. The exercise was repeated when it came to breakfast and adjudication. In the eyes of the prison administration it was one thing to refuse to leave cells for food and slop out but it was quite another when it came to adjudication and this they were not going to tolerate.

The first person to be adjudicated that day was the first blanket man, Kieran Nugent. Kieran was just across from me so I was able to hear all that went on. The PO or SO was at his door. Knowing there was the potential for confrontation, I suspect they didn't want to chance leaving the screws unsupervised. He requested Kieran to leave the cell for adjudication and while it was not a tone I was familiar with within the Blocks, it clearly was a request and not a demand. It wouldn't have mattered what way he put it: Kieran was not for moving. The PO/SO continued in a calm voice to explain he could do this the easy way or the hard way and with a tone I could only describe as pleading he appealed for the easy way. Kieran, in his own fancy way, told him to shut the door behind him. I was amazed! Kieran was receiving deferential treatment, a complete and utter anomaly for the H-Blocks. He was throwing it back in their faces and they weren't beating the crap out of him. The sound of scuffling followed, with Kieran shouting, and I managed to catch a glimpse of him being carried out. But the screws were not being aggressive in their customary way. Indeed, I could hear the appeals continuing, "Now Kieran, take it easy." Ten minutes later I heard Kieran shout as he came back to the wing, "That's it! Hunger Strike!" That was Kieran, doggedly committed but impulsive.

Kieran, I realised, being the first person on the blanket was a bit of a celebrity, even with the screws, and as such he was treated with some rare respect. A respect not accorded to the rest of us. I know had they opened my door, there'd have been no kid-glove treatment and I'd have been dragged out to the Circle. I was only with Kieran a few weeks therefore I cannot say if he continued to be treated with some respect nor could I comment on his treatment in the months before I joined the protest.

With the chamber pots at the point of overflowing, the admin arranged for slop out from our cells. An orderly accompanied by two screws came around with a bucket into which we emptied the pots. Neither the orderly nor the screws were too happy about this. It was some time before they brought food to our cells and when it did eventually arrive it was cold. This continued for the next couple of days, cold food, slopping into a bucket and washing in a basin of cold water. However, the screws read the mood, we weren't for giving way and they eventually conceded. We were allowed to wear a towel when leaving the cells. It was a great victory, a game changer and notification to the screws that we were a force to be reckoned with and it was in their interest to seek some form of cooperation if their regime was to run smoothly.

Stung by our success, the governor vindictively had Tom McFeely removed from the wing and put into isolation in the punishment block; the boards. I discovered later that this was carried out under Rule 24, approved by the Board of Visitors, which stated he was a disruptive influence and was, "removed from association with other prisoners for the maintenance of good order and discipline." This denied the fact that he was already held in solitary and therefore could not associate with other prisoners. Tom was kept on the boards for two months. He was later to take a case to the European Court of Justice about the inhumane conditions in the Blocks. While Tom was sorely missed it made no difference to our protest. The administration suffered from the delusion that if they removed who they believed to be key people our morale would plummet; we would be weakened and prisoners would begin to leave the protest. Not for the first time they underestimated our strength. There was leadership, commitment and strength in each and every one of us. If a leader was removed there was any number of ready and willing qualified replacements.

Life settled somewhat into a routine in my wing in H2. All meals were brought to our cells by an orderly using a trolley escorted by a screw. Each morning, one at a time wearing a towel, we would slop out, brush out the cell and wash. Twice a week we were allowed a shower that would be restricted to two minutes and timed by the screws. In the evening we would slop out a second time. Meal times and slop outs would mark out our day and break it up. We would live from one mark to the next and this helped us get through each day rather than face one big void.

III
1977 H4

It must have been early March when we were moved to H4. When we entered the Circle there were wheelbarrows, bags of cement, spades and an assortment of other tools lying about which suggested work on the block had just finished and we were the first inmates. Unlike my introduction to H2, there was no reception committee of baying screws, no hostility, only screws going about their daily business, not taking much notice of us except to inform our escort screws we were for D Wing. I was only in the cell five minutes when the door opened and a screw, who we were to name the Pipe, for no other reason than he smoked one, asked me if I would like a cup of tea. That knocked me for six. I was inclined to think it had to be a wind-up but his demeanour did not suggest that. I had to pinch myself. I must have been transported to another world where the screws were non-aggressive and civil.

Reciprocating his civility, I managed to say, "Yes, please," but was not totally convinced, and had a sneaking suspicion that there had to be a punch line. But a cup of tea it was. What made the tea even more amazing was it was not part of the normal meal time. First question out the door during the lock-up was, "Did anybody get tea?" We all did! Of course, the wind-up merchants, shouted, "Weren't the chocolate biscuits a real treat!" I almost fell for it but thankfully somebody did first. "I didn't get one!" cried a voice down the wing. That was just what the 'rakers' wanted to hear. They had a field day. "They must be picking on you." "Probably think you'll leave the protest. Get on the bell and complain." And on it went. As usual they went too far and it became obvious it was a wind-up.

Later that afternoon a governor came into my cell. He wanted to know what motivated me to endure the conditions on the blanket.

"My dog lives under better conditions," he said. He appeared to be genuine in his concern. He said that if I "put the gear on" I would be able to smoke, read books, watch TV and have weekly visits. To cap it all off, he declared, "And, you'll be out in twelve and a half years."

I thanked him for his concern but reminded him I was a political prisoner and would accept nothing less. I never met that governor again, but he left me with the distinct impression that he admired our stance. When lock-up came, JT shouted across and asked what the governor wanted. The lads had a real laugh when I told them he said I'd be out in twelve and a half years if I put the gear on. Not only were twelve and a half years beyond what any of us could contemplate but it was laughable that the governor could actually believe it would be an incentive to leave the protest. Little did I know then that I was to spend much more than twelve and a half years imprisoned.

We occupied two wings in H4, C and D, but they were by no means full. The admin still tried to separate us in alternate cells but as the numbers joining the protest increased this was becoming impracticable. On Sundays the two wings would be together for Mass. Initially, I, along with several others, chose not to go because it meant wearing the prison trousers. I'm not sure what made me come to that decision. I do remember having a conversation with Brendan McLoughlin and he was adamant that he wouldn't wear any part of the gear and I think I was all for going along with that. Obviously, I didn't think it through. There was also that look from McFeely when I carried the gear which still haunted me. I realised what a big mistake I'd made when JT arrived back from Mass and told me I'd been selected, in my absence, as OC. Just when I was settling in to H4, and saying to myself, I can do this, life dealt me another blow! Had I been to Mass I'd have turned down promotion. But now I was stuck with it. I did argue with JT that he was the experienced senior republican but he went to work on my weakness, my ego. "You're the man, you're dedicated, committed ..." and so on. Embarrassment stopped me from quipping, "McFeely might have a different view."

Where was McFeely when I needed him! Which brought another terrible thought. If I was seen to be organising and giving direction to the protest in the wing, would I, like McFeely end up on the boards? I almost wished I was back in H2. Every day I was being hit with questions from the lads which I rarely had any idea how to answer. For example, someone might have a medical complaint and would ask if it was okay to put on the trousers to see the doctor. I was asked if during adjudication we should stand for the governor or face being dragged to our feet, pinned to the wall and probably assaulted. I would be left pacing the floor with my decision-making capacity in a state of paralysis and cursing the responsibility that had been landed on me. I was naïve. Through time I realised the role did not demand that I was the decision maker but rather it required me to facilitate discussion to arrive at a decision. Together as a collective we dealt with issues and agreed ways forward.

Another Sunday, JT arrived back from Mass and told me we were to have a two-minute silence for our patriot dead and I was to shout out the orders to both wings. So, I asked him, just to confirm, if I had to call the lads up to their doors, fall them in, call them to attention for the two-minute silence and then give command to fall out. He assured me it wasn't a wind up.

At lock-up, as instructed, in my loudest voice to enable C Wing to hear, I shouted out the commands from my door. No disrespect to our dead but I did feel stupid. Easter Sunday is the day for remembering our dead, but I felt we could have found a more sensible way to do it. We could have sung a few songs, related some stories about dead volunteers and said a few prayers. In those early days, I think there was a need for militaristic parading to assert that we were an army and to defy the prison authorities. I have to admit, right back to my *Fianna* days, parading did fill me with a sense of pride and belonging. Proud was not how I felt as I stood at my cell door that Easter Sunday. I got into a bit of a panic about the 'two minutes.' How was I to gauge it? I thought about it that much I lost all sense of time! Indecisive, I fought with myself to give the command to fall out. Wait a few more seconds, I thought. No, long enough, call it now! On it went. Best analogy that comes to mind was when I was on the top diving board in Lisburn Swimming Pool fighting with myself to jump. Somebody down the wing had the good sense to cough which brought me to my senses and prompted me to give the command to fall out. The sighs of relief were audible. 'Two minutes' became a standing joke in the wing.

"I'm away to read fifty pages of the Bible. I'll only be two minutes!"

The screws leaving the wing for lock-up 12.30 to 1.30 would only be 'two minutes'.

I was never asked to do a two-minute silence again.

New lads coming on the blanket were interrogated for news, *scéal*. With no one taking visits and reduced to only the one letter a month, which was heavily censored, we depended on them to keep us in touch with the outside world. I suspect newcomers, realising the craving we had, just to keep us satiated made up some of the *scéal*. Not that it mattered, as 'fake news' served a purpose in keeping us entertained. We wanted to know everything – not just about the political situation and how the war was progressing. Who was Number One on *Top of the Pops*, who was winning Division One (later to be become the Premier), what was everybody wearing? Skinners and then parallel jeans had been the trend when most of us were out.

It was a bonus if the newcomer was from your area because there was the possibility of the latest local *scéal*, or even any local *scéal*. So, when Hector McNeill from Andersonstown landed on the wing I was in my element. He was on crutches because during an exchange of gunfire with the Brits he had been shot in the leg. This was his second time in prison. In the early seventies, while planting a bomb in a bar, Hector was overwhelmed by the patrons and came close to being kicked to death. The crowd had managed to wrestle the submachine gun from him and tried to shoot him but it jammed. He had plenty of *scéal* but even I didn't believe half of it. It was good to have him on the wing as he was a real raker who made us laugh. Hector could eat. I wouldn't say he was a scavenger but similarities were drawn with the seagulls that flew around the Blocks foraging. He let it be known that if anyone didn't like or couldn't finish their food, any food, no matter the condition, he would oblige by taking it off their hands. Prisoners could not finish some items of the food, not because they were full but they, unlike Hector, simply could not stomach it.

The food was transported to him by swinging between windows. The sender placed the item in a leg of the prison trousers, tying a knot at the cuff.

A Lurgan lad joined us in H4. After we bled him for *scéal* we asked him how he found the protest. "Wee buns!" he boasted. Naturally, we were glad that he found protest conditions so easy. We regularly checked on the newcomers to make sure their morale was okay because the protest was a shock to the system and it took several days to acclimatise. Bleeding the newcomers of *scéal* also served the purpose of keeping them occupied and the centre of attention, leaving less time to dwell on the misery of their new situation.

'Lurgan' appeared quite buoyant and took to the protest like the proverbial duck to water. He was married and therefore encouraged to take the statutory month's visit. There was no ruling on visits, anyone who wished could take them but the general consensus was only married men should. There was little enough to sustain relationships and what little there was available should be exploited. There were very few married men on the blanket and initially most of them, probably out of solidarity with the rest of us, refused the visits. Lurgan was the first person in the wing to take one. Despite our curiosity about what it was like to take a visit while on protest – was there harassment, did screws stand over the visiting box, was the search extreme – Lurgan had little to say when he came back. An hour or so later, I heard the screws coming down the wing and open his cell door. This was unusual because it broke the general routine of the wing. You soon get to know the times when screws come and go and the unusual was never a good sign.

Human beings are very adaptable to their environments. Limited to a narrow crack at the side of the door there was very little visibility but we found our hearing sharpened. We could identify a screw by the sound of his feet. If there was a group of screws it was difficult to distinguish the sounds but we would have a good idea how many were in the group.

Lurgan's door slammed closed. Two sets of screws' boots could be clearly heard but there was a third unfamiliar sound. It squeaked. New boots. Lurgan had put on the gear. And the new boots, getting their first outing, emitted that iconic 'squeaking' sound, as he headed out of the wing. New terminology entered our lexicon that day. Leaving the protest came to be known as 'squeaky booting.' Lurgan left quite a legacy because his statement, "Wee Buns" became synonymous with 'squeaky booting' and was to be quoted and requoted an infinite number of times down the years. When new lads were quizzed on how they found conditions, the questions would be designed to steer them towards the desired response, "Wee Buns". If it was said, the wing would erupt with howls, "He's squeaky booting!" It was all part of the craic. Actually, "Wee Buns" never did translate to leaving the protest and, on the wing where I was to spend over four years, D Wing, H5, we had a very proud reputation because it was very rare anyone did 'squeaky boot'.

For days the screws played on his departure, or rather overplayed. They all had stories about him being very happy in the conforming wing. "Speaking to him today and he was the picture of relaxation, smoking away, lying on the bed reading a letter from his wife." If it was to be believed, Lurgan must have been quite the celebrity with the screws as every one of them had first-hand stories.

"Saw him at the pitch playing football."

"He was watching *Top of the Pops* last night."

"Gave him his tuck shop today. Didn't know how he could eat so much chocolate!"

It was enough to make us wonder was Lurgan in the conforming wing or Butlins. It was beyond the screws to understand that their 'Butlins' stories didn't in the least entice us and, and far from being jealous, we felt sorry for Lurgan.

IV
TO H5

About mid-April, shortly after Easter, I heard the screws at Hector's door and the bolt shooting. Hector shouted out to warn us that he was moving. My cell looked out onto the front yard which enabled me to see the comings and goings. A van drove in and some prisoners spilled out from the main doors of the block and boarded the van. They were blanket men. I shouted down the wing that some of the lads were moving. Hector then appeared from the main doors and using his crutch hobbled across to the van with a bundle under his arm, which I was surprised to see was clearly part of the uniform. He was struggling to hold on to that bundle and use his crutch. I couldn't understand why he was even carrying it. It proved too much. As he stepped up to board the van, he lost his balance and had to let go of the bundle in order to grab the door to prevent him from falling. It flopped onto the ground and unravelled as it rolled, spewing out pieces of bread and cabbage. He had secreted cabbage sandwiches among the gear. How anyone could eat cabbage between two rounds of bread was beyond me, but that was Hector. The expression on his face as the bundle slipped away was something to behold. I thought he was going to cry. All that effort, lads swinging unwanted bread and cabbage, him making it into neat piles and secreting it in the gear, all gone to waste! Deflated, he scrambled into the van minus his sandwiches which were left for his co-scavengers, the seagulls. Vomiting sounds echoed over the wing when I told the lads he was smuggling cabbage sandwiches and we all roared with laughter about the mishap and Hector's expression.

More screws came down the wing, opening cells and informing us we were moving. It was clear they were emptying the two blanket wings but we had no idea to where. As I was driven out of H4 along with five of my comrades I was feeling upbeat. Hector's performance had put me in a good frame and a break in the monotony of the protest was always welcome. It got better. The van swung into H5 and as we drove down the yard the A-Wing lads were at their windows cheering us in. They were all blanket men. Such a change from the welcome in H2. A crutch, waving frantically, protruded from one of the windows. Hector was over his loss.

We encountered no hassle as we were taken into the Circle and escorted to D Wing where we were placed in separate cells. Immediately, we were at the doors shouting out to one another to find out who was in the wing. I was placed next to the last cell at the bottom of the wing looking out on the derelict exercise-yard side. The lads across the landing from me looked out onto the arrivals area and to A Wing, opposite, and kept us informed about the vans driving in and out, off-loading blanket men. Like the comrades in A Wing, they too were cheering. They also had the advantage of being able to communicate with the lads facing them in A Wing, some of whom were friends and from the same areas but hadn't seen each other for over a year. The place was buzzing. It soon became apparent that all four wings of H5 were to be a blanket block. It felt like we had achieved a victory. The screws attempt to enforce silence, while it had been a losing battle, was now gone. Although we were still in single cells (this would soon change), solitary confinement was dead and loneliness was no longer our bedfellow.

Blanket men were in every cell. We could communicate through the heating pipes and out the window. Conversation-wise, we were spoilt for choice: out the doors, where the whole wing could hear and join in; out the windows, which was only audible to the neighbouring six cells; and down at the pipes which was one-to-one with neighbours. Prisoners in cells facing across the front yard to the other wing could also communicate with each other. Even if I didn't participate in some conversations it was comforting and it was company just to hear other friendly voices. The place was alive and the air breathed solidarity and comradeship.

There was no time wasted in setting up command structures. An OC of the block was appointed and OCs in each of the four wings. A personal bonus for me was that my tenure as OC came to an end. I could slip into the background where I was comfortable and offload decision-making to the more experienced and able in whom I had every confidence, although decisions generally were made as a result of discussion. The screws gave tacit recognition to our staff because it made life easier for them. But there were the bigots who couldn't stomach any engagement as they had nothing but hatred for us.

Once the screws left the wing at the 8.30pm lock-up and were replaced by a night guard, the wings came alive with conversations until about ten. Then there would be a discussion or some form of entertainment such as a concert, a quiz or the retelling of a book, all of which had the effect of bonding the wing together.

The narrating of a book was very popular. Some of the lads had a real talent for this and would have embellished the stories to make them much more interesting. One or two of the storytellers were renowned for their abysmal delivery. They were that bad I found them entertaining but many would disagree and say it was like listening to nails scraping a blackboard. One of the more talented storytellers was Sammy Millar who went on to become a celebrated author.

Orderlies

The orderlies who maintained the wing stayed in Cell 26 (the 'big cell') at the top of the wing, close to ablutions and nearer the Circle. This was a double cell and usually held three to four prisoners who would be either loyalists or, more likely, non-politicals. They were under threat from the screws not to engage with us and when going around the cells with the meals they tended to have their heads bowed to avoid eye contact.

Before the protest escalated to the 'No wash, No slop out' there were some orderlies to whom we were deeply indebted as they risked a lot to help us. They would turn the volume up on the radio or TV when the news was on to enable the lads in the top cells to hear. Screws would scream at them to turn the volume down but, without making it obvious they were trying to help us, they would try it again some days later or would have the volume just loud enough that the blanket man in the top cell, if standing at his door, could just about hear. A lot of the lads were mad about football and the orderlies would sometimes rip out the back pages of a Sunday newspaper containing the results and fixtures and slide it under one of our doors.

They didn't have a lot of tobacco themselves but they did try to share some and took the risk of passing it through the door. For meals they could only divvy out what the kitchen delivered but the cornflakes which were kept in the wing canteen and replenished from the kitchen when finished, were at the discretion of the orderlies and they didn't let us down. We had bowls, with a capacity of about 500mls, and the orderlies filled them to the brim with cornflakes. It was the meal that I looked forward to most of all. It was either porridge or cornflakes for breakfast and two rounds of bread. Apart from Hector and a few others with *galvanised* stomachs, no one could tolerate the porridge. The two rounds of bread with a spread of cheap margarine were not very appetizing so I have to confess I made cornflake sandwiches and they were delicious.

A number of orderlies who were caught helping us were beaten up by the screws and sent out of the block. I don't know for sure if they were sent to the boards, but they lost remission, to act as a deterrent to others. Nevertheless, more cautiously, they would still help us and smuggle *toitin*.

Martin McKenna from Bawnmore in North Belfast was in the top cell and that left him with a lot of responsibility. He had to press his ear to the door and listen out for news coming from the radio and TV in the canteen and then relay it to the rest of us. Some others in the top cells could sometimes hear but Martin was best positioned being closest. More often than not he only caught snippets and so as a group the top cells between them would try to piece together what they had heard and make some sense of it.

I will never forget Sunday 24th April, 1977, during the midday lock-up, Martin having just listened to the news shouted down to me. Someone, he said, from Lenadoon had been shot dead by the Brits at the Hunting Lodge bar in West Belfast. He addressed me because Lenadoon had been the IRA Company I had been in and therefore he had a fair idea that I would know who it was. When he stated it was someone called Brendan my heart thumped. Dread came over me immediately because I felt it was in all probability Brendan O'Callaghan. I asked Martin if he had any more information and I think I must have held my breath awaiting the reply because when he added that he was aged twenty-one I let out one very big sigh of relief.

I knew Brendan well. He had been my OC in Lenadoon. No way was he twenty-one. He was married, had two children, had his own home and I was certain he was at least in his mid-twenties. I was very, very relieved it wasn't him and my thoughts turned to other possibilities. But I learnt I was wrong. He was twenty-one. It seemed implausible because compared to the rest of us in the company, who were between late teens or just entering our twenties, he was very mature. Martin, catching the name in a later news, revealed that it was Brendan. I found it difficult to take in that he was dead. Imprisonment bit hard that day. I felt helpless and longed to be outside with his wife and family. Not that I could do anything; but I just wanted to be there. I wrote a letter to his wife, expressing my deep sympathy with her loss, and had it smuggled out.[4]

Bears in the Blocks

Martin McKenna was also mainly responsible for keeping an eye out for screws walking down the wing during lock-ups, especially if we were 'shooting a line', which I'll explain later. If a screw appeared, Martin would shout out a warning: "Bear in the air!" I might have been okay with the 'in the air' bit, but the 'bear' was too much. What possessed Martin to christen them bears and for others to go along with it was beyond me. I do know that it originated from the 1976 song, *Convoy*, by C.W. McCall, about truckers who were evading paying tolls and the 'bears' were the police chasing after them; "Bear in the air" referring to a police helicopter. Maybe Martin really loved that song and that was his way of reliving it every day.

We'll never know because shortly after he was released, Martin was killed in a car crash.

I accept that a code was needed to alert the wing. But despite what some might think, the screws weren't stupid, and even accepting that some were, it didn't take long for them to catch on that "Bear in the

---

[4] When attending a commemoration on the fortieth anniversary of Brendan's death I was delighted when his son Paul approached me and showed me the letter I had written all those years ago. Not only was it confirmation that it succeeded in reaching the family but also that it meant something to them. The letter was quite rare because it was written on official headed paper in the days before we started writing on toilet and cigarette paper.

air" meant *them* and that something was *going down*! They loved being called bears so much so that occasionally they actually shouted it themselves. Why did we simply not just shout 'Screw' rather than elevating their status to 'Bear'? I could never bring myself to use that moniker and, like some others who had the same hang up, used the Gaelic *caoimhadeoir* (albeit, wrongly) or *bairdeori*. That said, there was one screw with whom I was happy with the term.

He was quite small and suffered from a Napoleon Complex. He compensated for his lack of stature with nastiness. We named him 'Teddy Bear', which he wasn't at all pleased about. The Class Officer (a screw in charge of the wing screws) had a bit of a rapport with some of the lads. He was hoping to use his influence and, along with Teddy Bear, came into the OC's cell to plea on his behalf. Teddy Bear said he didn't want to be a 'Teddy Bear': he wanted be a 'bear'! What a mistake! From that day forth he got 'Teddy Bear' with gusto, each and every time he approached the wings. Even some of the screws started calling him it.

Martin didn't escape this name culture. He became known as 'Polar Bear'. I'm not sure whether he named himself this, which was highly likely, or that the screws had reciprocated. Martin was well liked by one or two of the screws and they even threw him in an odd cigarette. I mean 'throw' because I witnessed them actually tossing cigarettes into his cell. Maybe they had to be on their guard and deemed it best to throw rather than risk being seen passing hand to hand. But I couldn't help feeling they were exercising their power over us. They were very selective who they gave cigarettes to and invariably they were the 'key men' in the wing. Whatever was thrown our way, the lads, of course, would always share.

A case of varicose veins

One of those key men was the Block OC. He was the first official head of all the blanket men. He informed us that he had to go to the hospital to have varicose veins removed because they had been causing him a lot of pain. We thought nothing of it as it was perfectly in order, at that time, to seek medical attention. However, the following day the screws were cock-a-hoop, spreading stories that he was in H8, the conforming block, and of course they went on large about how happy he was. Screws were always mixing. I don't think anyone believed them. We paid no heed and hoped he was recovering well. If anyone did have any doubt about the OC being in hospital, they didn't air it. I personally had every trust in him and never doubted him for one minute. It was another ploy by the screws to try to demoralise us and their taunts continued for days. I felt sure they were only setting themselves up to look stupid when he stepped back onto the wing from the hospital. There was some speculation among us that to avoid looking stupid, they would move him back into another blanket wing. Almost a week passed with my confidence in him unflinching until reality hit and sent my naive belief crashing.

One of the lads had spotted him on the visits, 'wearing the gear', proving the screws right and us wrong. Without exaggeration I can honestly say that experience was one of the watersheds on my road to maturity. I had looked up to men in the movement who held positions, had years of experience and were more senior in age than myself, never questioning their judgements and prepared to follow them whatever it took. That ship sailed that day. Republicans, whether in leadership positions or not, had in the future to earn my respect and confidence and I no longer followed with blind abandon. Most, if not all in the wing, were affected by that disappointing experience. Our wing was renowned by all the other blanket wings for being cynical and maybe even a little disrespectful of leadership. Our cynicism had its roots in the OC's departure.

Loyalists try the protest

With numbers on the blanket continuing to increase, the prison began to double prisoners up. I remained on my own for quite a while, not that I minded. H5 brought a mood shift with the majority of screws as they were no longer on a mission to apply pressure to drive us off the protest. Those screws who continued with the harassment, such as rationing our food, were in a minority.

A number of loyalists joined the protest. At the time I happened to be in a cell facing A Wing and I could see across to the cell where two of the loyalists were placed. I recognised one of them. It was the Bangor loyalist in the Red Hand Commandos who I had shared the cell with at court. I shouted across to him using his first name to make him feel welcome and hoping he would respond. I don't mind admitting that I felt pretty impressive in front of the lads, almost like an international diplomat, being on first name terms with an RHC. 'Bangor' was probably glad to have the opportunity to speak to me on a first-name basis because all the lads were listening and it was an ostentatious way of announcing, "I've always got on with you Provies." Our conversation lasted about ten minutes. I gave him some background to life on the blanket and asked him if we could expect more loyalists to join. The lads in A Wing, as with any newcomer, were anxious to interrogate him for *scéal*, therefore I let him go and wished him well.

We were very pleased with the arrival of loyalists because it added weight to our protest and the prison would become increasingly difficult to administer. Unionist politicians had much more sway with the British government than nationalist representatives (not that nationalist politicians were particularly interested in our plight) and so had the capacity to exert pressure. However, being in a bubble in the H-Blocks, I didn't fully realise that the unionist politicians and people would not support loyalist prisoners if it meant siding with us. Within a couple of days Bangor and the loyalists were gone. I heard their leadership ordered them off because their 'contradictory' position could not be justified to their community.

With nearly everybody doubled up my turn came. Brendan McLoughlin from Greysteel, Derry, became my partner – although he might use the term 'victim.' It was good to have another human being to talk to face-to-face. Brendan was a man of few words. It was me who did most of the talking and sometimes I couldn't help suspecting that he would have preferred to have stayed in a cell on his own. Slow to take a hint, I maintained my persistent chattiness.

Screws only opened one cell at a time but, because of the increase in our numbers, it was no longer possible to complete a full-wing slop out and wash. They had other options. For example, open more cells at the one time but they wouldn't consider that. Their solution was to allow one side of the wing to wash at the ablutions one day while the other side received a basin of water to wash in their cells, and this would alternate. The basins consisted of one inch of cold water, which every blanket man detested. It would have been enough to drive anyone on to a 'no wash protest.' We made our complaints but as usual they fell on deaf ears as the screws were not for opening more than one cell. Of course, when it suited, they did. If they were in a hurry to take a break or watch something on the television in the canteen, two and even three cells were opened (although three cells opened was very rare). Shaving in one inch of cold water was awkward and unnecessary. It was decided we would stop.

And so the iconic image of the bearded blanket man was born.

I found myself for the first time in my life interested in nature, not that there was much to see. I would stare between the bars of the window at the birds. Others, like Brendan, knew their names so I got to know wagtails, blue tits, sparrows, finches, starlings, robins, crows, blackbirds and magpies. I did know some of them before I went to jail but there were quite a few I could never have named. Some of the lads threw a little food out to attract them (but not Hector!) and to help pass the time. I disliked the seagulls because they came swooping in, scattering the smaller birds, and flew off as quickly as they came – show over! Whereas, the smaller birds would hop and fly about for longer periods. I was treated to a fantastic show one day, David Attenborough-style. One of the budding ornithologists identified a sparrow hawk and shouted out to me to look to the right at the fence. There it was perched on the fence slightly hidden within the coils of barbed wire, leaning forward like a sprinter in the Blocks, staring intently ahead and ready to pounce. It remained in that position, static for a couple of minutes and then like a rocket it shot out between the coils of wire and dived into the yard towards a couple of sparrows. The sparrows reacted immediately and flew upwards and simultaneously the hawk changed its trajectory and followed its prey. It twisted and turned, dived and swooped as the sparrows nimbly changed direction but I was robbed of the outcome as the hunt went out of my vision that was blinkered by the bars. It was a bit like the TV being turned off just when the final scene was about to unravel the plot. I felt cheated! While I could understand the hawk had to eat, I sided with the underdog and could only hope the sparrows made it away.

The mouse

One day, as my neighbours, Sean McKenna and Jake Emmanuel, were brushing out their cell a mouse ran in. It came from the yard door at the bottom of the wing beside their cell which was open. They said nothing, set the brush and scoop outside the cell door which the screw, unaware of their visitor, locked. Sean and Jake spent the next hour or so observing the mouse play and shouting out a running commentary to Brendan and me on its performance. I became a bit jealous and asked Sean who, being a country boy had no fear of mice, to send it in. I should have asked Jake, put him on the spot, because I knew there was no way he would touch it. And while he joined Sean with the running commentary, this was just a front because Sean told me Jake wouldn't get off the top bunk. Sean put the mouse inside the leg of the trousers, tied the bottom and swung it in to me. I lifted the small mat in the cell (which was about 100cm x 60cm), curved it so as it was wedged between the door archway, creating a semi-circular pen 60cm high into which I released the mouse from the trousers.

It didn't disappoint. I felt a sense of solidarity with the mouse as it ran around its pen searching for an escape route. Having no luck with that it began to run vertically up the door but it could only reach 40 or 50 cm and fell back down again. Its attempts to escape ran to double figures before it stopped. I could only assume it was exhausted, although I have no idea how a mouse exhibits exhaustion. I had accepted that the entertainment was over and the mouse had conceded defeat when to prove me wrong it jumped up again and returned to its attempt to scale the door but unfortunately for him or her, had the same result. I almost willed it on but the best it could manage was about 50cm. I had to admire the mouse; it took its breaks but always returned to the attempts to escape. There was a message in there somewhere.

Shouts were coming from other cells that they wanted a piece of the action, so I grabbed the prison trousers that were always unceremoniously dumped in the corner, pushed the end of the mat in to allow a gap and covered the gap by opening the leg of the trousers. Sure enough, the mouse ran through the gap into the trousers. I stood on the top of the leg, closing its escape route and entrapped it by tying the bottom of the leg and swung it into the next cell. The mouse was swung from cell to cell, spending about twenty minutes in each, until eventually he was given his freedom later that day.

Sean McKenna

Sean, although only twenty-three, was a veteran republican. At the age of seventeen, he, together with his father, also called Sean, was in the first batch to be arrested by the British Army on 9th August 1971 and interned. His father was one of the famous 'Hooded Men' who was tortured and, as a result of that torture, Sean senior died a few years later. Young Sean had been taken to Ballykinlar Army camp where he was subjected to beatings before being interned on the Maidstone Prison Ship. He was released in 1975 and immediately reported back to the IRA. He was very active in the South Armagh/ Newry area and was regarded as public enemy number one by the Brits. He was pursued relentlessly.

The SAS unit tasked to seize him, Sean told me, included the infamous undercover soldier Robert Nairac, who was later killed by the IRA. The SAS crossed the border during the night and captured Sean in a cottage in County Louth. There was no outcry by the Irish Government about the illegality of the incursion, the infringement of sovereignty. Once they had trailed him into the North he was then arrested. Sean spent his remand time in the Cages with political status where he was second in command. Upon sentencing he lost political status. Fortunate for us, but unlucky for him, he was sent to the Blocks where he became our OC.

Since Sean was my next door neighbour, he was literally stuck with me. Most of our conversations took place out of the windows. Sean was quiet and not one for shouting out so, apart from the wing discussions and the conversations with his cell mate Jake Emmanuel, in the main his geographical position limited him to conversations with my cell and my other neighbour. Brendan, like Sean, was a country lad, so they talked about country life and farming. When the country lads started, even if we Belfast lads found it interesting, we would wind them up by telling them to "stop talking about shovelling shit." Sean had a lot of experience operating along the border and I wanted to hear about some of his close encounters and his final capture by the SAS, but he wasn't very forthcoming. He wasn't one for skirting too close to 'LT' (loose talk) and even when I pointed out that the Brits knew some of the details of his activities, he would respond that they only knew *their* version. Sean hadn't much interest in schooling, but he was very intelligent which I felt was an awful waste. I found that quite common in the Blocks: guys with 'brains to burn' had left school at the first opportunity. I was brought up in an environment where education was a priority. My father, a teacher, believed in the power of education to change things rather than by the gun. I believed in both and put one on hold while I engaged with the other.

Sean was a very strong character and the only weakness I detected was his inability to refuse to sing when prompted during the wing concerts and that's when I really wanted him to be strong and stand up to the pressure because he had to be one of the worst singers I had ever come across. Like Sean, I hadn't a note in my head but, unlike him I knew when to stop. The restrained chuckling after my performances, rather than clapping, were tell-tale signs – enough to let me know singing wasn't my forte. I know that came as a relief to the majority, and those who tried to persuade me to sing only did so in the knowledge that no matter how bad they sang, if I did, they wouldn't be the worst singer that night.

Mass

Learn from your mistakes and that, as far as Mass was concerned, I certainly did. I looked forward every Sunday to those forty-five minutes when I was out of the cell, mixing face-to-face with lads who I otherwise would never see, unless through the gap in the steel door, or heard their voices through the metal pipes or from a window. It was especially good to talk to lads from my own area of which there were quite a few and to swap whatever bits of local *scéal* we picked up. I think the canteen at Mass time could best be described as bedlam. This wasn't H2; the screws weren't going to tell anyone to shut up. They withdrew and stood outside, manning the grilles, although the din of the multitude of conversations were enough to have them retreat. Once the Mass started, apart from some of our staff who spoke in whispered tones at the back, we were respectful and, in the early years at least, gave ourselves fully to the service.

When the *sagart* (priest) entered, some of the lads would corner him and ask for cigarettes or tobacco. I use the term 'corner' because, while they were respectful, it must have seemed like an ambush to any unsuspecting *sagart*s celebrating Mass for the first time in a protesting block.

The regulars, some of whom included Fr Alec Reid and Fr Gerry Reynolds from Clonard Monastery, Cistercians from Portglenone Monastery, and Fr Faul, soon knew what to expect and, all due respect to them, most did bring some cigarettes. The prison chaplain was Fr Tom Toner assisted by Fr John Murphy and being in the Blocks from day one, they grew up with the situation and appeared to take it in their stride. Once the cigarettes were extracted, the *scéal* came next. What was happening in the outside world?

There was no point asking the Cistercians as we knew more than they did. Fr Faul was good for the football results but he didn't always get them right. He had the habit of saying 'duck' rather than nil. Liverpool 2 Man United duck! GAA results tended to be limited to the championship, not the national league, and very rarely did we hear about hurling except for the All-Ireland Final. While it never entered my thinking back then, *sagart*s coming to the Blocks for the first time were probably nervous and I'm sure not helped by the raucous din when entering the canteen and seeing emaciated Ben Gunn-type characters with long hair, scruffy beards, and wearing only trousers.

I recall one *sagart* overdoing it with the Holy Communion hosts. Only at the last communicant did he realise he still had half a chalice full of hosts. He had to eat them all. His face became beetroot red. I don't know if this was due to the enormity of the task before him or because we were staring intently, curious as to how things would unfold but ready to spring into action if he started to choke. It was the closest I've ever seen to the scene in *Matilda* where Bruce Bogtrotter had to eat the giant chocolate cake. We were very pleased and in admiration when he just about made it. I'll not say it was a miracle but obviously God was on his side.

Fr Murphy was literally a godsend. For almost two years I didn't take visits and he became an important link between my family and me. My parents regularly went to see him at his parish at the Rock, Stoneyford, and he would update them on how I was doing. I've no idea what he said but I'm sure he would have censored anything that would have caused them anguish. Fr Murphy was apolitical and only concerned with his pastoral role, which I respected. Neither my family nor I ever asked him to do anything that stepped outside that role. He was a great comfort to them during those very difficult years and he was the bearer of good and bad news for me. Through him I learned of my sister's marriage and that I was an uncle for the first time. On the downside he broke the news of the death of my grandfather and then an uncle.

'Spud,' as we referred to him, was a very pious man, an expert on theology, devoted to his vocation and a quiet man who shunned publicity. Even during the no-wash/no slop out days when the cells reeked, he continued to visit us and during the hunger strikes he was with the hunger strikers on a daily basis.

Smokes

Cigarettes/tobacco were distributed as fairly as possible, or so I was led to believe. For some of the lads, who would have sold their granny for a smoke, the temptation was too much, and they would have taken a little extra and rolled a thicker cigarette than the rest. Possibly, the thought that everybody else was at it eased their conscience. During the first eighteen months of the protest, when few were taking visits, there wasn't a great amount of cigarettes/ tobacco to be had. Not that there was much to be had throughout the protest. A drop here and there trickled in from *sagarts*, friendly orderlies, from the few lads taking visits, and screws. That's not to suggest the screws were philanthropic or had moments of weakness when they felt humane. It was rare that they threw a cigarette into a cell.

The source from the screws was the discarded butts be it in ashtrays, bins or on the floor. The lads, smokers or not, scanned the wing for butts when they slopped out and discreetly picked them up. If they spotted something but were unable to it pick up, once back in the cell word would be passed along the pipes. This gave others time to put together a plan. Screws would be distracted while one of the lads swooped in to grab the prey. You hit the jackpot if you could empty an ashtray. But they were difficult to reach as they were usually placed under the nose of a screw on duty at a grille. Screws didn't always do their 'duty' and there were moments when the grille, or more importantly, the ashtray, was left unattended and the contents liberated.

Some of the experts or, more appropriately, the 'brass necks', didn't need ruses. They were that cool they scooped up the contents right under the noses of the screws. One day when I was slopping out before the previous cell had finished, I saw a pair of legs hanging out of a bin. One of the lads was literally scraping the bottom of the bin, rummaging for butts and whatever else was available. Ashtrays were emptied into the bin so it was the mother of all jackpots. A popular method when slopping out was to set the water gallon on the spotted butt. The bottom of the gallon was wet therefore the butt would stick to it.

The majority of us did not know how to roll cigarettes so the one or two who did, took charge – willingly, took charge, as it had its perks. JT was the main man on one side of the wing and on the other, when he arrived around October 1977, was Joe McDonnell. However, ever suspicious that their eye could be wiped, it wasn't long before the ardent smokers learnt to roll. Proper cigarettes were 'straights', butts and tobacco were collectively known as *toitin*.

Whatever *toitin* had been gathered, if indeed any, was swung to the roller. He would dismantle the butts and straights and re-roll their contents into thinner cigarettes. The miracle of the loaves and fishes had to be performed. Four or five rolls could be made from a single straight. For cigarette paper we used pages from the bible and toilet paper (that thin it was like school tracing paper). We had the luxury of real cigarette paper now and again and they were referred to as 'skins'. Once the *toitin* was rolled the swinging swung into action.

'Swingers' were made from boot laces (although within a few months the screws removed the boots from the wings) and from thread harvested from blankets, prison trousers and shirts. The swinger went up the line, each smoker taking a roll or if we struck really lucky maybe two. It was possible to light everybody's roll with one light, which in the early period, usually meant a match. However, it was more usual to have a source of light on each side of the wing. Either a lit roll would be swung from cell to cell or whoever had the light would have the person in the adjacent cell swing in his roll to be lit and swung back and this would be repeated the whole way up the wing. Through time we learned how to make wicks and I learned to roll.

Shooting a line

To connect with the opposite cells on the same wing we would shoot a line. We'd remove a small button from the prison-issue shirt and knot thread through the eyes of the button. The button would be flicked out of the bottom of the door either with the finger or a piece of comb. The cell directly opposite would do the same, until the two lines overlapped and intertwined. Once connected we could import and export contraband! The lookouts at the top of the wing, Polar Bear and company, would be at their station when the line was being shot at the bottom of the wing.

Teachtaireachti (communications to or from the IRA leadership; or personal letters) were a regular feature of the line but always secondary to the *toitin*. There were times when the screws would hide, allow the line to be connected and race down the wing to grab it once the rolls or whatever else was being transferred, only to miss by the tip of their fingertips the line being withdrawn into the cell. While it was very rare, there were one or two less funny incidents when they actually did succeed in grabbing it. Occasionally, if we spotted a determined screw, we would set up a dummy line and while he was observing that line the official one would go unnoticed or if not unnoticed, the screw running for and wrestling with the dummy would have been distracted and bought us enough time for the official line to transfer the goods. It was not unknown for a parcel containing excrement to be attached to the dummy line: a fitting reward for the screw's efforts.

While the roll was just a portion of a cigarette it was the most satisfying and relaxing smoke I have ever known. Every roll my comrades and I lit and smoked was a defeat for the system.

Bobby Sands and Joe McDonnell join the protest

I was delighted when in October 1977 Joe McDonnell, Seamy Finucane and Bobby Sands came on the wing. They had been sentenced weeks earlier but had been held on the boards in Crumlin Road Jail because of a fight with screws.

Seamy and Joe were able to update me on the local *scéal* and I had high hopes that Bobby would start a Gaelic *rang* (class). Seamy was transferred to A Wing after several weeks and sometime after that to H4. He would have you believe he was transferred because he was 'such a key figure' but I maintain it was just his bad luck! I didn't see him again for another five years until we ended up together again in C Wing, H7, where a bit of history was made. Joe was at the far end of the wing from me and it wasn't until over a year, when I was moved one cell away from him, that I had the full benefit of his *craic* (and he mine, I think). He was a great man to have on the wing as he was a very strong character and the screws, who he stood up to, treaded carefully when approaching him.

Bobby burned with energy and exuded a confidence and a determination that propelled him, and the rest of us, above the boring, monotonous drudgery of the blanket. If I was to describe him in one sentence, I would say he was the type of person who not only made an impression wherever he went but also made a difference. If there was a God handing out talent, he was over-indulgent with Bobby. He was well read, a great narrator and debater, a brilliant singer, musician and a *gaeilgeoir*.

Importantly for us, he was a leader, an organiser and a strategic thinker. It wasn't until after his death on hunger strike that I found out how talented a poet and writer he was also. Bobby gave another dimension to the entertainment at night. He narrated books from memory and he drew from a huge repertoire covering everything from politics to fiction. He organised quizzes and sing songs and did one-man shows. The hairs on the back of my neck rose up when he belted out, and I mean belted out, *The Curragh of Kildare*. His voice carried to the far wing and they fell silent when he sang it. I loved him singing *Band of Gold* by Freda Payne and when performing his one-man shows that was always my request.

When I hear that song, I think of him.

"Now that you're gone all that's left is a band of gold."

It brings me right back to those nights in D Wing, H5, when we forgot our surroundings as his singing transported us to another world. Bobby, if not leading the political debates would have been in the thick of them, some of which became quite heated. Discussions ranged from how we were going to win, to how Ireland would be governed after unification. We were confident we would win. It was just a matter of how it would pan out.

There was a lot of debate about maintaining a parliament in Belfast as well as Dublin. Some felt it would serve only to facilitate sectarianism, others felt it would ease unionists' fears and make a United Ireland more acceptable. In the main, debates were conducted by the same half dozen lads who appeared to have some political knowledge. At least that's how it appeared to most of us who barely had a political thought in our heads. The one-eyed man is king among the blind. Like me, I'm sure others were afraid to open their mouths in case they came across as stupid. Most of us had joined the IRA as a reaction to unionist misrule and British oppression and a desire for a United Ireland. There was no depth to our politics but that was to change.

Toitin being a priority in our lives Bobby came up with an ingenious idea to smuggle it in. Our friends and families bought birthday cards, the ones with padding, which they removed and replaced with *toitin*. The altered cards successfully passed through security. Every week we were celebrating *another* birthday milestone without getting older! Too good to last it was eventually rumbled and padded cards were placed on the banned list.

Paddy O'Hagan

Football, or to be precise 'soccer', was very popular in the wing. However, to many, particularly the country lads, *real* football was the Gaelic sport. Soccer gave us something to discuss, predict and argue over. I had always supported Chelsea but I had a liking for Nottingham Forest because of their player Martin O'Neill. We had gone to the same school. My brother and his were in the same class, and I had befriended and shared some of my classes with one of his other brothers. So, the connection was there, though not the football skills. I sometimes would have watched Martin play soccer in the schoolyard at lunch and think to myself, I could do that. No one else seemed to think so.

On Saturdays orderlies would turn up the volume of the radio at five o'clock – but the screws made sure that didn't happen too often. Even when it was possible to overhear the results it wasn't easy for the top cells to remember them all and mistakes were made. I was glad I wasn't the one passing on the results because football was that sacred to some of the lads, getting them wrong was a hanging offence.

I remember poor 'Paddy O' (O'Hagan) from Greencastle, Tyrone, who knew nothing about football unless it was Gaelic, and he had to read out the results after an orderly had slipped them into his cell. Unfamiliar as he was with the game, he made mistakes pronouncing the teams and this brought both puzzlement and laughter. "Everton 2. Leechester 0!" he shouted.

"Leechester! Who's Leechester?" came the response, despite them knowing. His pronunciations of West Bromwich Albion and Wolverhampton Wanderers had the wing in stitches. His cell mate, 'Sean T' (Treacy), who likewise hadn't a clue about soccer, was shrewd enough to stay out of it and let Paddy read out the results and take the flak. Paddy O and Sean T, who we named 'The Brothers Malone', whether they were caught up in the 'soccer atmosphere', or just wanted to be one of the lads, ended up taking an interest and supporting teams. This was the case with most in the wing. Lads whose only interest was Gaelic football adopted teams. They took their cue from the 'panel', that is the 'experts' who debated the ins and outs of the game. These included Micky Loughran (Fat Mick) supporting Man United; JT, Leeds; Livvy, Nottingham Forest; Finbarr McKenna, West Ham; and Bobby Sands, Aston Villa. The Panel, usually Livvy or Fat Mick, from time to time would have called Paddy O up to the door to hear his take on the soccer scene.

Paddy, whom I seem to recall became a Villa supporter, would be asked an assortment of questions. "What's your prediction for Villa at the weekend?" "Are you happy with Saturday's result?" "Do you think the team will improve/slide/be relegated/win a trophy?" The sort of questions asked on BBC's *Football Focus* of a pundit, because Livvy and Fat Mick elevated Paddy to one. He was their trophy. They had turned him. This *culchie*, who probably hadn't much of a clue what size or shape of ball was used, who knew more about milking cows, was now a soccer pundit! Of course, he wasn't *really* – but for the *craic* he played along and the lads never failed to ask him about Leechester.[5]

---

5 Paddy and his family suffered greatly from the conflict and from life's misfortunes. He served an eight-year prison sentence. After his release loyalists broke into his home and shot dead his wife Kathleen, who was seven months pregnant, in front of their five children. Three years later his youngest son died in a fire in a shed. In 2002 Paddy died of a heart attack and in 2008 another son died in a motorbike accident. Then, in 2020, Patrick, thirty four, died suddenly at home.

From the outset we had petitioned for reading material and invariably met a brick wall. After about a year into the protest Fr Toner succeeded in wresting a concession. We were to be allowed religious magazines and this went a long way to putting the hours in and providing some respite from the boredom. Without a doubt the most popular magazine was *The Word* published by the Divine Word Missionaries. It contained interesting contemporary articles that would not have been out of place in mainstream non-religious magazines. There were interviews with celebrities, such as writers and musicians, and articles about life in Third World countries.

A poor second came *The Messenger*, which was very *definitely* religious, containing stories of the lives of saints, which I have to admit were interesting. Realising that we were receiving some sort of intellectual sustenance the magazines were withdrawn, effectively banned. By then, I was an expert on saints and all the more convinced that sainthood was not for me, not that the thought ever entered my mind. There were some religious books too and one or two gems slipped by the censor simply because of the title. Lucky for us no one told the censor 'never judge a book by its title.' One such gem was about the Abbé Edgeworth which was historical rather than religious. The Abbé, an Irish priest from Longford, was with Louis XVI during his last few days and accompanied him to the scaffold when he was guillotined. I couldn't help feeling sorry for Louis, even though my support was with the revolutionaries.

There was a very strong religious fervour that permeated through all the blanket wings. How much exposure to the written word limited to religious magazines and the Bible contributed to that I cannot say but the most influential factor obviously was our dire situation. What else could we do but pray for a miracle that the gates would fly open and we would be reunited with our loved ones. Or, failing a miracle that we would at least win political status and the protest would end. If God dished out miracles on the basis of the quantity of prayers offered, we'd have won it hands down. Not only were all the protesting wings (bar one) saying rosaries every night, but our families, friends and supporters were praying for us on a daily basis. Many of the lads had rosary beads, wore miraculous medals and scapulars.

The all, bar one, was of course our wing, the 'cynics'. There were one or two lads who suggested the rosary should be said but they were roundly shot down. While it was never actually said, I think the lads in our wing regarded themselves as very strong, and religion, or more precisely praying, was perceived as a crutch, a crutch they didn't need. The very rare incidents of 'squeaky booting' did testify to the strength. However, I'm sure every wing regarded themselves as very strong and the communal recital of the rosary strengthened their bond.

V
FOR THE LONG HAUL

Christmas 1977 came but there was no good will in the form of any concessions. Not that we expected any. It's a day when there is a sting to imprisonment as the separation from family is felt but the strong bond between us helped to alleviate it. Sing songs and quizzes were organised and it was the one day in the year when we had no complaints about the food.

Back in February I never would have imagined that the protest would still be going on at Christmas. I was still on that learning curve and had a long way to go. It was a journey that took another jolt as the New Year approached and Sean McKenna, reflecting on a full year of protest, asked the question what we had achieved and were we anyway nearer our goal. I was taken aback. We were political prisoners; we were refusing to be criminalised and we would never, ever, wear that gear. How could he even question the effectiveness of the protest! It was what we had to do – period. His reflection actually angered me. I suppose it was because not only was I convinced we were taking the right action, but I firmly believed we would win and now, someone who I respected, was breaking into my safe and secure world and shattering it. Sean, by posing the questions, was saying that it wasn't enough. We were in a rut. The screws had accepted our protest and were more than content to let us continue for years to come, possibly confident that it would fizzle out as the realisation dawned on us that it was ineffective.

Locking us up 24/7 actually made the screws' job easier. I was very defensive. Yes, the screws did appear to accept our protest in H5, there were very few incidents but our numbers were increasing, and H3 now had blanket men. We had few incidents because the screws knew we were well-established on the blanket, but in H3, where new blanket recruits were now housed, they were employing their brutal tactics once again, which suggested they were concerned about the growing numbers. As our numbers increased so too did our morale. But if the flow was reduced to a trickle and there was a swing to 'squeaky booting' the governor knew this would have a major negative effect on morale. Therefore, the different regime in H3, I'm sure, was no accident and the direction would have come from the top.

Sean's questioning made me, for the first time, take a critical look at a protest that previously I had just accepted. No doubt this is what it was designed to do. I was still confident that we would win, as wearing that uniform was never an option, but gradually, I began to realise the validity of Sean's point: something extra was needed, but what it would take and whether it came from inside or outside I wasn't sure.

Entering another year of protest, I believe there was a realisation that we were in for the long haul. Married men were still being encouraged to take visits and we overwhelmingly agreed with this decision. However, during discussions there were some voices raised as to why just married men and what of those in long-term relationships and, even, what about our mothers? I remember Willie 'Deek' Johnstone from Belfast's New Lodge stating that he was engaged, therefore, "nearly married", and so why shouldn't he take a visit. JT, always ready, never short of wit, suggested he should, "nearly take a visit."

For me, refusing visits wasn't just to do with not wanting to wear the gear but I felt if we took visits the protest would take on a permanence and psychologically it was important it remained a temporary measure.

Food punishment

Rationing and tampering with food was another weapon employed by the screws. They would use it sometimes as a reaction to the IRA's operations: for example, after a screw was shot. When the IRA bombed the La Mon Hotel (killing twelve innocent civilians), our rations were cut for a number of days.

The screws also stole some of our rations. I recall one day when they cut us to half a fish. Joe McDonnell when handed his plate challenged the screw, the 'Red Rat'. Joe was fearless, he didn't mince his words and the screws, wisely, were cautious when dealing with him. The Red Rat was actually apologetic, closed the door and flew up the wing only to return with a spatula in his grip on which a fish rested.

"There you go, Joe," he grovelled, offering the fish in the hope of pacifying him. But the response was not what he expected. Joe asked where was everybody else's fish, and the Red Rat had no answer. Joe told him to stick his fish where the sun didn't shine and the Rat slunk away like a scolded school boy. It was great to have men like Joe to confront the screws head on, showing leadership and coming out on top. His victories were our victories and his strength strengthened us.

On the boards

On Holy Thursday I was taken to the boards. It must have been for something petty like ripping a page out of the Bible (for rolls) or maybe caught with some form of contraband, like tobacco. I can't remember what it was but as I was to find out it was a bad day to be caught. Three days was the standard time spent on the boards, unless the 'offence' was judged to be more serious, such as striking a screw. Easter was a holiday period therefore there would be no adjudications (i.e. kangaroo courts) until Easter Tuesday, which meant I would be there for at least five days. I was placed in the bottom cell, right next to the yard door which during the day was kept open, meaning I was getting the brunt of the cold air sweeping in. No doubt I was strategically placed in that cell with the yard door probably kept open for my benefit. It was that cold I had to stop pacing the concrete floor as my feet were blue and in pain. Yet, I had to keep moving because to stop meant I would freeze, so I walked up and down on the six-foot wooden board, raised a foot above the floor that served as a bed. With no one to communicate with, cold and restricted to a six-foot piece of wood, it was a very long day and I was relieved when the mattress and blankets were handed in at half eight. I immediately jumped on that mattress and buried myself in the blankets. Ecstasy – heat; there were no other words. My sleep was disrupted several times during the night as a result of the dilapidated condition of the mattress. Unlike the foam mattresses that were the regular issue in the Blocks, this was made of straw, and pieces of the straw, which were more like needles, had pierced through the material and were pricking me. I just couldn't seem to catch a break! Actually, I did get a break the next day when they moved me to a cell which did not get the full brunt of the chilled wind. I didn't know their thinking on the cell move. I only know it was not through any act of kindness and possibly it was the turn of the next victim for the cooler.

In relative and real terms, it did turn out to be a Good Friday. The cell was warmer (but still cool); I was able to pace the floor and that night a couple of lads from the Cages (the political status end of the camp) ended up a few cells from me. They gave me *scéal* on what was happening in the outside world and how things were in the Cages. We fed off each other. They got first-hand information about morale and life on the blanket which they could bring back to the Cages and I was able to bring back their *scéal* to the Blocks.

Over the next few days the boards began to fill up with prisoners from the Blocks. On Easter Monday an orderly, on request from one of the Cages' lads, slipped an *Irish News* under my door. The Cages' lads had not yet faced adjudication, therefore they still had access to parcels. When all was said and done, apart from the start, the boards were turning out all right. A full *Irish News* to read and it was the Easter Monday edition! I was able to read about the republican Easter Parades across the North. I folded the paper as tightly as I could and hid it in a prison sock that was lying in the corner with the rest of the prison gear. It was a long shot, but I had to make the attempt to smuggle it back to the block.

The following day the governor arrived to do the adjudications. I was brought before him naked, no concessionary towel, and, of course, was found guilty. I never heard of anyone ever being found not guilty. To my surprise, he backdated my three days so I was to be brought back to the block that day. I thought it better not to push my luck and ask him to record I was owed two days and so the next time I was back and sentenced to three I would only need do one. His decision must have been influenced by the fact that the boards were almost full, and he needed the cell for the next victim.

Shortly after the adjudications I heard cell doors opening and locks shot as prisoners were brought out to be returned to the Blocks. My door opened and who was it but my old friend Eddie Wylie, now promoted to Senior Officer.

"Right, McCann," he said. "Grab your gear and get out." Obviously, Eddie was not to know that I was still traumatised from the day McFeely gave me that look as I sat in the back of the van with that mark of shame, the gear, sitting on my lap.

"I'm not lifting that gear," I replied with chest out, doing my best to pretend that I was tough.

Wylie screamed, "You *what*!"

As if he was taking this as personal and his honour was being challenged, he made a lunge at me. I took a swing at him. I don't know if this was an instinctive defensive reaction because I doubt if my brain would have given it the go ahead. Possibly, subconsciously, Livvy had something to do with it. When any of the lads were assaulted or beaten up by screws he would always ask, "And what did you do when you were hit?" In other words, did you fight back and if you hadn't, you'd probably be left with the feeling that you had let yourself down. Wylie and I ended up wrestling on the floor. He shouted out to the other screws and they came rushing in and trailed me away. Wylie walked out, followed by the other two screws. I was left to consider what had happened and, more worryingly, what was to come next. What had come over me! I was now facing about three months on the boards for assaulting a screw.

"Damn you, McFeely," I said to myself. "This is all because of you!"

I heard the keys jingling. I bounced up, heart thumping, trying to steady myself for whatever was to happen next. The door swung open. Wylie stomped in, face red and smoke belching out his ears. Poking his finger towards me with each word he spat out, he bawled, "Don't you ever, ever, take a swing for me again!" Yes, I could live with that one. No coaxing required. Then to my unbelieving ears he yelled, "Now, get to fuck out!" I didn't need a second invitation. With gusto I was out the door, pinching myself, and thinking, did he really say that? In double-quick time, leaving the screw escort in my tracks, I was out the front doors and into the yard where the van was parked to take me back to the block. As I was just about to enter the van, I heard a loud thump. I turned around and saw Eddie, who had just kicked the front doors open, with my gear in his arms. With what I can only describe as fury, he tossed the gear up into the air with all the venom of the pent-up rage inside him. It flew in every direction all around the yard.

"There's your fucking gear!" he screamed. What he hoped to achieve by this, I was at a loss. I can only say I didn't take any offence. In fact, I have to say, Good on you Eddie Wylie! You did exactly what every one of us wanted to do. Toss it away. Respect.

I'd say my escort felt very much demeaned as he then had to scurry about the yard picking it up. I literally floated into the van feeling ten feet tall where I was greeted with the sight of the rest of the lads – with the gear on their laps. All eyes, screws and prisoners, turned to my escort as he followed me in holding my gear, which cast him more in the role of my valet. Redemption. McFeely, get a picture of this, I thought. I hope the lads, by my action, were not made to feel vanquished the way I had once. My stance was not worth risking a beating, or worse, making others feel inferior. It was silly of me but whether it was my ego or Tom rankling me, I just had to purge that demon.

The day was to get better. Back in H5, once the screw left my gear in my cell and the door was shut, I immediately grabbed the socks to check, just on the off chance that the *Irish News* might have got through, and lo and behold there it was! The screw, unbeknown, had smuggled it back. I was absolutely chuffed with myself with the day's outcome. A full *Irish News* for the wing, *scéal* from the Cages and exorcism of the guilt from carrying the gear, what more could I ask for. Wing humour being wing humour, instead of kudos for my achievements, I was told I was useless because I didn't bring any *toitín* back.

At the time I couldn't work out why Eddie Wylie did not charge me with assault. Years later, when in H7, where he was the SO and I got to know him, I had a better understanding why. He fancied himself as a bit of a lad and the screws did look up to him. How would it look if I, a skinny runt, was brought before the governor charged with assaulting Eddie (who was over six feet tall)? Eddie's ego and reputation were more important than charging me. If a screw was assaulted the common practice was they would seek their revenge and the prisoner would be in for a hiding. Eddie could easily have followed this practice without impugning his reputation and the fact that he didn't suggests that perhaps some respect is in order.

Arrival of Brendan Hughes

Easter 1978 fell in late March. But earlier that month a number of political status men from the Cages, among them Brendan ('the Dark') Hughes, arrived in the block. There had been an altercation on the visits which resulted in a fight back in the prison yard with screws. The Dark and others were stripped of their political status and sent to the Blocks. Not only had the Dark been totally innocent but, as confirmed by one of the screws, he actively tried to stop the fighting and in doing so saved some screws from very serious injury. The Dark was Camp OC of the Cages and the Blocks and it was obvious the admin had used the fight as a pretext for removing him.

He arrived into A Wing, H5, and we were very glad to have someone of his stature join us. Teddy Crane, who came with him, was placed in the cell with me. The two of us were moved to the top of the wing where for some odd administration reason the top three or four cells were to be allocated to Young Prisoners (YPs). It was part of their pretence that they were going to operate a regime in accordance with the book yet in parallel with that they made their own rules up as they went along.

The average age of the blanket men was nineteen and H5 already had two YP Wings (who we named the Yippee wings) but it wasn't enough for the rising numbers. After a few months they had to abandon the move and blanket men were moved to wherever there was space. At this stage of the protest there were approximately two hundred and fifty on the blanket. In Armagh Prison the women were allowed to wear their own clothes but for refusing to do prison work the republican women faced a raft of punishments, including lock-ups, strip searches, and loss of remission.

The Dark's presence caused a bit of a buzz throughout the block. There was a feeling that something was in the air. A strategic thinker, he would bring some direction to the protest that had seemingly lost momentum. The speculation increased as the Dark and Bobby Sands, in cells across the yard facing each other, communicated continuously in Irish and some code. Once they got up to their windows that was the signal for others within hearing distance, afraid of missing anything, to have their ears cocked to the conversation. A pin could be heard dropping. The problem was very few of us had Irish, we had no idea what was being said, only that it concerned us, and this became a big incentive to learn the language.

A couple of days later, Bobby called everyone up to the doors, told the scouts at the top of the wing to be vigilant for screws (not Bears!) as he had matters of importance to reveal and discuss. The protest he said, which really meant the Dark *said*, was ineffective and leading us nowhere. There it was again, that word 'ineffective'. I could just about take that from Sean McKenna who had spent months on the protest, but from the Dark, whose coat was still swinging in H-Block reception, that was too much! It got worse. Bobby, acting on the Dark's behalf, asked our thoughts on putting on the gear, going into the conforming Blocks with the aim of wrecking their system from within. The lads were vehemently opposed to the idea. Putting on the gear just could not be countenanced. Likewise, the thought that we couldn't win was just not in our thinking. Bobby, playing the devil's advocate, tried to reason it out but no one would listen. The Dark came in for some negative banter.

"Tell him to do his whack!"

"Is he missing his cream buns and newspapers in the Cages?"

(Deprivation had us exaggerating and elevating the conditions in the Cages.)

Not that the Dark heard this, nor did we really doubt his commitment. It was just the idea of giving in and putting on the badge of a criminal that had us livid. Even if the Dark had been on the protest from day one, we would have rejected the idea – but his cause wasn't helped by being only in the door.

Despite the negative reception to his idea the Dark was not going to allow things to remain as they were. We were soon to learn that he had a strategy to make the protest effective. Excitement grew as we awaited this to unfold and the shouting, as *Gaeilge*, between Bobby and the Dark intensified. There was to be a gradual escalation in the protest. Every Monday there was a step up. It began with refusing to brush and mop out our cells. The following Monday we refused to accept the basins to wash. What a relief that was. Just about everybody hated those basins with their one inch of cold water! The screws dreaded Mondays because they didn't know what was coming next. We, and not they, were now in control of events. We refused to wash, we refused to slop out and so the 'No wash, no slop out protest' came into being. Our morale was sky high, we felt like we were winning and in contrast the screws were totally demoralised.

When the governor came into the wing to do the fortnightly adjudications he was met with a cacophony of noise as we banged the chamber pots against the steel doors. Prior to escalation, to give it an air of officialdom, a table was set outside the cell door for the governor to adjudicate the prisoner. This was the compromise from the days they had dragged us out naked to the Circle. Compromise was now over. They had to abandon the practice of the table as the wing was awash with noise and we refused to stand at the door. The governor had to enter the cell where the prisoners would ignore him and because it became that farcical, they moved this silly procedure to every month instead of two weeks.

Directions were continually shouted across from A Wing to Bobby and he would *scairt* across to Seanna Walsh in C Wing. (A would shout to B). Hoping to disrupt the chain of communication Bobby and other *scairteoirí* were moved. Fat Mick, who had some Irish, replaced Bobby as *scairteoir*. Most of the commands that Mick had to *scairt* began with *Na Bí* (Don't be). *Na bí ag cuir na braillíní amach* (Don't be putting the sheets out), *Na bí ag fluiche amach* (Don't be slopping out). From that Mick became known as Micky Na Bi.

Beatings intensify

As conditions deteriorated, orderlies – whether they could no longer work in such squalid conditions or simply were refusing orders – were replaced with those who appeared to be motivated by the same hatred towards us as the screws. The environment became hostile, extremely

86

tense. Beatings that were rare in H5 now became a regular occurrence. Slopping out in particular became the main friction point. The orderlies hated going around the cells with a bucket and the screws hated it just as much. Spillages, deliberate and accidental, occurred. Urine could be splashed on orderlies' hands, on the boots and trousers of the screws. Heated words would be exchanged which often led to violence, at the wrong end of which would be the prisoner.

As all blanket men will testify, the worst aspect of the protest was listening to someone receiving a beating. The scuffling, yells, the dull thud of a head banging against a wall, the smack of fist and boot on skin. Soul-destroying to listen to, and the sense of helplessness was agonising. Lads would shout out, berate the cowardly actions of the screws and let them know we knew who they were. Venting anger and frustration, comrades would throw the contents of a chamber pot around screws identified as abusers. Of course, this led to more beatings but, despite the obvious repercussions some of the lads, enraged, felt compelled to retaliate.

Events moved at a fast pace, in a direction of which we weren't always in control. There was an incident in C Wing and Seanna *scairted* that the screws were taking the furniture out of the cells. As I recall it, there was also a window broken. So, in order that no one could be singled out, the order came to smash the windows and the furniture. Teddy and I being in the top cell didn't manage to smash everything as we were the first in the wing to be invaded by the very irate screws. The chair in particular was difficult to smash because as I swung it against the floor it kept springing back up. In our defence I have to say that we did manage to smash the window and throw most of the broken bits of furniture out into the yard. The yard, littered with broken furniture, was like a collection point for a Twelfth of July bonfire. The screws removed what was left in the cell and to my surprise and relief we were not assaulted. This was possibly due to the fact that the screws were exhausted racing around cells salvaging what was left. However, C Wing did not fare so well. A number of men there received bad beatings.

The windows were now without glass. In the cell we had two mattresses, six blankets (three each), a chamber pot, water gallon and, to contemplate the error of our ways, a Bible.

We were jubilant. We were taking on the system and we felt victorious. The sense of permanence and normality that had befallen the protest previous to the escalation was now gone. We felt that an end was now in sight and that we were clearly on top. When the Dark was asked by our wing how well did he think the protest was going, he famously said, "We're on the pig's back." (This is an expression from the Irish *ar mhuin na muice*, which is used colloquially to mean 'well off' or 'in luck'.)

However, we were to learn that we had underestimated the Brits' determination and overestimated our impact. Just like 'Wee Buns', 'the pig's back' became part of the wing lexicon to mean the *direct opposite*! During those periods when events either didn't go as anticipated or went against us, quite often the words, "We're on the pig's back", could be heard echoing in the wing.

With the windows out and the mattresses on the ground we felt a bit like campers. It was easier to hear and swing to adjoining cells. This brought a dramatic increase in the conversations between the sides of A and D Wings that were opposite each other across the yard. The lads on our wing in the cells opposite us, whose windows faced onto the derelict exercise yard, at times became a bit annoyed with this because while the chatter stopped around 10pm to allow for a wing activity, they hadn't been a part of exchanges and it did affect that sense of a unit or even a family. Isn't that what affects solidarity within a group, when some have more than others? The side looking across to A Wing not only had the advantage of being able to talk but to see the faces of the lads opposite. This side could also see all the coming and goings to the block – arrivals of governors, screws, orderlies, chaplains. Confined to a cell 24/7 this did make the day that little bit more interesting. I suppose they could be referred to as the 'sea view' rooms.

Spy holes and hoses

The spy hole, or hatch, on the cell door, was really a slit made of glass measuring about 30cm by 4cm and was covered on the outside with a hinged metal flap. Screws would lift the flaps when doing their checks and in the early hours of the morning they'd bang them down to wake us. They were usually too lazy to do checks at night, but they had to hit the buttons at the far end of each wing every hour (or was it two hours?), otherwise an alarm would go off, or so we thought. We discovered later that if the button wasn't pressed the Central Control Room would radio through to find out why. If there was no answer then the alarm would go off. Compelled to walk to the bottom of each wing the screws would use their batons to whack the cell doors as they made their way to and from the buttons. It was quite a shock to the system to be suddenly awakened by the loud bang of wood on metal, if indeed we were asleep. Sleep deprivation was just another weapon in their arsenal. Thankfully, they could not sustain the banging, possibly because some of their number were sleeping and they had to think about the orderlies. However, it was a tactic always at their disposal and was used periodically. While blind hatred could explain their behaviour, there were other explanations. For example, they could be retaliating for a prison officer having been shot by the IRA, or because we had escalated our protest another notch.

We discovered that the button for the cell bell (inserted in all cells for emergencies) could be unscrewed and pulled out. Once extracted we learned it was a bar, about 15cms long, rather than a button, and we used it to smash the glass in the spy slit. We'd then put it back in (for use another day) and the screws were baffled at how we were able to break the glass. With the glass gone we could lift the outside flap and see the cell opposite, and they us. We could literally see the whites of each other's eyes. Communication having been restricted to sound it was a bit of a jump to have visibility and this caused some excitement. To explain, it was like your old black and white television being replaced with a colour set.

There was a downside to this. One night, C Wing *scairted* across that the screws were in the wing, hosing the cells. They were using one of the fire hoses that were at the top of each wing. Bobby, who was still in our wing at the time, *scairted* across to the Dark for direction. As always, the communication was conducted in Irish so I had no idea what the response was until it reached me *as Bearla* (in English), having travelled from cell to cell, via the pipes. "Do nothing!" came the command. Teddy and I looked at each other in bewilderment. We concluded they're having a laugh or there's been a mistake in translation. There was no need for Ted to ask me to check if the message was correct. I was on to it right away, rapping the pipes to next door and praying to God it was just a joke. I could hear the pipes being knocked from cell to cell as the message went down the chain and then back up again.

"Just lie there and do nothing," was the message again! I wanted to contest this but it was in the early hours of the morning and even at the best of times I probably would have been told to fuck off. The lads just wanted to sleep. Sleep? How could they? I was crapping myself, and Ted was the same. We were the first cell at the top of the wing and odds were we would be visited first. There was nothing for it but to lie down and pull the blankets over me. Ted did likewise and like me I'm quite sure he lay awake, alert to every sound in the wing and fearful of what could happen. I held out the hope for a while that the lads were just mixing but as the minutes passed the hope faded. We didn't have to wait too long before we heard the screws.

The cell flap was lifted, revealing a rectangle of light. Ted and I pretended to be sleeping. Outwardly, it displayed that we were unaffected by their harassment. We weren't trembling or shirking in a corner. Inwardly, anxiety levels were sky high at this act of madness. The screw peering through the hatch began sniggering and laughing, like a schoolboy desperately trying to maintain composure in order not to come to the attention of the teacher.

"Look," he said, excitedly, but in a whisper to his partner, obviously anxious not to wake us up. "They're sleeping." I recognised the voice. It was Monty, a wee squirt of a screw. I would not have put him down as one of the worst but given that he was acting as if he had just won the Lotto, he was clearly determined to drench us, but I hoped that he would be satisfied with just a few bursts of the hose to wake us up. The hose was aimed through the flap and a jet of freezing cold water hit me directly on the head. It took my breath away. I didn't move. "Lie there and do nothing," was the order. My head felt like it was being squeezed with a clamp. My body tensed, I gripped the blankets, trying with all my might and will power not to move but it just went on and on. I was on the verge of giving in when he turned the hose on Teddy. I had my back to Ted but I knew that he too didn't move. My breathing and racing heart beat were just beginning to abate when unbelievably that little squirt turned the hose back on me. This was too much. I couldn't catch my breath. My head was going to explode. It went on and on. It was if I was drowning. Unable to endure it any longer I jumped up and covered the hatch with my arm. Monty and his partner were in fits of laughter. He was, after all, as bad as the rest. It must have been his size that kept him in check. I was livid. Why did we put ourselves in a position where we couldn't win? Worse, the screws had been handed a victory because by jumping up, as much as it kills me to say it, was me breaking. Giving in. They had their victory and entertainment. It would have made more sense to have blocked the hatch with my arm or blanket before they had the chance to put the hose in.

There we were, the two of us, left standing shivering in the cell and not knowing where to turn next. We needed warmth but the blankets and mattresses were soaked. Exhausted, we had no choice but to get back on the sodden mattresses and put the soaking blankets over us. For a while we continued to shiver and I felt we'd be lucky if we could stick it out until the morning, and if we did, I also felt that we would be carried out with pneumonia. The thought then hit me that maybe this was what the Dark envisaged and perhaps "Do nothing," wasn't that mad after all. It had the potential of making the news and exposing some of the torture we were being subjected to, and, possibly, at the very least could have ended the dreaded hosing. As it turned out, despite the soaked mattresses and blankets, we did heat up, survived the night and didn't contract pneumonia. It took us a couple of days to dry everything out, but we managed.

If this was in the Dark's plan it didn't work, the hosing not only continued but got worse. However, a lesson was learned.

We would never again lie down and just take it.

A few days later Seány McVeigh in C Wing smacked Monty and was trailed off to the boards.

Any time the cell door opened there was the potential for confrontation because basically they were at war with us. The main trigger for violence was slopping out. The screws hated escorting orderlies from cell to cell with the slopping-out bucket (as much as we hated it ourselves) and therefore I suppose it was inevitable that it would come to an end.

Protest escalates

It wasn't surprising that in response to the assaults and to minimise our injuries we simply stopped slopping out. It was a continuation of that downward spiral that had a momentum of its own. However, it did come as a shock when the order came to put the excrement on the walls. I felt that even within the brutality and inhumanity in the H-Blocks there had to be limits to the lengths we would go. Screws and some orderlies had poured urine back and thrown faeces into the cells, but I wasn't convinced our response was the inevitable and correct one. It was total anathema to me, going against everything I was taught while growing up. It was undignified, uncivilised and animal-like. It was the most difficult IRA order I ever had to follow – but follow it I did. It most certainly wasn't a fist in the air moment that other escalations had brought; just the opposite. I had to dig deep, as no doubt all my comrades did and, while it did become easier as the weeks, months and years passed, I was never comfortable with it. I could understand that we were prepared to do whatever we could to achieve our demands and avoid hunger strike. Hunger strike in all probability would mean death, death of one or more of my comrades, therefore I wasn't really in a position to have qualms over a bit of shit on a wall.

Our living conditions were that bad – no washing and surrounded in our own waste – that most of us believed the prison could not sustain the situation and it would only be a matter of time before they had to give way. We were 'on the pig's back.' Time being weeks as we felt under these conditions the body could not escape ailments and that it could lead to an epidemic. However, time was to tell us how wrong we were and that we had underestimated the durability and adaptability of the human body. There were no epidemics or serious illnesses and time was also to demonstrate that what was at first regarded as abnormal and inhuman became normalised and acceptable.

We threw waste food in the corner and out into the yard where we watched seagulls scramble for whatever was available. Rats also came out scurrying about for our offerings. We named one of them Ben and adopted him as one of our own. I've no idea how we could have done this because I couldn't tell one rat from another! Hours were spent watching Ben (or at least an increasingly plump rat pretending to be Ben) furtively darting to and from the yard, avoiding the boots of the screws and their hoses. The rats had an advantage over us in that respect as they could run.

The screws and the orderlies used a high-pressure hose about 15-16cms in diameter, which was the same as that used by the fire-brigade. It was another weapon and a very potent one. During their daily hosing of the yard they turned it on us. Sometimes it was just a quick spray which was enough to soak the cell and the mattresses. We had to be quick enough to squeeze into the corner, evading the worst of the jet, with the mattress held a foot or so off the ground and clamped between the wall and our bodies to keep it off the waterlogged floor. There were times when the hoses were set to full force – and had me regretting smashing the window. Ted and I would have no choice but to sacrifice one of the mattresses to block the window. The other mattress, between us, we held precariously above our heads with the blankets on top. We used all our strength to hold the mattress against the bars as the jet had considerable force and was enough to knock you off your feet. The jet forced the mattress to belly and the water would run down, spilling into the cell and covering our feet. When the hosing was finished one of us would continue to hold the mattress up while the other used the lid of the chamber pot to bail out the cell, scraping the water out under the door. We would sleep that night as best we could on the one mattress head to toe.

The Red Rat was one of a number of screws who revelled in hosing us. I remember him coming in one morning, walking up the yard, and singing, to the tune of the *Teddy Bear's Picnic*, "Because today's the day/The Provies are having their hose down!"

"Fluiche amach!"

Each night, around nine or ten o'clock, after the lines were shot across the wing, the OC gave the order to *"Fluiche amach!"* which meant we were to empty the urine from the chamber pots out onto the wing landing. Like most new situations it took a while to perfect a system. We experimented, funnelling it out the side of the door. That was a disaster! Then we poured it under the door using the chamber pot lids to scrape the back flow out again. Depending on the floor level, quite a bit of time could be spent scraping it out and inevitably it trickled back in again until the screws had squeegeed the wing dry. Next, we came up with the idea of building a dyke. We squeezed bread under the door and sealed it with margarine, leaving a gap to pour the *fluiche* out and quickly sealing it once completed. It was a marginally better system, but sealing those last few inches was testing, depending on the level of the cell floor. Finally, we overcame this difficulty by building a semi-circle wall of bread and margarine, into which the *fluiche* was poured and from there it flowed onto the landing. A little might be left in the pool but at least it didn't seep back into the cell.

The dykes weren't without their problems. Firstly, they were made from bread and bread was the staple part of our diet. The food at times was so bad that it was the bread that kept us alive. While needs must we weren't happy about donating some of our ration for the dyke. Through time we had dyke building down to a fine art and reduced what was required to two rounds of bread – a round each. Our biggest problem was one we had no control over – the screws squeegeeing. The night guard had to squeegee the *fluiche* out of the wing before they went off duty the following morning. When we first began pouring out the *fluiche* it was a battle royal with the screws squeegeeing it back into our cells. This was devastating during those early days when we either had no dykes or had not perfected them. We had to be alert, ready to lift up our bedding to prevent it being soaked in urine that was driven back in. The screws knew we couldn't stay alert all night and some timed the squeegeeing in the very early hours to catch us out – and catch us out they did.

Just like the banging of the doors, to be suddenly awakened with a wave of urine splashing in was quite a shock. While the screws had their fun, they realised that pushing the *fluiche* into the cells meant it would inevitably come back out again. They had to sweep the wing clean and how far they were prepared to do battle with us was related to their bigotry. The bigger the bigot, as long as we were being given a rough time, the less the concern about squeegeeing the wing two or three times.

Screws who were indifferent just wanted to get the clean-up done as quickly as possible; they weren't going to create more work by driving the *fluiche* into the cells. Thankfully, even the worst of the bigots lacked the staying power and after several weeks of battle their desire for an easier time, by simply sweeping the *fluiche* straight out the door at the end of the wing, without the detours, gradually became the sensible option. That's not to say they stopped it altogether. They didn't; and too many times lads lured into a false sense of security were caught out.

Gerry McConville (at this time my cell mate) and I were dealt a particular bad hand. We ended up in the bottom cell beside the yard door where the screws pushed the *fluiche* out. By the time the *fluiche* had been squeegeed down to us it was like a tidal wave. Too many times a *tsunami* of urine came crashing into our cell, bursting through the dyke, spraying us and soaking our bedding. Unfortunately for Gerry and myself, the screws were prepared to push it into the end cell because while they knew we would scrape it back out, it wasn't as if they had to squeegee it the whole way down the wing again. Since they had to come down the wing again to test the button, it was only a matter of grabbing the squeegee and with two or three shoves the *fluiche* would be out the door, or back into our cell!

VI
SUMMER OF '78

We threw waste and unwanted food in the corner. I never was a great fan of vegetables, especially cabbage, of which there was never a shortage. Twice a week the dinner would consist of potatoes and cabbage and somewhere in there would be a bit of meat which we referred to as 'spot the meat'. It was very thin, like you see in the cheap packets of sliced ham for sandwiches, and full of fat. We dreaded the 'fry' (well, maybe Hector didn't). It consisted of dry soda bread, a hard-boiled egg and a slice of 'hairy bacon' and as a rule was stone cold. After a couple of weeks maggots, in their dozens, crawled out of the waste. They littered the floor – got under the mattress, on the mattress, all going in the same direction, towards the pipes. We scooped them up and threw them out the window for the birds but there was always more crawling about.

At night, if I felt something tickly, perhaps imagining it more times than enough, I'd jump up, shake out the blankets and turn up the mattress. I don't know if it was because of the maggots, the rotting smell or for reasons of hygiene, but one Sunday while we were at Mass, masked screws shovelled the waste out of the cells. Disturbing the piles released a foul gas and it was really bad, even for us hardened to the worst of aromas. It had our eyes watering and our stomachs turning.

Another unrelenting enemy came from within. At first, I didn't know what the cause was until one morning when I awoke and saw a number of the little creatures crawling on the mattress. The sight of these worms and the thought that they had been (and their cousins still were) inside me, revolted me. But it explained the exasperating itch: although infecting the gut threadworms lay their eggs around the anus from where they hatch. How was I ever going to endure this? However, just like other challenges associated with the protest, at first it seemed impossible but through time the body and the mind adapted, and while never easy, it was accepted.

That was the first and last time they removed the waste while the wing was occupied. They introduced a new procedure. A wing would be moved to an empty and clean wing on average every fortnight. The screws, kitted out in what I could only describe as space-suits, would move in with power hoses and chemicals, clean the vacated dirty wing and shovel the waste out.

B Wing was moved to H4, leaving one wing empty, making it possible to clean and move wings on a rotational basis.

Wing shifts meant leaving the cell – which left us vulnerable to assault.

Our time spent with no windows was not deemed to last, although it did last much longer than either we or the administration imagined. The usual regimented routine of life in the block was broken one day with the arrival of a squad of Trade Screws. They decamped outside A Wing, which had just been shifted to the empty B Wing. We, in the cells facing A, stood at our smashed windows gazing over, curious to discover what they were at, and appreciating the opportunity to watch something different from the norm.

They grabbed their tools and set to work chipping away the remnants of glass left in the windows. Then, to our disappointment, off-loaded sheets of Perspex from their van, making it obvious to us that this was to replace the glass windows. The disappointment must have registered on our faces because the screws appeared to become buoyant and began a slanging match.

"What's you Provies going to do now, eh?" they jeered. "You'll not be able to break these windows!" To prove the point and to rub our noses in it one began banging the new Perspex window with his hammer and triumphantly shouted, "Look, you can't break them, see! They're unbreakable." These words were hardly out of his mouth when with another hammer blow the Perspex smashed! We roared with laughter and some of our wits weren't short of a few comments to rub it in to them. There wasn't another word from the Trades, but while we had our moment of fun, which had lifted us, reality soon descended. We didn't have hammers. The Perspex did look final.

The following day, experiencing our first wing shift, we were moved into A Wing. I don't recall any incidents of brutality which were to become characteristic of these shifts. There was no longer anyone in the wing facing us and the Perspex did spell the end of the communication out the windows.

However, we still had the pipes and shuttering holes to communicate with adjoining cells, not to mention out of the doors.

A couple of weeks before we were moved to A Wing, we discovered there were two shuttering holes at the bottom of the walls that ran lengthwise down the cells. The shuttering holes had been filled in with cement and were thus a weakness, in comparison to the solid walls. They had been painted to blend in with the rest of the wall. Careful tapping revealed their position and we set about hacking the cement out with the brass bars that we unscrewed from the cell bell. I wouldn't say having hacked through the holes and seeing our neighbours was on par with the euphoria when the French and English met digging the Channel Tunnel, but it was a cause for celebration and again we had undermined the system. We discovered also the area of the walls around the pipes was filled with cement which we dug out. In some cells the holes that were created were wide enough to put an arm through. Paul McGlinchey in C Wing learned this to his cost. He put his arm through to Benny Lynch and his cellmate Gerry (O) McConville in the next cell and they tied it to their pipes. He spent the whole day like that!

The screws alerted to the sound of our excavating organised a search party to hit the wing. Being in the top cell I was able to hear a senior officer instructing them to find whatever tools we used to hollow out the holes. Before the door opened, I replaced the brass bar into the aperture for the bell but it wouldn't screw in! While the bar was fully inserted and as such looked just like the bell button (as it was supposed to), it would not engage the threads with the internal screw that secured it. Our cell was hit first so I had little time attempting to secure the bar and while I stayed with it right up until I heard the keys in the door, I didn't succeed. Panicking, I threw some margarine from the waste tip in the corner onto the bell button to cover the marks left from the hammering and to dissuade the screws from touching it. Regrettably, they did touch it. My heart sank as I watched a screw twist the button and pull it out to reveal that it was a bar. Talk about the cat that got the cream. Out he raced holding the bar aloft like a trophy shouting, "Sir, sir, look what I've got!"

I could hear the senior office congratulating him in terms that I felt were so over the top that anyone listening might be forgiven for thinking he was being nominated for the Victoria Cross. It left me feeling really bad. The bar was caught in my cell. I had failed to secure it. It was my fault that all the bars in the bells were subsequently removed. Did I confess this to the lads? No way. They'd have tortured me. I probably would have been branded for life with a name like 'Buttons'. The guilt was bad enough without being reminded about it every day. My conscience was eased somewhat with the belief that they would have found it in one or more of the other cells. The bars were gone, a confession wasn't going to bring them back.

The windows, with no 'hammers' (or even a brass rod) to smash them, were going to be a permanent fixture and that meant an end to the swinging. Luckily, we had dug out the shuttering holes so we could still pass things from cell to cell. However, we knew it would only be a matter of time before the administration found a way to block them. Indeed, within a few weeks the Trades were back and welded metal plates around the pipes and over the holes.

Burning the windows

However, before that happened, we were already a step ahead as we had found a solution to the Perspex. Yes, it may have been unbreakable but it was flammable. All that was needed was a flame and I had become quite the expert at that. JT had been the source of a 'light' for the wing but one day when the screws introduced a metal detector it went berserk when waved near his ass. He was taken away and told he either shits the lighter out or the doctor will use forceps. JT chose the former.

Necessity being the mother of invention we came up with other ways to get a light. We experimented with different methods of creating a spark and making tinder that would ignite until we had it perfected. About an inch of the plastic handle of a fork, knife or spoon was snapped off. This was heated until one end began to melt then a flint was embedded. A flint was too small to be held steady on its own while being struck so the inch of plastic handle was just enough to secure the necessary grip. The flint was struck by a sliver of glass recovered from the broken windows and hidden in a mattress. This produced a good spark and we named this device a 'splunker'. A 'splunk' was a light. For tinder the fibres from towel threads were pulled apart to produce something akin to cotton wool. A paper hanky was twisted into a taper and the fibre placed on top. Once the spark hit the fibre it ignited which in turn lit the taper. The paper hanky came from our monthly parcel, although parcel is too grand a description. Initially, we were allowed one parcel which was limited to a bar of soap and three packets of paper hankies. With the no-wash protest soap was no longer required and why they allowed in the hankies, given the muck we were surrounded in, I've no idea. Not that I was complaining because they came in handy for tapers. The initial light came from a red head (a match with most of its stem broken off) which had been smuggled in along with *toitin*. Later, the lads smuggled in the wheel mechanism from lighters to produce a spark.

When the command came to burn the windows, I took out my *splunker*, set the taper alight and held it against the Perspex. Disappointedly, as the taper burnt down to my fingers the Perspex showed no signs of lighting and only turned black where the flame touched it. I tried again without success. Then one of the lads shouted out that his window was alight. He had placed some sponge from his mattress beside the window and set it alight. The sponge burned long enough for the Perspex to catch fire. My cellmate, 'Portadown' (aka Kevin Keegan), ripped off some sponge, spread some margarine on it and I set it alight and placed it beside the window. Sure enough, within a couple of minutes up went the Perspex. It burnt with such ferocity that we had real concerns for our safety as thick black toxic fumes filled the cell and choked us. I'll not deny the thought did cross my mind to hit the bell, except there was no bell as the screws had taken the brass rods out. Was I going to be the author of my own downfall? But that thought was only fleeting. There was no way I was going to call for help from any screw. Wasn't I an RTP, I hoped? Thankfully, as the window burned and melted away leaving an opening for much needed fresh air to enter, we were able to breathe again. Success was sweet; that feeling of victory at again having beaten the system.

I used the splunker to pass a light next door to Jackie McMullan and Gerry McConville (my soon-to-be cellmate), but they weren't having much luck. Several times I had to pass lights in and I have to say, feeling chuffed with my success, I did rub in their lack of success. Jackie was good measure for it as he was forever mixing and I wasn't for letting his failure pass. He wasn't alone: several of the lads didn't manage to burn out the Perspex. The following day the screws smashed what was left as they knew it was only a matter time before they were burnt out and they didn't want any more damage. The burning had scorched the walls and melted the gutters.

We decide to take visits

To ensure there was ongoing communication with *Taobh Amuigh* the block camp staff encouraged us to take visits. While the majority followed the request (it was never an order), initially I couldn't bring myself to do so. At that stage I had been on the blanket over a year, I had never taken a visit because it meant temporarily wearing the gear. I still held out some hope that a few more months would see us gain political status and, when that day arrived, I could take personal pride in never having worn the gear. The idea of wearing the prison uniform was still too much of a leap for me. It wasn't until the end of 1978, faced with another year of protesting, that it began to dawn on me we were in for the long haul. So, I decided it was time to take the visits.

The visits were good for *scéal* which we craved and, in the view of many, and more importantly, the supply of *toitin*. There was an expectation, whether a smoker or not, that you would smuggle back a *bairt* (a small parcel containing tobacco). As soon as someone was back from a visit the first question they were asked was, "*An bhfuair tú é?*" (Did you get it?) The wing held its breath awaiting the response, praying it would be, "*Fuair mé é!*" (I got it!) Loud cheering and celebration would accompany a positive result. If it was negative, "*Ni Fhuair mé,*" abuse would follow. "Waster." "What are you taking visits for anyway?" This was just banter, part of jail life that we all knew not to take personally, even when we were at the end of it, which we all were at some time or other. There was no room for sensitivity and with the ongoing banter thick skins soon developed.

Bangling

It wasn't easy to '*fuair*' a *bairt* on a visit as the screws kept a very tight eye on blanket men. The operation depended not only on the prisoner but, and more importantly, on the visitors. If caught, the visitors would be banned from the jail and the prisoner sent to the boards. We had our experts, both prisoners and visitors, and *bairteanna* got through. We did have our dry periods but usually there was a trickle of *toitín*.

Our wing touched lucky with the arrival of 'Dikel' Gorman and Seany Bateson. They were appealing their case, which meant they were entitled to three appeal visits a week and both were experts at '*fuairing*' *bairteanna*. Their presence spelt the end of the 'Famine' and the beginning of the 'Feast'. They were placed at the top of the wing in the cell next to me, which meant they were now in the first cell in the wing. If there was a raid their cell would likely be hit first, providing me with some warning, giving me time to conceal *splunker* and *toitín*. As a result of my position next door to Dikel and Seany, I was landed, or some might say *gifted*, the role of controlling the wing's *toitín* supply. They did not know how to roll *toitín* so they would pass the *bairteanna* through the shuttering holes to me and I would roll for the wing. Sometimes they would have 'skins' (cigarette paper), but more often than not I would roll the *toitín* in toilet paper. From one square of paper I could make eight rolls. I have to admit I really loved that role. It was like having employment and just like employment it gave a purpose to my life. Normally, the *toitín* production line flew into service once the screws locked up for the night at 8.30, but now with a regular supply, I threw caution to the wind and rolled during the lock-up after dinner. The shuttering holes meant the rolls could be passed quickly down the line from cell to cell (but only on our side) to provide the lads with their after-dinner smoke.

Learning Gaelic

I was that busy I had to 'contract out' some of the work to Jackie, the other neighbour, who was an expert roller. The role gave me power and I unashamedly used it to the hilt to wind up Jackie. I would keep him waiting for the *toitin*, hoping I could get him to plead, although he was always too proud. No matter, I knew he was eating his heart out waiting. "Any chance, Big Jim?" he'd ask, all sweetness and light. "Busy, Jack. Try me later." Or I might suggest, "What's the word, Jack?" and if a 'please' was extracted it would not have been in a mannerly tone. He was a wind-up merchant and I was only getting my own back. When he first moved next door, I asked him if he would teach me Irish as I knew he was a bit of a *gaelgeoir* (Irish speaker).

"No problem," he said and told me to clear a space on the wall to write out vocabulary. We used the metal end of a toothpaste tube to write on the walls and when that went, we used the tip of a miraculous medal. Like the eager beaver I cleared a space and couldn't wait to start – but Jackie could! After several polite, well-mannered appeals he did eventually come to the pipes to begin a *rang*. As he gave me the words in Irish and their meaning, I would ask for the spelling and I would write them down quickly, anxious to be the good student and keep him on board. It took about four or five words for me to realise that he was winding me up although what had me mad was that I should have caught on after the first word, it was that ridiculous, and the spelling was even worse! I felt stupid but at least no one knew.

This was not the case for my cell mate Portadown. He loved singing and in fairness to him, although at times it drove me mad, he had a good voice. Foolishly, he would ask Jackie for the lyrics of songs and of course Jackie would oblige, but he would make changes and, again, to the point of ridiculousness. I remember one of the milder ones was with *Henry Joy* which goes, "He kissed his sister and went aloft…" Jackie changed it to, "He kissed his sister Gwendalot…"

Names of lads in the wing were inserted into songs but Portadown just thought this was an amazing coincidence. Emboldened with his success, Jackie took it too far and Portadown eventually caught on. However, to our amusement, he continued to belt out songs doctored by Jackie and to this day I suspect he is still singing about Gwendalot. Portadown brought laughter to that hell hole and for that we will always remember him fondly.

After the Feast came the Famine. The appeal visits were stopped, the supply dried up, the *toitin* rolls became thinner and thinner until non-existent. I lost my power, joined the unemployed and had to content myself that it was good while it lasted.

In desperation Jackie suggested we try making a roll with potato skins. We had nothing to lose and plenty of time on our hands to kill. The skins kept from the dinner were placed on the pipes to dry until flaky. This was crushed and rolled into the toilet paper. It did light and burn like a cigarette but the taste was stomach-turning. After four of five puffs I couldn't take anymore as I felt that I was going to be sick. Seany, equally desperate for a smoke, was aware that we were going to experiment with the potato skins and wanted to be included. Jackie had a little bit of *toitin* left, just enough for one last roll (at least that's what he told me). He suggested we pass it into Seany and tell him it was potato skins. He fell for this big time. He jumped up to the door and excitedly announced to the wing, as if a scientific breakthrough had just been made, that they must try potato skins, they were fantastic, even better than the real thing.

Jackie and I and our cellmates were in stitches, the mix went much better than expected and we knew what was shortly to unfold as the lads set about drying out the skins in anticipation of a smoke, "better than the real thing." Sure enough, as the wing filled with the sickening smell of potato skins burning, the discontented shouting began. "Disgusting!" "It's making me sick!" and abuse was hurled at a very confused Seany Bateson. "Bateson are you sick in the head?" "Is this your idea of a joke?" When the smoke settled, so to speak, we confessed to him. Shortly after that Seany and Dikel were moved out of the wing.

Breaching the Sterile

We were moved to B Wing which looked across an unused area (known as 'the Sterile') to C Wing and both were at the back of the block where there was no coming and going, unlike looking out onto the front. However, it was good to have occupants in the wing across from us again and even better that it was the 'Yippee' wing.

There was nothing wrong with the Dark's wing. However, we had faced them for over a year and it was good to have the opportunity to shout across to others. I was particularly pleased because facing me was an old friend, 'Gilly' (Brian Gillen) from Lenadoon. Although I had spoken to him at Mass a month earlier, we still had a lot of catching up to do. If there was local *scéal* to be had, he had it. The problem was he had no filter. Some things were better left unsaid or at the very least couched in diplomatic language. Not with Gilly who shot from the hip. There was no soft landing on hearing bad *scéal*. One night he called me.

"McCann! Get up to your window."

I got up to the window and shouted, "What do you want?"

"Your girlfriend got married."

I was speechless. I knew the wings were waiting my response. I had none to offer. I got down from the window stunned. I didn't care what the rest of the lads were thinking. They obviously knew I was taking it bad.

The lack of screw movement at the back of the block provided the opportunity to try something new. Comms, *teachtaireachtí*, from the IRA outside and the staff inside would circulate on an ongoing basis. If wings were on the same side of the corridor (A and B, for example), comms could be easily passed when prisoners came together for Mass but it was much more difficult to pass to the far side of the block (C and D): separated by the Circle; the yard at the front and the sterile at the back, separating B and C. It wasn't unknown for comms to be smuggled out on visits from one side of the block and smuggled back to the other side.

C Wing had a comm for our OC and it was decided we would try to make a line between B and C. It was left to the cells at the top of the wings to try because the bottom end was where the screws entered when checking the yard and if they appeared this would leave no time to pull the line in. Whereas they would have to make a thirty-yard dash to the top of the block and that would leave enough time to pull it in avoiding capture.

The distance between the wings was about twenty-five yards. This would mean our wing would have to throw a line that would reach at least 13 or 14 yards, and likewise C Wing would have to make a similar throw. The idea was the lines would intertwine, the connection would be made, and one side would pull the other in and tie the two together. For the line we used the thread from the hem of a blanket. The problem was finding a weight to attach that was heavy enough to be thrown a distance and small enough to go between the bars. Chicken bones, from the rubbish tip in the corner, were tied together but it was difficult to throw them between the bars and the distance couldn't be achieved. Next, we tried making a ball from the sponge ripped from a mattress, but it was too light and while it did roll a little after landing, the throw only went a couple of yards.

Then I had a long-overdue brain wave. For weight I squashed a couple rounds of bread into a ball, covered it with sponge and wrapped thread around to hold it together. We now had our ball which was heavy enough. Standing in the middle of the cell, aiming the ball between the bars and throwing it with all the force I could muster wasn't easy. More times than enough it would hit the bar losing its momentum and drop outside the cell or bounce off the bar back in again. After many attempts, I did manage to throw well over half-way and winding several yards of line around the ball enabled it to roll further once it hit the ground. This made it easier for C Wing who could now concentrate on aiming their ball over the line rather than covering distance.

Throwing the line across to C Wing became my job. I felt a sense of accomplishment each time we linked up and sent the comms and *toitin* back and forth. The process took quite a bit of effort and was time consuming, not that I was in any rush, but the smokers were. With the ball hitting the bars nine out of ten times or falling short of the distance, having to be hauled back in again and rewound, unlimited patience was required. Sometimes the line severed due to hitting the side of the bar and the ball would fly out with no line attached so another ball would have to be made. At the very least it would take half an hour before we were successful. One night the line had just been connected with C Wing when the shout came from a bottom cell there was a screw coming into the yard. The two wings fell so completely silent that the screw could be heard rattling the keys in the gate and opening the latch. He knew something was up because there was no buzz of conversation and shouting characteristic of the block after lock-up. There was no order to keep quiet, it just instinctively happened as everybody stopped whatever they were doing and focused on the screw. They knew the line had just been connected and they also knew some would be waiting anxiously on *teachtaireachts* and maybe a bit of *toitin*. Lads would often smuggle a number of *teachtaireachts* through the visits and they wouldn't be just for themselves but for comrades from their local area or comrades who didn't take visits. If the screw detected the line, not only would he break it but he would more than likely hover about, in hiding, awaiting a second attempt. I had spent such a long time and effort making the connection I didn't want to pull the line in.

Taking a chance, I stood up on the pipes and held the line up to the top of the bars above my head. I tugged the line to motion to my opposite in C Wing to do the same. The screw walked slowly up the yard scanning the ground as he went, knowing there was something up. He concentrated that intensely on the ground, with head bowed he walked under the line as the two wings held their breath in disbelief. It was comical, we wanted to laugh, but knew that might give the game away. He turned at the top of the yard and came back down still scrutinising the ground. Once again, unaware, he walked under the line and, equally unaware, entertained us for a second time. When he disappeared through the gate the wings erupted into spontaneous cheering. The *teachtaireachts* and *toitin* were tied to the line and pulled across triumphantly. I was chuffed with myself!

Mirror searches

Wing shifts, when men were routinely brutalised and degraded, were something to be feared. The level of brutality inflicted was related to the make-up and mood of the prison staff involved. There were occasions when we all made it through unscathed but more often than not at least some of our number were assaulted and trailed from one wing to another. Removing the cell cards from outside our doors signalled a wing shift. Nerves wore thin as we didn't know what was ahead but knew what they were capable of. Ears were cocked to the doors hoping with the first doors unlocking we would not hear the sound of shouts and scuffling. If those unwelcome sounds did echo in the wing, we knew what to expect and it was a long torturous, distressful wait until it was your turn. The ordeal did not always end with placement in the cleaned wing because we could be made to spend long hours in bitter cold conditions before blankets were returned.

The ordeal was to become much worse with the introduction of the much hated 'mirror search'. During the shift, one by one we were taken into the ablution area where in the presence of three or four screws we were told to remove our towel and squat over a mirror. We refused. What warranted such extremes? Yes, some of us had *splunkers* and some *toitin*. But was that such a danger to jail security? We would have *teachtaireachts* and comms but they knew we inserted them into our bodies which neither a mirror search or a metal detector would reveal. For over two years all blanket men had to endure the mirror search on wing shifts and going to and from visits. I would be interested to know exactly what they found for the thousands of times it was used. I don't believe security motivated them but rather it was designed to humiliate us and break our resolve.

The screws would grab our arms, kick our legs apart, manoeuvre us over the mirror and kick the back of our legs causing them to buckle and we would go down. That's the least we could expect to happen. Depending on the screws present it could be, and at times was, much worse and it wasn't just a matter of physical assault, there were also incidents of sexual assault.

We in H5 were more fortunate than our comrades in H3 and H4 as we had Kevin Lappin for our Principal Officer. Not only did he not conform to an environment where hate and brutality prevailed, he stood up against it and prevented a much more brutal regime being inflicted upon us. When we expected a wing shift, we hoped and prayed he was on duty and, if not, we could be in for a rough time. I recall one day when he was overseeing a wing shift, he was called away. Everyone going through the mirror search from when he left until he was back was beaten. As a measure of how much he was appreciated we named him *Daidí na Nollag* (Daddy Christmas).

I was shocked when I heard that JT had *bangled* a lighter. I know I'd have done without rather than do that. It was so uncivilised. But that was then, and as the years moved on my comrades and I had to adapt to an uncivilised environment. It was survival and needs must. From time to time I had a *bairt* to look after. Initially this would have been a *splunker* and *toitín*. I stopped smoking towards the end of 1978 but kept my role as *splunker* and *toitín* roller for a few more months until others willingly took over.

The Cages' men arranged for pages of Irish history to be photocopied and miniaturised and smuggled to us. Being deprived of reading material, I had a real thirst for knowledge and along with Gino McCormick and one or two others we took charge of them until forwarding to another wing. A pen was another item that had to be concealed. We smuggled in refills which we strengthened by wrapping thread around them. Parker refills were ideal and needed no adapting. We kept in contact with our family and friends by writing on toilet paper. When folded and wrapped these *teachts* in cling film at the finish were no bigger than a mint imperial sweet and usually easy to smuggle out.

The summer of 1978 we were on a high. We believed we were winning, that we had the prison administration on the back foot, conditions were unsustainable and it would only be a matter of time before political status was conceded. We received a great boost with the high-profile visit of Cardinal Ó Fiaich to the jail and his famous interview to the media afterwards when he said: "One would hardly allow an animal to remain in such conditions let alone a human being. The nearest approach to it that I have seen was the spectacle of hundreds of homeless people living in sewer pipes in the slums of Calcutta."

Frank Maguire, the MP for Fermanagh and South Tyrone, also paid us a visit. Little did we know then what a pivotal role he would indirectly play during the second hunger strike.

Don Concannon was a Northern Ireland Office Minister when Roy Mason was Secretary of State. He came to see conditions for himself, although not only was he no friend of ours, his party, Labour, had been responsible for removing political status. As he walked down the wing, my cell mate, Portadown, shouted out, "Lump of shit on the air!" (He knew better than to shout 'bear'. I had taught him well.) The wing erupted, banging doors, shouting, "Up the 'RA!" and the order was given, "*Fluiche amach!*" (That is, pour out the urine.)

As the *fluiche* poured out into the wing, Concannon, already flustered by the din we created, and not wanting to get his shoes wet, navigated his way out of the wing at lightning speed. That is – he bolted! The governor who accompanied him could not keep up. We kept the shouting up as Concannon went down the yard. I like to think it was one occasion he would never forget. His big red face did suggest we had rattled his cage. What I couldn't understand was what did he expect? Didn't the governor warn him off?

Boredom, curiosity and just a way to pass the time would have me jump to the window each time I heard the gates in the front yard opening. Like jail life in general, it was usually routine, the same faces coming and going at their predicted times. But now and again something came along to break that routine and that's what happened one day when the keys rattling in the gate had me, on cue, jumping up just in time to see David Capper, a BBC reporter, arrive in the yard with a film crew. Word quickly went down the line to let the lads know. The crew turned their camera towards the wing and we just began cheering and waving and some gave a clenched fist salute. Like others, I panicked, a bit worried about what I would say if they came to my cell, and that was a strong possibility given that I was in the first cell. The OC said just state the obvious, we are political prisoners and we demand political status. Thankfully, they didn't come to my cell.

VII
WINTER OF '78

Having no windows had its downside with the hosing and screws throwing things back into the cells but the benefits of improved communication, including the lines, plus the fresh air, outweighed the disadvantages. But the tables were turned very much against us when the winter came. The blanket protest was littered with tough incidents and periods but the 'Winter of '78' had to be the mother of all endurance tests. This is not to relegate the horror of forced washing and *an Seachtain Donna* (the Bad Week) in H4 when prisoners were subjected to an orchestrated and intensive period of beatings. It is accepted that while the random beatings were horrendous and agonizing to listen to, the fear, tension and anxiety can be multiplied tenfold when they went systematically from cell to cell brutalising prisoners. As previously mentioned, all blanket men can relate to the sound of a bolt being shot (cell door opening), the scuffling, banging, shouting, the thuds of heads and bones knocking on walls and the smack of flesh being thumped, the anger and helplessness listening to comrades beaten and the anguish and torment awaiting your turn. But when it was over, it was over, and it actually strengthened us because we had withstood it.

However, there was no respite from the bitterness of winter. It was at its most severe in the middle of the night, depriving us of sleep and leaving us praying that we could make it through to a morning that could never come quickly enough but seemed like an eternity away. As relatives and friends of ex-POWs will confirm, the winter of 1978 has become part of prison folklore. When weather turns severe, as regular as clockwork, they will have to listen to ex-*Fir Pluid* rhyme off the well-worn expression, "Did I ever tell you about the Winter of '78?"

To keep the wind and snow from the cell either my cellmate or I would sacrifice one of our blankets to serve as a curtain. The blanket was held up by wedging it between the bars by bending the lid of a chamber pot at one end and a water gallon at the other. To compensate, whoever donated the blanket, (we took turns) would be allowed to place their mattress along the back wall beside the heating pipes. Sometimes the weather was so cold the water in the water gallon turned to ice. Apparently, the Lisburn area during this period recorded a temperature of −25 °C which was the lowest that night throughout Britain and Ireland. The gods were really testing us.

During the day, with all three blankets wrapped around me, I would not venture off the mattress because the floor was bitterly cold. If I was brave enough to stand up at the window to talk to a neighbour, who was mad enough to do likewise, a blanket would be wrapped around my waist, two over my shoulders and my feet would not leave the mattress.

It was common practice to walk up and down the cell. It provided some exercise and peace of mind. With the *fluiche amach* and the condensation, the underside of the mattresses became wet so placing it on its side became obligatory to allow it to dry out, as well as leaving space to walk. A blanket would then be folded in four lengthwise and laid on the floor to walk on, avoiding placing feet on the cold floor. Some, not happy being confined to a blanket runner made moccasins from a blanket enabling them to walk the cell from end to end. Cutting a hole in the blankets to make a poncho was also quite popular. However, these practices came back to bite us. Blankets were changed from time to time after a wing shift. Shock was how Gerry McConville (my new cellmate) and I felt when they threw us in blankets that were no bigger than towels. Obviously, the lads' tailoring had something to do with it. Thankfully, Gerry and I did receive one blanket each that was regulation size otherwise we would not have survived the winter. Reduced basically to one blanket and, what only could be described as two hand towels, this was not sufficient to keep warm. At night my comrades and I suffered in the sub-zero temperatures. The towels were too small to cover my body so I would curl up into the foetal position and grip them to prevent them slipping off, but they did. I would shiver with the cold and the pain in my feet was excruciating. It was impossible to sleep as the cold and pain were inescapable. I just wanted some warmth! I didn't care about sleep deprivation because at that point sleep was only important to escape the cold for a few hours but there was no respite. It took all my reserves to fight hard and make it through to the next day and it was a test that I would never want to endure again. I'm not sure I could.

The cold – not the beatings, hosing and deprivations – was the most difficult, painful and testing time during the whole of the protest. I was very, very relieved when a saviour, a genius, a champion, came up with the wonderful, fantastic, life-saving idea of making a sleeping bag. Using the tine from a plastic fork I sewed up the one good blanket (and thank God for it) turning it into a sleeping bag. I placed the towels inside the bag and because it was in a confined space they did not slip off. The bag trapped my body heat and I was able to get some sleep and survive. Necessity really is the mother of invention.

Matt Talbots

Another blanket change brought the introduction of the dreaded 'Matt Talbots'. When we first received them they were flat, like cardboard, and had an oily smell. Through time these cheap blankets softened somewhat but they never lost their itchiness and were aptly named 'Matt Talbots'. Matt Talbot, or the Venerable Matt Talbot, lived a strict penitential regime, wearing hairshirts, chains and ropes and slept on a plank of wood. (He would have been at home on the boards.) He was a reformed alcoholic and he offered his suffering up to the lost souls and alcoholics. Fr Tom Toner, the chaplain, who temporarily won us access to religious magazines, would have been proud of the knowledge we gained. (Although we were *no* fans of Matt Talbot; apparently, he was a blackleg during the 1913 Dublin lockout!) If Matt had gone shopping for blankets, these would have been his choice, and I'm sure there were penitential double points there to be had. They itched like mad! Clearly, the prison administration did their homework on how to make life insufferable.

A Visit

Towards the end of 1978 I decided it was time to take a visit. We were about to enter another Christmas and New Year on the protest and while I couldn't see any further than six months, reality was beginning to dawn: political status wasn't coming any time soon. It did feel strange putting the uniform on, but I had no sense of compromising my principles. It was a *tactic* to assist communication and provide some comfort to my family. Prison policy was to walk blanket men to the visits rather than transport them in a minibus, as they did other prisoners. Possibly this was because they did not want us to have contact with anyone. The screws kept a very close eye on us, at times to the point of harassment. My legs felt strange walking but I was glad to have the opportunity.

My mother, father and sister were in the visiting cubicle when I entered. They were a bit emotional. I don't know what their impressions were of me. I never did ask them. Neither did I ever ask what way they were treated by the screws on that day or any subsequent visits. I doubt if they would have told me, but I do know they were waiting quite a long time. The visit was tense, not helped by the screw hanging over the cubicle. When my sister, Patricia, managed to pass a *bairt* to me undetected, the tension eased somewhat. The pressure was on me when the visit ended because while I had the *bairt* I had not secreted it. With a screw stuck to me like Velcro, that wasn't going to be easy. Thoughts of the boards and the lads' slagging that I was a waster descended.

To my surprise my luck was in for a change. The visits were running late, the screws probably thinking about their break called for a minibus and three blanket men and I were told to jump in. Rules can change if the screws feel they'll be going over their time – even if it's minutes! Sitting at the back of the minibus with my three comrades from H4 I was able to secrete the *bairt*. Once it was safe, I felt so good. Success: the lads would get their smoke and there would be no slagging. I was dropped off at the front gate. The lads were up at their windows awaiting me as I walked down the yard. They only wanted to know one thing – did I *fuair*? I was pumped up with my success, floated down the yard in triumph and apparently, as the lads told me later, shouting *"Fuair mé, fuair mé!"* continuously in an excited tone.

Forced washing and shearing

After a wing shift the OC would do a roll call to ascertain the injuries. There were occasions when there was nothing to report but it was more usual to hear at the very least reports of bruising and abrasions. The situation was something similar in H4 where there were bad and not-so-bad shifts, although they endured a torturous period (*an Seachtain Donna*) when the screws really excelled themselves with their brutality. H3 fared much worse. They had a cruel PO who was on a mission to break the protest and was renowned for his brutality. Despite multiple fencing we in H5 were able to communicate with H4 by *scairting* because, while we were quite a distance apart, our Blocks were in parallel. It was more difficult to *scairt* to H3 as they were at a different angle and if the wind was blowing the wrong way it wasn't possible.

In early December 1978 H3 *scairted* across that five men had been forcibly washed, were badly beaten and two were taken to hospital, among them Martin Hurson from Tyrone. We felt that the washing would neutralise the effect of the protest and after much discussion the decision was taken to fight back. Feelings were mixed about that. To say the least, it frayed nerves. We knew if you lifted a hand to a screw you paid a heavy price. In another sense, we were proud with the 'fighting talk'. We would take them head on, show our strength and commitment and let them know what they were up against. The order was *scairted* to H3 and H4, *"Buail orthu"* (hit them), but the response from H3 was, *"Nil muid ablta a chluinsint"* (we can't hear). Our block persisted with the *scairting*, sometimes changing the command from *"Buail orthu"* to *"Troid iad"* (fight them) in the hope that they might better able to hear.

An eerie silence fell over all three Blocks as the *scairting* continued. No doubt the command had everybody's thoughts caught up with what was in store. The attempts to communicate the command to H3 were unsuccessful. Although, difficult as it could be to communicate, there was a feeling that it was the acceptance rather than the hearing that was the problem that night. Through the visits we were to learn that the H3 OC had changed the order to 'passive resistance'. Given the extent of the brutality that was the norm in H3, he felt to fight back would risk very serious injury and even death. All prisoners in H3 were dragged from their cells, thrown into a bath, scrubbed with scrubbing brushes and doused with bitterly cold water. Their hair was forcibly cut and their beards shaved.

Meanwhile, in H5 (and no doubt in H4) it was very tense as we awaited the inevitable battering. Whoever was on the yard side at the front of the block were on constant alert for tell-tale signs that the forced washing was about to begin. Any reports about changes or increase in staff had us bracing ourselves ready for the battle ahead. The anxious waiting went on for several days until H4 *scairted* that the forced washing had started in their block. With H3 finished and H4 started it was apparent that they were going to take one block at a time. Realising the pattern, the tension merely dropped a few notches in our block but the anxiety continued as we waited our turn.

H4 bravely fought them. Each night they *scairted* across their casualty list and while it angered me and fired me up to get stuck into the screws, it wasn't good for my nerves. For some reason the forced washing ended in H4. I don't know if the lads there broke it by their heroic action or maybe the prison authorities were worried about the grave consequences of letting sadistic screws run loose. There was also speculation that PO Kevin Lappin refused to implement it but I doubt if that would have stopped it as it would only have been a matter of removing him to another post. I suspected it was a combination of reasons. We were never told that the forced washing had stopped so we sweated it out for another few weeks but, as Christmas approached, we began to settle, suspecting, hoping, there may have been a reprieve.

Christmas Day arrived. Some of the lads were shouting, "Happy Christmas!" Others were telling them to "Fuck Off!"

At Mass we were with the Yippees. Morale was high and everyone appeared to be in a good mood. Paul 'Pidgey' Priget had the Yippees practising carols all week and he was all biz that morning as if he was organising a major production. All he had to do was conduct the carol singing but he took it that seriously you would swear it was a career-breaking moment. I suspect that's why the lads let him do it. They got a kick out of him losing himself. That was Pidgey, full of drama and one of the most popular characters of the Blocks.

Fr Faul was the priest that morning and never one for letting us down (at least not at that stage) he had a couple packets of cigarettes which the '*toitin* chiefs' divided among the two wings. I, who still had a role at that time, was handed the share for my side of the wing. When Mass ended Pidgey took his place at the front (where else) and counting us in, "One, two, three," began conducting the carol singing with such serious focused intent that anyone could have been forgiven for thinking he had the Vienna Philharmonic before him.

To a man we all responded, putting our whole heart and soul into, 'Angels We Have Heard On High.' It was quite emotional and Fr Faul was moved to tears.

It was more than a Christmas carol; it was a statement.

We were still here; we were stronger than ever and we were determined to win.

So good on Pidgey! We had needed that. It made us feel so proud and the bond between us that morning was palpable.

The day kept getting better. We had the traditional turkey dinner and it was warm. Not only was there no hassle from the screws but you could have knocked me down when after the dinner, the cell opened and we were asked if we would like a cup of coffee! That was a first. Never before had I ever had a cup of coffee in jail. They didn't have to ask twice. To crown it off *Top of the Pops* was on the TV in the canteen. Being in the top cell the volume was loud enough for me to hear. There I was relaxing with a cup of coffee listening to

Olivia Newton John and John Travolta singing, 'Summer Nights'. I was in seventh heaven. All I needed to make it just perfect was a smoke. A real smoke, not one of those skinny *toitin*, wrapped in toilet paper. And didn't I have a dozen straights on me! I had stopped smoking a few weeks before but this was a one-off. Opportunities to have a real cigarette with a cup of coffee while listening to *Top of the Pops* weren't going to come along every day in the Blocks. I fought with myself – will I, or won't I? Just this once wouldn't do any harm, and after all it was Christmas. Another voice demanded, "Where's your will power – no excuses! If you've stopped, you've stopped." While I was wrestling with my conscience, word came up the line. The lads wanted the straights swung down. The chance to have a smoke with a cup of coffee was too much and they were not prepared to wait until lock-up.

The screws, not worried about being on duty at the best of times but more so because it was Christmas, had withdrawn to the canteen (and possibly the Circle) so there was no risk. With heavy heart, I wrapped all the straights together and swung them to the next cell. I couldn't give myself a slap on the back for showing willpower because I wasn't sure if I had done the right thing. The urge for a smoke was never stronger than that day; and up to the point when I'd quitted, each and every time I lit up a *toitin* it felt like a victory, that I had beaten the system. I never did smoke again.

VIII
1979 – MORE BRUTALITY

January arrived and the scouts were still reporting any change of movement at the front gates as the threat of forced washing still hung over us. Unexpectedly, word came through one day, not that we were to be force washed but were to have photographs taken. In keeping with the spirit of resistance the OC told us not to cooperate. They came to me first which was okay because it was always best to get it over and done with rather endure the wait and all the horror entailed.

I sat on the mattress with my back to the wall facing them, refusing to move. While I was worried what price the resistance was going to be, I didn't question it. We were 'protest incarnate' to quote Chekov's prison story, *Gusev*. A couple of screws pounced on me, grabbed my arms and trailed me out. I managed to struggle one arm free and gripped the doorway, preventing being trailed any further. At that, my other arm was released and Jimmy the Bigot, who made up for his lack of stature with bitterness, grabbed me by the hair and dragged me out. It felt like he was going to rip half my scalp off, so, trying to ease the pressure, I grabbed his hands as I was trailed into an empty cell. Once in the cell he let go and I lay on the floor surrounded by four or five screws. I refused to move and they dragged me up and pinned me to the wall holding my arms out like I was being crucified. The screw with the camera raised it to take a photo but I dropped my head. Jimmy the Bigot fired up, began swearing and warning me to keep my head up. There was an SO outside the cell, who I assumed was in charge and was unknown to me, but he couldn't see all that was going on because the door was only slightly open and the screws in the cell blocked what little view he had. Jimmy the Bigot, who appeared to be calling the shots, told me, in his own polite way, that he would beat the head off me if I didn't comply. He must have been a bit slow because after a couple of years 'not complying' I'd have thought the penny would have dropped. That wasn't to be but he nearly dropped me with a huge punch to the face.

I tried to shake it off like they did in the cowboy movies and gave a look that suggested, "Is that the best you can do?" He told the screws to grab my hair and pull my head up in readiness for the photo to be taken. The photographer aimed the camera, the screws let go off my hair just on the point the snap was to be taken but I was quicker on the draw and dropped my head again. This was the signal for the blows to rain in and I noticed the SO still outside but in response to their 'chastisement' his head was bobbing about trying to get a glimpse of what was going on but not intervening. The exercise was repeated. Screws grabbed my hair, let go when the snap was about to be taken but I successfully dropped my head.

The Bigot, obviously taking this personal, took a step back, told them to hold my head up again and punched me hard. It was a lot more difficult this time to give my, "Is that it?" look. The process was repeated, except the photographer took the picture while they held my head up. With the picture taken, they let go off my hair. But I wasn't stupid, and I automatically dropped my head, knowing they would photograph me if I thought they were done. That sent the Bigot berserk. As he took another step back to have a good swing at me, I couldn't help thinking – déjà vu – Jimmy B in the Crum! – except this time there was to be no ducking. Beatings, of course, are always traumatic but it is much worse when your arms are held and you cannot protect yourself. The punch came again, hitting me square on the face and the blood poured from my nose. Undeterred, he threw a second. But this time I managed to move just enough for his fist only to glance my head and he hit the wall with a thump. I detected some chuckling from the screws at the Bigot's misfortune. Thankfully, my ordeal ended with that. My resolve remained intact – just about. I was dragged back out, by the hair again. As I lay licking my wounds (blood from my mouth and nose and swollen eye), I heard the rest of the lads being dragged out to face the same treatment.

When it was over the OC did the roll call for the injuries but the tradition ended there because for the first time, instead of taking it on the chin, we were told to demand to see the doctor. This was a new departure.

Surprisingly, after the requests were made, later that day, we were allowed to see him. The doctor cleaned the blood around my nose and noted some of my injuries and asked what happened.

Our OC then instructed us to request a solicitor. This was a further change in policy and in my view was instrumental in reducing, but not eliminating, the frequency and brutality of assaults. The screws were not held accountable for their actions but this move had the potential to change that. Republicans traditionally refused to recognise the courts, were loath to use the law, tainted as its institutions were as apologists for state torture and killings, internment, and Bloody Sunday. In my view, we understandably entered the process tentatively and half-heartedly. It took a number of years for the possible benefits of challenging the system through legal action to become apparent, but it came too late to address the systemic brutality in the Blocks. Pat Finucane, solicitor, was permitted to see myself and others and he took statements about the incident. He said that he would have loved to have seen the photographs they took that day. No doubt, like much of the other incriminating evidence, they were shredded.

The next move of the prison administration was to single out the men in each wing who they believed were leaders. The Dark, Bobby Sands and others were moved to H6. I can only assume they believed we would be left leaderless, that morale would drop and there would be a drift off the blanket. Once again, they failed to understand that we were led by our principles and politics and were committed to them. Leadership was within us all and positions vacated were easily filled. If anything, the move to H6 indirectly worked to our advantage. It brought a wealth of experience together to analyse the protest, come to conclusions and draw up strategies. That said, it was plain that there was only one direction left.

The forced washing had not been completely abandoned. The new tactic was for the doctor to parade around the wings and select individuals. The unfortunate individual would be dragged to the boards where he would be subjected to the usual brutality of the forced washing. My cellmate Gerry, regrettably, was selected. The position remained the same: we were to resist. Although I wasn't selected it would involve me because, while it was tempting to turn the other way as they dragged Gerry out, screaming and kicking, I could not just be a spectator. Like it or not, I would have to help him resist and I wasn't looking forward to that because I knew what it would incur. Every time we heard the jingle of keys our hearts thumped. Each time a van drove into the yard we were up on our feet bracing ourselves, gathering courage, ready to meet the rush of screws into the cell. The anxious wait went on all day. With nerves worn thin, lock-up came at 8.30pm after a day where the minutes went like hours but confusingly, and most unusually, the unwelcome visit did not happen. Had we to face another day of torture waiting? We got our answer later that night when the Yippee Wing *scairted* across that 'Gerry O' had been dragged from his cell, beaten, taken to the boards and forcibly washed. Gerry O and my cellmate were both called Gerry McConville. Obviously, the screws got the wrong one!

Gerry and I were moved to the bottom of the wing. Apart from a brief shift to H6 we remained at the bottom in every wing until the end of the protest. It had its disadvantages with the *fluiche amach* but, for me, being one cell away from Joe McDonnell more than compensated for any disadvantages; disadvantages which included the wing shifts.

There were no half measures with Joe. If he set his mind to something he stuck to his guns and pursued it relentlessly. During wing shifts there was passive and, I would say, even token resistance to the mirror search. Not with Joe. The refusal to bend when held over the mirror was met with boots. Legs would buckle and the prisoner would fall. It didn't take much of a kick to buckle my legs, but Joe was something else. He tensed his legs and it was as if he had iron rods in them because the screws would kick like mad to put him down. The problem with this was it effectively fired the screws up. If the screws went around the wing in anti-clockwise direction, opening cells one by one during a wing shift, I had a better chance of getting through it relatively unscathed because I would be before Joe. However, if it was clockwise, coming after him sometimes meant rough treatment with screws still incandescent from their experience of Joe.

A year or so after the protest ended a screw told me that Joe was the toughest prisoner he had ever come across. After the shifts, when the OC did the injury roll call, Joe, whose legs more time than enough would be black and blue, could never understand why the legs of others, like myself, were not. There was no point explaining tokenism to him. He didn't do it.

Windows blocked

Having braved the winter, we were now looking forward to the benefits no windows would bring with the better weather. Unfortunately, this was not to be as there was a new development. The prison installed what we called 'horse boxes'. The box, roughly 5ft x 4ft x 2ft, was attached to the outside wall. The front, 2ft out from the bars had a Perspex window at the top that allowed us a view of that 'little tent of blue' (to quote Oscar Wilde), but if we stood on the pipes, we could see the wing facing and the yard. There was no base on the horse box so if something was dropped out the bars it would fall to the ground.

On the inside of the cell window a metal grille was welded to the wall covering the four bars (concrete slats). The grille crisscrossed to make diamond shapes that were just large enough to push a finger through, but no more. The authorities must have believed that would spell the end of the swinging but they forgot the old adage: necessity is the mother of invention. We set to work. Pieces of mattress sponge, attached to a line, were pushed out the grille and the adjoining cell tried using an improvised hook to pull it in. When that failed, both cells then tried a sponge attached to a line hoping both would intertwine.

Modesty prevents me from saying who came up with the idea of kites-cum-parachutes! Suspension lines (string) were attached to each of the four corners of a square of toilet paper (the canopy). The suspension lines were tied together and attached to a longer string (the bridle). The toilet paper was folded and pushed out the grille. Holding the string the prisoner would blow the paper causing it to open like a kite/parachute. This would then be blown out and the wind would catch it like a kite. The adjoining cell would follow the same procedure, the kites would intertwine and with the connection made the kites would be pulled in and lines tied together. So, the answer was 'blowing in the wind.'

Joe McDonnell was commander in chief of the *toitin* on the exercise yard side of the wing. He shot the button to join with the other side and distributed the *toitin* on his side. Neither Gerry nor I smoked and since we were the last cell there was no need for a line for the *toitin* train but it was required if passing *teachtaireachts*.

Gerry McConville

Gerry was my cell mate from early 1979 to late 1982 when the protest ended. I was lucky to be twinned with such an easy-going person. He was from a well-known republican family. His mother Madge was arrested in 1942 after a shoot-out in West Belfast when an RUC man was killed. Her friend and comrade Tom Williams was subsequently sentenced to death and hanged. Through lack of evidence the charges against Madge were dropped but as she left court she was arrested and interned in Armagh Jail. While she was in jail her brother Seamus 'Rocky' Burns, who had escaped from Derry Jail, was shot dead by the RUC during a gun battle. Madge married Tommy, a former internee, and they had seven children of which Gerry, my cellmate, went to jail and his sister Mary (who later became a Sinn Féin councillor). Madge herself was again interned in the 1970s.

During the day, as was typical with blanket men, we would participate in *rangs* out the door, chat with neighbours at the pipes and window and, of course, with each other. Some of the lads played chess, scraping a board on the floor and using paper for the pieces. Neither Gerry nor I knew how to play so we satisfied ourselves with draughts. The chess players could be a little too vocal shouting from cell to cell for my liking! "Move my queen to B4!" got up my nose sometimes. Maybe it gave me, with my draughts, a bit of an inferiority complex. If Gerry had known how to play, I would have gladly taken lessons from him, but his interest lay in Celtic FC and horses, in neither of which I had any interest. I wasn't prepared to take lessons from others as it was an opportunity to be 'set up'. I've no doubt I would have been given all the wrong instructions.

Unlike others, Gerry and I very rarely paced the floor. Most of the lads would put their mattresses on their side against the wall. The reasons for this were twofold. It gave them space to walk and it dried out the mattresses. We didn't care if the mattresses were wet at the bottom as long as it didn't seep through. We relied on the wing shifts to receive dry mattresses. Quite often the orderlies who shifted the mattresses didn't care who owned what. Gerry and I would have a good old snigger when two dry mattresses were thrown in the door while some of the lads would be in a fit because they ended up with our wet ones. We never owned up. Why would we, it wasn't going to dry out the mattresses, plus we got a kick out of listening to the rant and not being part of the controversy.

Most of us were thin, maybe even emaciated, but not Joe McDonnell. He actually put on weight. It could only have been due to lack of exercise. Certainly nothing to do with food. We named him 'Fat Joe' and '*Seosamh Ramhar*' the Irish equivalent. It was like a ritual every single night. Shortly after lock-up, or if there was *toitín* once Joe had shot the line and distributed to the smokers, he would call me up to the window for a yarn. Finbarr McKenna would often join us. All who were in those bottom cells, Brendan McLaughlin (who we named 'Andy Capp'), Teddy Crane, Willie Campbell, Sean Laverty and Gerry, if they were bothered to listen, would butt in and now and again and nine times out of ten it would be something sarcastic. Joe and I having been in the same IRA Company (although not at the same time) had a lot in common, but we had never actually met while on the outside. Ironically, through our conversations, we discovered our paths had crossed numerous times.

We had also both been in a local bar on the night a Brit patrol entered, which resulted in a riot and Micky Fitzsimmons being shot. (Micky was now on the blanket in H4). We talked a lot about our families, friends, experiences, and the life to come.

IX
JOE MCDONNELL

Joe was big into the future. A favourite conversation of his was when the 'brown bags' would be thrown into the wing. 'Brown bags' was a metaphor for political status. The bags contained our clothes which had been taken from us when we refused to wear the gear. Joe, using his experience from internment when the men in the Cages organised communally into *cliques*, had it all worked out. We would have our own clique – Finbarr, Gerry, Ted (if he didn't opt for the Short Strand squad), Joe and myself. We tended to be very parochial at that stage: all West Belfast men – apart from Ted who would be on 'probation' before being considered for adoption! Parcels would be organised so there was consistency and not a feast or famine. Handicrafts were to operate along production lines, roles assigned where, who else but Joe, deemed best! Above all, what he longed for and never doubted it would come, was that big day when he would put on his own clothes and see his wife and children again. Joe refused to take visits because it meant wearing the gear.

There was never a dull moment with him. He was a great raconteur, at times irreverent, but he wasn't one for taking hardship that seriously. No matter how bad or hard a situation Joe had the knack of finding some humour. There were many difficult times, especially with wing shifts, but on the heels of these lows Joe, rallying the troops and not allowing us to feel sorry for ourselves, would famously quip, "There's going to be bad days for these good ones."

As intended, his humour never failed to lift us.

I learned all about his life, he less so about mine, because he had all the interesting stories. He grew up in Slate Street in the Lower Falls, had five brothers and three sisters, the youngest of them Bernadette died at six years of age. I don't think Joe got over her death because he talked about her that much and named his daughter after her. I could feel the affection when he reminisced about carrying her around on his back, bringing her to the cinema and the sweetie shop on the corner. It was the same with his children, Bernadette and

Joseph. He spoke passionately about them. Goretti, his wife, to keep him informed, ran around half the country petitioning relatives and friends of blanket men, to smuggle *teachtaireachts* to him. Ironically, Joe knew more about the world outside than the rest of us, who were taking visits. He had several of us donkeys (as I called ourselves) smuggling *teachtaireachts* in and out for him. His main donkey (but, clearly, not his best!) was Raymond McCartney, from Derry, who was on appeal and thus entitled to three visits per week. Goretti would visit Raymond and, as well as exchanging *teachtaireachts*, would hear first-hand news of Joe. All went well until Raymond 'got' Goretti caught with a *bairt* and she was barred from visiting. He would argue that it wasn't his fault (it wasn't), but I got too much satisfaction keeping him going to admit otherwise and continued to blame him, even to this day!

Joe's sister Maura would have done a lot of the running for him too and she would have visited another brother, Frankie, who was also on the blanket, in H4.

Joe took great pride in sharing news about his family and in particular the children. Hours were spent at the window relating how well they were doing at school and what was special in their lives – birthdays, football teams, pop stars.

I remember one bitterly cold night he shouted to me to get up to the window as he had received a *teachtaireacht* and, as usual, was just busting to tell the *scéal*. I was on the mattress, wrapped up in blankets and huddled against the pipes. I wasn't for moving. There was only one thing on my mind – staying warm – and it wasn't *scéal*. Joe could be quite persistent, quite stubborn. He kept calling and it really bugged me when he used an exaggerated pleading voice. He knew what he was at. My conscience was pricking and I just wanted to tell him to fuck off! Then, to crown it off, Gerry turned to me and said, "For god's sake, get up and talk to him. You know what he's like when he gets *scéal*!" That was it, my conscience couldn't take anymore. Mumbling some chosen words under my breath I reluctantly got up to the window. With an Arctic wind blowing into my face, teeth chattering and nose ready to drop off, I was to learn the dead exciting news that his mother was knitting his children Aran sweaters for Christmas and Bernadette was getting a pair of

128

roller skates. I think I had to count up to ten to stop myself from telling him to take a flying jump. Yes, I know, that would have been heartless. What Joe could never understand was the passion he had for his children was not shared, especially in sub-zero temperatures. Blue with the cold, I fought hard to feign some interest and conjure up some small talk, just enough to pass myself. After about twenty minutes Joe, pleased with sharing his news, duty done I wished him good night and returned to my spot by the pipes. As I sat defrosting, I felt good with myself for giving in, listening to him and pretending I was interested. My admiration for him went up a notch and I thought to myself, if I have children I would want to be as passionate as he was for his.

Joe did not like a quiet wing. We would talk every night until it was time for a wing activity which, while sing songs and quizzes did take place, it was more usual for a book 'to be told'. If there was nothing arranged and the conversation out the windows had burnt itself out, he would try to persuade someone to 'tell a book'. If he had no joy with that, he would call on the old faithful and ever reliable Tony (Scatter) O'Hara. Tony, from Derry, was the brother of Patsy who would later die on the hunger strike. In fairness, he never let Joe down, although the wing would have preferred he had.

His famous story about the 'Duke' from the Grosvenor Road (*London* not Belfast) was – to be kind – passable the first time, bearable the second time, but after that there was general agreement it was fucking torture. Joe was the only dissenting voice. Those less kind said they would rather listen to the pumping of the new industrial Hoover, introduced by the admin to deal with the pools of urine. To harass us the screws would deliberately leave the machine running, the loud vibrations making it virtually impossible to hold wing activities.

Sticking up for my comrade Scatter, I would have preferred to listen to him – but it would be a close call. While the wing groaned at the mention yet again of the Duke, Joe cheered. I think he generally fell asleep before the end of the book. I write 'I think' because I certainly did. Joe, as a rule, said goodnight before he bedded down. I don't believe there were too many 'good-nights' when the Duke was on. Either I was asleep and didn't hear him or, more likely, both of us were asleep. Just like in *The Waltons*, Joe ended the night with, "Goodnight, Big Jim," and I had to return the salutation. He called me 'Big Jim'. I think I must have reached five foot eleven by then.

Humour was ever-present but sometimes it could be razor sharp. I'll not deny there were one or two occasions that it caused me to call it a night. Joe would shout out his customary, "Goodnight, Big Jim," but I, feeling slightly aggrieved, would not reciprocate. That was my way of getting my own back as I knew he wouldn't rest without the goodnight. I suppose it was his way to check if everything was alright. It was my way of letting him know it wasn't! He would keep shouting until I, feeling a bit silly only because others could hear, would give in. If I dug my heels in Gerry, the voice of reason, would tell me to wise up and he'd remind me that Joe would not settle until he knew all was okay. I liked that side of Joe. He would feel real hurt if he thought someone was offended or upset by something he said. Gerry told me that Joe had asked him at Mass if I was taking the slagging about an ex-girlfriend bad and if that was the case he would never mention her name again.

The prison authorities soon realised that moving what they believed to be the leadership out of the wings and up to H6 had made no difference to the protest. They abandoned the idea in September and the lads were reintegrated into H3, H4 and H5. Joe, like the rest of us, had heard there was some talk of hunger strike coming from H6 and he wasn't at all pleased. Not that he was against hunger strike. On the contrary, he was adamant that if there was to be one then all the Blocks and not just H6 should be privy to the plans and have the opportunity to volunteer. At Mass he made a bee line for Tom McFeely, who had just returned from H6, and let him know that they had no right to think they could go on a solo run. From talking to Joe later, while he didn't reveal all that had been discussed between them, and reading between the lines, I did gather that McFeely fully accepted his points and that Joe would be involved in any future plans.

I look back on that day as a turning point. Firstly, because hunger strike became a reality and featured prominently in conversation. We referred to it, *as gaelige*, *Stailc Ocrais* or simply the *Stailc*. Secondly, Joe became central to that conversation. On Sundays he joined a small group of staff who discussed plans in whispered tones at the back of the canteen during Mass. Joe was determined that a *stailc* would involve him. It was obvious our protest had gone stale again. The highs of 1978 had fizzled out with no movement by the British government. There was no other way to turn but to resort to a *stailc ocrais*.

Christmas cake

Another Christmas arrived but this time there was no *Top of the Pops*. Being in the bottom cell I probably would not have heard it even had it been on the TV. I know it would have been a treat for the lads at the top of the wing and I would have been really jealous! While not in keeping with the Christmas spirit, I was glad in a way that the green monster did not bite that day – or so I thought.

I have a sweet tooth and I really missed chocolate and confectionery – which were not part of the prison menu. Christmas Day was the one exception when we were served a piece of cake. I can honestly state that I looked forward more to that piece of Christmas cake than to the dinner. I'm sure the shock registered on my face when the door opened and two plates were handed to me, minus the customary and much-expected, dearly-longed for, piece of Christmas cake. I know I swore when the door banged behind me. I was in a rage, while Gerry found my antics very amusing. He didn't care much for the cake and he would have been prepared to give me his. I called next door to Ted and Andy Capp to check if they got theirs. They did – and this made me even madder. I could just about take it if we were all deprived but not if I was singled out. Due to the mixing that was embedded in our culture I asked them to get real and be serious and tell me. "Right hand up to God," and to swear on the graves of beloved grannies if they really got cake?

I was such a slave to my sweet tooth that it blinded me to how ridiculous I appeared, but it was great entertainment for them. Joe shouted to me that they did indeed get it. Ted suggested I bang the door and ask the screws for the cake. Mad as I was, I hadn't totally taken leave of my senses and I wasn't going to grovel to any screw or give them the opportunity to laugh in my face. Joe told me to forget about it, that Sean (his cellmate) and he didn't like the cake and he would swing theirs down to me. That made me feel better. I settled down to eat what was on the plate and awaited the arrival of Joe and Sean's much appreciated present. The minutes turned to hours without the delivery. My rage had gone, I was able to think straight again and began to suspect that they were still at their mixing. Joe and the rest were probably waiting on me bouncing up to the window and asking what was keeping my promised parcel. They would break into fits of laughter and say, "Dead on. Did you really expect to get our cake?"

I wasn't going to play their game, they weren't going to have a laugh at my expense, so I did not react; well, not outwardly. Inwardly, I was seething. After lock-up, as usual, Joe called me to the window for a yarn and asked if I enjoyed the cake.

"Dead on, Joe," I said, in a voice that I tried to make sound that I couldn't care less and didn't fall for their stupid mix. Joe was surprised and he assured me with all sincerity that he did send the cake my way. As he was telling me this, I heard giggling coming from the cell between us making it obvious what had happened. Joe, finding the funny side, in mock anger remonstrated with Ted and Andy Capp. "You can't have your cake and eat it in this bloody place!" he cracked, but I was in no mood to laugh. Sensing that I was annoyed, despite I thought doing a very good job of covering up, he told me not to worry, I would get his cake next year. Not being able to see any further than six months that did little to soothe me. I restrained myself from "going off on one" with Ted and Andy because I knew that would only add spice to their pilferage. The cake was mentioned no more and Joe and I, mostly Joe, spent the night discussing how great the following Christmas would be after the 'brown bags' were thrown in. I still had some optimism, but time had diluted it.

My resolve never to wear a prison uniform hadn't wavered. It was never an option but I could now see the parallel with Sean McCaughey's jail experience and realised that I was wrong; society, or, more pertinently, government, was not more civilised. Joe on the other hand remained very upbeat. He was animated, talking about sitting around a table, wearing our own clothes with our party hats on, eating Christmas dinner and watching *Top of the Pops*.

1980

With the arrival of the New Year, the writing was on the wall for *stailc ocrais*. We had exhausted all means at our disposal to press the British government to concede to our demands. On the outside the RAC (Relatives Action Committee) had marched and protested around the country, highlighting our cause. Their committees more or less morphed into the National H-Block/Armagh Committee which extended the campaign and broadened the support base. The committee came up with the idea of framing the solution around 'Five Demands', which really amounted to political status but without using those exact words as it was thought the British might find it easier to concede.

It was agreed that the Pope's visit scheduled for October 1979 offered an opportunity to raise our profile and so it was decided a *stailc ocrais* would commence that would reach the thirty-day mark when he arrived. However, due to the opposition from the IRA outside (and I believe the Catholic Church), the plan had to be abandoned.

We knew that a *stailc*, while we sought to avoid it, was the only avenue open to us. I wasn't aware of the full details of the plans that were being laid by the group huddled together at the back of the canteen during Mass but Joe did tell me that a *stailc* was imminent.

There was to be ten men on the strike, one of them Joe. At the time I don't believe this was well-known and I doubt if I was supposed to know. I think it was a case of Joe needing someone to confide in and I was sworn to secrecy. At this period, convinced he was to go on *stailc ocrais* as well as psyching himself up, he prepared Goretti for what was ahead through a series of *teachtaireachts*.

However, the *stailc* was delayed for two reasons.

When Cardinal Ó Fiaich heard about our plans he appealed to the IRA staff to put off the strike and allow him to follow the diplomatic route. He began discussions with the British Secretary of State for the North, Humphrey Atkins. He also held a number of unpublicised meetings with Sinn Féin representatives. To facilitate progress the IRA announced that from 1st March it would cease its armed attacks on prison officers.

Meanwhile, Belfast republican Martin Meehan arrived in the H-Blocks. The RUC and the British army, anxious to get Martin off the streets, had him set-up on the lying testimony of an informer whose reliability was questioned even by the judge. Nonetheless, he found Martin guilty and sentenced him to twelve years. Martin, much aggrieved at the blatant injustice, reacted impulsively by going on *stailc ocrais*. There were many men in the Blocks wrongly convicted and Martin should not have expected justice, something he later conceded. His solo run around his own case precluded the start of the bigger *stailc ocrais* for status. As things turned out, Martin ended his *stailc* after sixty-six days.

Ó Fiaich's talks dragged on through the summer. There were rumours of concessions and we debated among ourselves (as if the rumours were true) would the concessions be enough? The talk was that we were going to be allowed our own clothes and, given the symbolism of a prison uniform, I believe most of us thought this was significant. Sanity demanded we did not abandon hope.

Joe, in keeping with his character, had the craic going about the 'brown bags' being on their way. I'm not sure how far he believed the rumours or if, as I suspect, he grasped these opportunities to keep our morale up. Even when we learned the talks came to nothing, he wasn't perturbed, laughed it off and was as bubbly as ever.

We were offered 'civilian-type' clothing – which would be issued by the prison administration only. The Brits knew in advance it would be totally unacceptable. Their motivation was to appear to be flexible rather than find a solution. The clothes included pastel-coloured jumpers and trousers that must have come from Rupert the Bear's wardrobe. Of course, even had they provided us all with Armani suits it still would have been unacceptable. Only our own clothes would do to establish our status as political prisoners. All avenues had been exhausted. There remained only one course of action open to us – hunger striking.

X
THE 1980 HUNGER STRIKE

Our public relations machine went into full swing. We wrote *teachtaireachts* to celebrities, politicians, churchmen and newspapers, explaining the conditions we had to endure in our fight for political status. We also pointed out the anomaly that we were arrested and held under special legislation, interrogated under special measures (ill-treatment at best, torture at worst) to extract confessions, sentenced in special Diplock Courts and yet once sentenced the 'special' label was removed and replaced with 'ordinary criminal'.

We provided the H-Block Information Centre at Sinn Féin's Belfast headquarters with *teachts* which they sent out across the world; and we used whatever personal connections we had. I sent my sister, Patricia, in Saskatchewan a *teacht*, which she succeeded in having published in the local newspaper. On the back of that a local radio station then interviewed her. There was a feeling we were approaching the end game and every last piece of publicity was sought as it could make all the difference.

A *teacht* from the Dark was read out to all the wings announcing the *stailc* ocrais. There was a finality about it which left myself and others with the deep impression this could be his last words to us. Symbolic of the signing of the 1916 Proclamation, seven were to begin the strike on October 27th. They were the Dark (Belfast), Tom McFeely (North Derry), Leo Green (Lurgan), John Nixon (Armagh), Tommy McKearney (Tyrone), Sean McKenna (South Armagh) and Raymond McCartney (Derry). Joe was not included but he accepted the rationale of the seven and the geographical spread. I don't know if he was privy to the details before their announcement, but I suspect he knew something because he expressed neither surprise nor disappointment. I'm sure he was relieved that others were taking the burden on and that he had done his bit by offering his name to go forward.

When the decision had been taken to go ahead with the *stailc*, volunteers were requested. I put my name forward as did over one hundred others. Why did I do this? It was my protest as much as anybody else's. I agreed with hunger striking as we had nowhere else to turn and giving up was not an option. I felt I couldn't take a back seat, but I did hope I would never be required.

Within a short period of beginning the strike, Raymond McCartney was moved out of the wing along with the six others to a clean wing in H3. Later, Raymond and his six comrades were moved to the prison hospital. Through our communication system and the support from outside we were kept up to date on their progress.

On December 1st three women from Armagh Jail joined the strike – Mairead Farrell, Mary Doyle and Mairead Nugent. I knew Mairead Farrell quite well. We were from the same area and her cellmate, Sinead Moore, who I kept in touch with through *teachts*, kept me updated as to how both of them were getting on. All the republican POW women in Armagh wrote regularly to the lads in the Blocks. Joe and Mairead would also have written to each other occasionally.[6]

We received news that Sean McKenna's health was deteriorating quite rapidly. Whether this prompted the tactic of increasing the strike or whether it was part of the plan all along I don't know but on December 15th thirty more men joined the strike. I was to be one of the thirty. I'm sure I was nervous but the only feelings I can remember were pride and honour. There were better men than me to represent our struggle, as was to be proven later, but nonetheless I was chuffed. Joe, on the other hand, could not mask his disappointment with not being selected. The feeling was that he was excluded because he had a wife and children and since the staff had a wide pool to select from it made sense to choose those who had no responsibilities. Making light of his disappointment and possibly feeling somewhat rejected, in conversation that night I will forever remember Joe saying that he had lost the run of himself thinking that he could be part of history. How could anyone believe, he asked, that he could possibly be part of group like Pearse and Connolly? I know his comment, typical of him, was tongue in cheek but he never would have imagined just how

---

[6] Mairead Farrell served over ten years in Armagh Jail. She was released in October 1986. Seventeen months later she was shot dead by the SAS in Gibraltar, along with IRA Volunteers Dan McCann and Sean Savage.

wrong it would prove to be – and that he would go down in history and be spoken of and remembered in song and poetry forever.

The next morning I refused food and later that day I was asked to attend the doctor in the Circle. This became a ritual for the next three days, to have my temperature, pulse and weight measured. I only recall my weight, which was 63kg. Standard practice for all *stailceoirí ocrais* (hunger strikers) was salt tablets added to our water gallons. Joe was very attentive. So much so that I had to remind him that I wasn't an invalid. He spoke through Gerry as if I was incapable of speaking directly. "Ask Big Jim does he want someone to tell a book?" "Ask Big Jim is it ok if I have a yarn out the window with Finbarr?" "Ask Big Jim how he is feeling?" And so it went on. I'm not sure if my headache came from lack of food or Joe's over-attentiveness.

I was surprised when a screw, called Parnell, leaving in my water gallon, asked me if I wanted the light on or off. Screws weren't in the habit of offering us choices. They generally used the lights to harass. Parnell, however, was English, and was not tainted by bigotry. He was actually an asset to have on the wing, especially when doing night-guard. He was a fan of Pink Floyd and fond of an illicit smoke. On night guard he brought in their albums and blared them all over the wing. It was a real treat listening to *Shine on You Crazy Diamonds, Wish You Were Here*, and other big hits. A big favourite was *Is there Anybody Out There?* It was a number we could relate to because in a way it summed up our plight. To add to the entertainment Parnell would get high on cannabis and dance his way down the wing to hit the button. I watched him one night in action. As he danced, he neared the button, but it was as if he was attached to an invisible elastic rope. With his arm and fingers outstretched, desperately straining inch-by-inch to hit the button, he went flying backwards up the wing again, hands flaying in the air, panic in his face like he was being dragged into the abyss. Undeterred, back he came, dancing, but as he neared the button, the straining against the invisible force was repeated, but with the second attempt he was an agonizing few inches short before he was propelled back up the wing again. This was repeated a third time when he eventually hit it and did a victory dance as he exited.

On December 18th the Blocks became very tense – the *scéal* was that Sean McKenna's condition had turned critical. We were on edge awaiting the outcome: would the Brits concede our demands or was Sean going to be allowed to die. There was excitement that night when after lock-up the lads on the yard side began exuberant cheering. Bobby Sands had entered the block along with an escort, Fr Murphy and a PO. This *had* to be good news because it meant that the prison authorities were recognising our structures, as Bobby was the OC. However, according to the lads on the yard side Bobby appeared subdued and did not resemble someone who was the bearer of good news. Bobby went to the other two wings first and spoke to the OCs and there was another cheer when he entered our wing, his old wing. Gerry jumped up to the door to catch a glimpse and impatiently I asked him to tell me was Bobby in good form.

Gutted, absolutely gutted was the feeling I had when dejectedly he informed me Bobby had tears in his eyes. I thought either Sean has died or the *stailc* has collapsed. Bobby went into Jake Emmanuel, the OC's cell, and left within a few minutes. Jake Emmanuel then informed us that the stailc was over. The Brits had offered a thirty-page document that contained the basis of an agreement, but it was too early to ascertain what that meant and more information would follow. Sean McKenna had been taken to hospital where he was receiving medical attention. This was not the ending we had anticipated. The *stailc ocrais* was supposed to deliver a clear outcome but we were none the wiser. Gerry offered me his chips that he had wrapped up in toilet paper and set on the pipes to keep warm. I didn't say no. It wasn't the celebratory meal I had hoped for, but food was food. (Gerry wasn't pleased. He bemoaned the loss of his chips for months after. Indeed, he was still talking about them forty years later!)

Over the next couple of days Bobby was escorted around the Blocks and allowed to have meetings with our staff. The fact that this was happening gave us some hope that there was movement. We each received the thirty-page document but its contents, unless liberally interpreted, did not reflect the basis for a settlement. One of the lads met Bobby on the visits two days later, Saturday 20th December, and was told there was going to be another *stailc*. Our hopes over the following days went up and down. The *scéal* we heard was that an offer was on the way on the 18th as Sean McKenna's condition became critical. The Dark, knowing that a document was on its way, decided to call off the *stailc*. Sean, however, was clearly committed to hunger striking to death. According to blanket man Tom (Dutch) Holland, who was in Musgrave Hospital recovering from a perforated ulcer when Sean was wheeled in, the doctors appealed to Dutch to tell Sean the strike was over because he was refusing treatment.

Gerry McConville told me that many years later he was drinking with the Dark in a Falls Road bar. Sean McKenna – who, apparently was searching for the Dark – approached the table and said to the Dark, "Why did you not let me die?"[7]

Christmas low

Sinead, from Armagh Jail, wrote to me enquiring what was happening. I wasn't in a position to tell her much other than Bobby was in negotiations with the Number 1 Governor, Hilditch. I didn't mention the possibility of a second *stailc* because speculation about that had been dampened down. An apparently reliable source had it that *Taobh Amuigh* had completely ruled it out. The information that we were receiving was that Bobby had been told to get a concession, more or less any concession that could be held up as a victory or, more to the truth, could be used as a face-saver. Bobby was placed in a very difficult position. We were angry because it was almost as if he had to go cap in hand to plead for what was rightfully ours and pleading was never part of our make-up. Speaking for the wing I was in, our experience a couple of days before Christmas left us in no doubt the prison administration, probably under direction from the British government, were not for compromising.

---

[7] Sean never recovered from the *stailc*. I was with him several times later in different Blocks, but it was pitiful because he was only a shadow of the man he had been. Years later Sean took his own life on the anniversary of the ending of the first *stailc ocrais*.

A few days before Christmas Fr Toner came to the wing to relay to Jake, the OC, a compromise that had been agreed. We were to report sick. This would be accepted given our years on the blanket and therefore we would not be available for work. Once we were no longer in breach of any prison rules, and allocated the status of sick, we would be issued with pyjamas, so no wearing of the monkey suit, and we would be entitled to full privileges. In other words, we would be out of the cells, able to associate with one another and be permitted a Christmas parcel. This would allow time for the negotiations to take place in a non-protest environment. We were to be moved into a clean wing the next morning, which would be furnished, and we were not to soil the cells or break the furniture. We had no objections and that night the wing was upbeat with the prospect of celebrating Christmas together. The craic was good with the likes of Micky Na Bi declaring he couldn't wait to get his party hat on, eat a Mars bar and watch *Chitty Chitty Bang Bang*.

The following morning the screws collected the cell cards (that contained our details) from outside our cells, the routine that signalled a wing move. For the first time ever, we were relaxed about a shift as we were confident it would run smoothly and there would be no need for the usual roll call to ascertain injuries.

Yet, oddly, breaking the routine, the familiar sound of the shooting of the locks that announced the shift, did not follow the removal of the cards. The wing was silent as our ears were cocked to every sound that might reveal what was to happen next. We waited and waited but there was nothing. Being in the bottom cell it was difficult to hear but I believe the screws left the wing. Some twenty minutes later I could hear the jingling of the keys as the screws entered. They walked down the wing, replacing the cell cards. There was to be no move. No explanation was provided. Micky Na Bi would have to wait at least another year for *Chitty Chitty Bang Bang*. As usual we laughed it off, made jokes about the pyjamas and we rounded on Micky, telling him we'd rather spend time on the boards than watch *Chitty Chitty Bang Bang*.

It was becoming abundantly clear: not only was there no good will from the prison authorities, but they were bent on taking a hard line. Not that we expected anything else, but we resented the fact that Bobby was being made to deal with them.

Christmas Day arrived. If nothing else, we could look forward to the food. No *Top of the Pops* and no Pink Floyd as Parnell wasn't on duty. There was, however, my favourite Christmas cake. Lightning, thankfully, did not strike twice. When the plates were handed in I think I had my foot in the door ready to stop it from being shut, just in case there was a repeat. I was happy as the door banged behind me. I sat down ready to tuck in with the cake secure. I could hear next door opening and then banging shut. Then onto Joe's, the screws continuing their rounds. But breaking the pattern I heard muffled conversation followed by Joe's door shutting and the sound of feet returning down the wing. Our door opened and to my surprise a screw held out two pieces of cake. I was off the mattress in a flash and grabbed them out of his hand barely before he could blink. Joe had kept his promise from last Christmas. I was so moved by this. The cake could not be swung because of the grilles so Joe dug deep to ask the screw to bring them to me. This took a lot because not only would he not talk to them unless confronting them but to ask a favour went totally against his character. I felt very privileged. When Joe shouted down to check if the cake arrived, I thanked him and told him it really was a Happy Christmas. This was to be Joe's last Christmas on earth and I was to be the proud recipient of his last Christmas present.

Triumphalism

The prison admin which had accommodated meetings, ferried block OCs to H3 where Bobby consulted with them in the big cell, now stopped all movement. Governor Hilditch insisted that if Bobby wanted to speak to him, he had to put on the prison uniform. Feelings were running high in our wing and no doubt replicated across the protesting Blocks. Why were we taking this? In a last-ditch effort to resolve the impasse, and possibly on instruction from *Taobh Amuigh*, it was decided that two wings, Bobby's and ours, would de-escalate the protest. All of us would come off the 'No

Wash, No Slop-Out' protest and it was arranged that we would be moved into clean, furnished wings. Furthermore, ten comrades in each of the two wings would present themselves for work – but only of an educational or vocational nature or wing maintenance (which had always been acceptable to us). This gesture on our behalf was an invitation to the prison authorities to also de-escalate and take the opportunity to gradually introduce a regime that did not criminalise us.

Families left clothing in for the men. But the authorities refused to accept them. There was no give, no meeting half-way, no goodwill gestures. It was sheer triumphalism.

It was now January 1981. The governor stated that he would decide what work we did. The twenty men, he said, would be moved out of the segregated, protesting wings and into the mixed conforming wings.

We were furious. Furious that we were put in a position where we could be mocked. Furious that we were required to go on bended knee before the bastards. The prison authorities, the NIO, the Brits, could not have read the situation more wrong. They took our gesture, our negotiating, as weakness. They smelt blood and went for the kill. They weren't interested in compromise or solutions, they wanted surrender. We weren't weak, we weren't on the point of surrender, and their actions actually served to strengthen our resolve. I doubt if even *Taobh Amuigh* could understand how faced with such adversity the bond between the *Fir Pluid* intensified. The Brit intransigence united us, removed all indecision and made the decision for us – hunger strike! *Taobh Amuigh* wanted us to get a face-saver and have done with the protest. If we had been offered our own clothes, the protest would have ended. Although I'm quite sure we would have gone into their various workshops to wreck them.

The order came to smash the place up. We did it with relish. All the anger and frustration from the ending of the *stailc ocrais* came out in us as we went to town on their property. The wing was awash with banging and crashing as adrenaline-filled bodies shouting, screaming and cheering smashed furniture to smithereens, purging the undignified experience Bobby and ourselves had been subjected to. It was as if a giant had been awakened. It was invigorating, therapeutic. Our pride was restored. We were fighting back. Our message was clear – we would never be defeated! Bring it on.

Riot squad

As the dust settled and there was nothing left to smash, the adrenaline receded, replaced by a foreboding. It wasn't long before the shout came that the riot squad was in. Grilles banged, keys jingled, a lock shot and the shouting began. My nerves were shattered as I awaited my turn to be dragged out – and from the commotion I knew this was going to be a rough one. Two at a time they trailed us out aiming kicks and punches as we were run up the wing. In the Circle we had to run a gauntlet of screws, well fired-up, kitted out in riot gear, shields and batons in hand. Both Gerry and I managed to stay on our feet and evade most of the efforts to batter us. Some of the lads weren't so lucky and were dragged along the ground leaving them easy targets for the blows. There were plenty of bruises and while there were some suspected broken bones, miraculously, it turned out there were none.

We were thrown into cells that had pools of water on the floor as they were still in the process of being cleaned. I was relieved that we had made it over in one piece so I didn't care about the pools. We faced across the yard to the Yippee wing and they had heard the uproar, which I'm sure wasn't easy to listen to, and were anxious to discover if we were okay. We assured them we had made it through and hoped it wouldn't be long before we received our blankets and mattresses.

It was winter and we had only a skimpy towel that was more for modesty than to provide protection from the cold. When the Yippees told us the riot squad had left, it dawned on us it was going to be a long night as we were not going to get the bedding. I was very tired but I had to keep moving because to sit down was to freeze. Gerry and I spent the night jumping up and down and treading what little floor space was not covered with water.

I was never so glad in my life to hear the screws coming on duty that next morning. It signalled the end of an exhausting night and brought the prospect of receiving blankets. When the doors opened and they handed in porridge, it was the most welcome meal ever, even beating the chips that Gerry begrudgingly gave me when the *stailc* had ended. With every spoonful I could feel my body de-frosting. Following that, the blankets were thrown in and I immediately buried myself in them. It felt really good, almost heavenly as the warmth enveloped my body and I relaxed. Of course, it was too good to last. Within twenty minutes the shout came, "Wing shift!" We were on the move again.

We were loaded into vans and transported to H6 where there was a reception committee waiting on us. One at a time we were taken into the ablutions area where half a dozen screws, with expressions on their faces clearly signalling they were pumped up and were ready to get tore into us on the pretext of going through a mirror search. I refused to bend and, more in hope but not at all confident, I anticipated the customary few boots to the back of the legs. Their brutality exceeded even what I thought they were capable of. As they laid into me with boots and slaps, dragging me about by the hair and shoving fingers down my throat, I got the feeling they were in competition with the screws in H5 as to who could be the most brutal. They won that one by a clear margin.

The nightmare over, I was thrown into a cell and, as was always the case but all the more that day, it was such a great relief to hear that door bang closed. Gerry was already there crouched in the corner. I don't think we said much to each other although I may have muttered something about it being a rough one. I huddled in the other corner, exhausted, feeling sorry for myself and I have to admit really down. The wing was dead. I suspect that others were feeling the same.

A voice broke the silence. It was Joe. Unbowed, he started into his usual banter: "There's going to be bad days for these good ones," and so he went on, making light of our ordeal, rallying the troops and not allowing anyone to feel down. Such a lift I got from his flippancy. He knew what he was at. He sensed morale was low and something was needed to lift the gloom. Showing leadership, especially when it was most needed, he continued as if nothing had happened, and I'm sure the screws were left wondering what more could they possibly do to break our spirits. Joe put everything into perspective, they had done their worst, we had been battered, deprived of sleep and heat but we were still here, we were still strong, and we were still determined to accept nothing less than to be treated as political prisoners. Around half four the bedding was thrown in. Exhausted, I crawled on to the mattress.

Bobby's wing was also smashed up and, like us, they were also beaten. They were moved to H6, opposite us. There were a lot of messages shouted back and forth with lads asking for each other. Although I was on the yard side, facing them, I was too tired to join in. I found the greetings a bit much and even nauseating. It was as if some just wanted to be noticed, to have their names broadcast.

Joe was the worst offender for shouting and putting the mix in. He changed a lot of the messages that lads on the blind side of the wing wanted to be *scairted* across the yard. For example, if 'Tom' asked Joe to shout over to 'Seamus' and tell him he was asking for him, Joe would *scairt* across, "Tell Seamus Tom said he was surprised he was still on the blanket."

Of course, Bobby's wing, like all protesting wings, was well acquainted with banter.

Bik McFarlane came in for special abuse from Joe. He wanted to know if he was the 'lunatic' who wanted to be a priest. While he made some very irreverent comments, Bik took it in the spirit it was meant. Bik was only getting what I had been getting for years. All week Joe was in his element getting *scéal* from the H3 lads and keeping the craic going.

XI
THE 1981 HUNGER STRIKE

After a week we were moved back to H5. Morale had picked up as preparations for a second *stailc ocrais* were under way and our pride was restored now that the negotiations with Hilditch were over. Bobby was to lead the strike which was to begin on March 1st. Two weeks later, Frank Hughes would join, followed by Raymond McCreesh and Patsy O'Hara one week later.

There was total respect and admiration for Bobby. He knew and we knew that because of what had happened in the first *stailc*, tragically, it was difficult to see how he could escape death. A group of twelve were to be on standby, ready to replace any *stailceoirí* who died. Seanna Walsh *scairted* to our wing the names from our block who were on the list. The names of those in other Blocks were not disclosed to us. Joe was Number 1; Brendan (Andy Capp) McLoughlin, Number 2; Martin Hurson, Number 7; and I was Number 11. Once again it was an honour to be considered but I was relieved that I was number eleven rather than in the top five.

My reasons for putting my name forward were the same as the first *stailc ocrais*. This was my fight for political status as much as anybody else's. I didn't particularly want to go on *stailc*, but after years of exhausting all avenues of protest, I knew there was no option. Giving up was never an option. Joe, on the other hand, was very upbeat and proud that he was Number 1. He had been hurt when he wasn't included in the first *stailc* and now his pride was restored. He was under no doubt, as we were, that he would now go on *stailc*. His only question was – did he replace Bobby or the first *stailceoirí* to die?

The 'No Wash, No Slop-Out' protest was to end on March 2nd. This part of the protest had run its course so there was no point continuing with it. The focus would be on the *stailc ocrais* which we were confident would win us our demands. It took a couple of days before we were all washed. The screws were in no hurry to accommodate us. That first shower was heaven. It wasn't just the feel of water and the cleanliness – but washing away years of protest, mirror searches, beatings and deprivations. Yes, the blanket protest would continue but the ugliness and brutality aspect had ended. No more wing shifts and no more feeling the cold. We now had the luxury of beds, sheets and pillows. Ironically, some of the lads accustomed for years to lying on a mattress on the floor could not take to beds and continued to sleep on the floor for some time afterwards.

It was a big relief to get rid of the worms that had tortured quite a lot of us, some of us for years. I had the ass scratched off myself. There was quite a queue to see the doctor on March 2nd and, ironically, with just a mug of cordial-like liquid that he dispensed, the years and months of scratching ended.

It was very strange at Mass seeing the lads clean-shaven and with their hair cut. We hardly knew each other and couldn't stop laughing. Cormac Mc Airt took on the responsibility for cutting our hair. When it was my turn, he asked me what style would I like. Silly me, who really should have been wise to Cormac, another one of the wing's notorious rakers, I walked straight into the trap and told him, "Bowie style". Only when he started chuckling and repeating, "Bowie style" in an exaggerated way, did I realise my mistake. Cormac only had one style – short, back and sides. Of course, he told everyone, and I was tortured for weeks with, "Hey, Bowie!"

Bobby begins stailc ocrais

I'm not sure how it looked to those outside the prison but for us the *stailc* did not seem to generate the same response as the first one. The media more or less ignored it. It was worrying that the campaign was so flat.

Raymond McCreesh was moved into our wing shortly after he began his strike. I recall him asking for a newspaper one day (*stailceoirí* were entitled to this) but the screw sneering at him asked why, as there was nothing in the papers about the *stailc*. We were very protective of our comrades and some lads responded by hurling abuse at the screw. Realising the depth of feeling and high emotion, he had the sense to hightail up the wing and stay out of the road when we were slopping out. What really annoyed us was that he was right, but we didn't want Raymond exposed to this.

Frank Maguire's death in the first week of the *stailc* and the unexpected moving of a writ for a by-election in Fermanagh and South Tyrone changed everything. In a brilliant move, *Taobh Amuigh* put Bobby forward as a candidate. It was a gamble, but we had nothing left to lose. Up to this point we were receiving little or no publicity, but this propelled Bobby and the protest onto the front pages. The turn out on the day of the election was high and we were told that the contest between Bobby and Harry West, leader of the Ulster Unionist Party, was tight. The next day seemed to drag on forever as we anxiously waited on the result. If there had been such a thing as a fast forward button that would have been the day to use it. The wing was as tense as I had known it, but optimistic.

At this stage we had a small crystal set radio which Gino McCormick guarded with his life. The radio, which we code-named the 'Maggie Taggart' (after a BBC news reporter), was only safe to be taken out during lock-ups. Gino relayed the news to us after the *One O'Clock News* and reported that our side were confident they had got our vote out. I recall, it was around half four when the result was expected. The order was *scairted* around the three wings that there was to be no cheering if Bobby wins. To do so would alert the screws that we had a radio and they would go on the rampage searching for it.

"Bua Bobby!"

None of us will ever forget that historic moment five minutes later when Gino got up to the door and *scairted*, "Bua Bobby!"

Even now, thinking back to that moment, the hairs on the back of my head stand up. The place spontaneously erupted. We were that ecstatic we couldn't control ourselves. We cheered, yelled, screamed, banged the doors with the chamber pots and I'm sure there were some tears. It was one of the best most unforgettable moments of my life and I know this was shared by my comrades. The people of Fermanagh and South Tyrone were with us and by extension we knew the nationalist people were with us. It was an endorsement of the fact that we were political prisoners. But above all we felt it would save Bobby's life. He was an MP and as such, we initially assumed, the British government would not want one of their members to die.

The world's press descended on Belfast. Bobby and our struggle reached the world stage and we were winning.

With hindsight, I can say this was a turning point in Irish history. Thatcher and her government's intransigence handed us a victory that not even countless IRA military operations could have achieved, and it gained us support throughout the world.

Raymond McCreesh

The following day both Raymond ('Raymie') McCreesh and I had visits. As usual, because the screws would only allow one cell at a time out to the showers, by the time we were called for the visits we still had not been washed. This worked to my advantage because they had to allow Raymond and me out at the same time, giving me the opportunity to have a yarn with him. In contrast to myself, who was still bubbling from the election result, Raymond was very subdued. He just wasn't himself. I had noticed at Mass he had difficulty kneeling down and struggled to get back up again. Trying to lift his spirits I went on about Bobby's victory and that we were going to win. Raymond was deeply religious and he had rosary beads and a large scapular of Padre Pio around his neck. He had taken them off to wash and I lifted the scapular and told him he had no need to worry, Padre Pio would keep him safe. I felt much better when he smiled, but I couldn't help but feel that he did not share my optimism.

While I was between the grilles awaiting the escort for the visit, I was shocked to witness Raymond struggling to make his way to join me. He could barely walk. Every step was an effort. Two screws did show some concern and were reassuring him there was no rush and he should take his time. I knew there was no way he was capable of walking to the visits as was the procedure for blanket men. I assumed he had only to make it to the front of the block, which would have been difficult enough for him, and a van would take him the rest of the way. I was really angry when I later discovered they actually had expected him to walk all the way. Not surprisingly, he collapsed en route and transport had to be called. That was the last I saw of Raymond. He did not return to the block but was taken to the prison hospital. The wing was disappointed because we did not get the chance to give him a good send-off before he left for the prison hospital to join Bobby and Frank.

The Yippee wing had given Big Frank Hughes a good send-off the week before. A concert was arranged and Frank made an emotive and spirit-raising speech. He took over the concert and it became a 'one-man show'. Our wing, in total respect and awe, fell into silence and listened to this giant of a man who hadn't a note in his head sing with all his heart song after song. The screws, probably intimidated by his show of fortitude, placed the industrial vacuum outside his cell and left it running. Our respect and admiration for Frank only grew, as, unperturbed by the roar of the vacuum, he sang even louder!

Information about the four lads who were all now in the prison hospital trickled through to us from a number of sources. One of the main sources was Patsy O'Hara's brother, 'Scatter', who was in the wing with us. The reports suggested that the lads were being treated with some humanity. A Medical Officer and an orderly, in particular, were mentioned for their care and respect. We sometimes wondered if the lads, not wanting to cause us anxiety and anger, censored any bad reports.

With the No Wash protest ended and the *stailc* in progress the prison authorities made the late concession of allowing us reading material. Twice a month we were permitted newspapers, although this was subject to the censor, and certain newspapers were prohibited. The years of denial had made us ravenous for material and information about the outside world. So, it was a very welcome development, but it brought a noticeable change in the vibrancy of the wing and how close-knit we'd been. While debates continued, the communal concerts, quizzes and 'books' ended and there was less communication at the windows and at the pipes.

Even Joe, who would spend hours at the window relating stories of his colourful past and cajoling me to reveal experiences which really should have gone with me to the grave, lost some of his characteristic consistency. Not that he stopped, and I was glad for that, for Joe could never have been described as boring. He would have made a great *seanchaí*, a traditional storyteller. Above all, he just loved sharing news about his family, and the excitement and pride which this invariably brought him was manifest.

Weeks into the *stailc* Finbarr and I were called up to our stations at the window. Joe was buzzing. He had just received a *teacht* from Goretti and he was over the moon to learn that Bernadette, his daughter, was going on a holiday to America. The trip was organised by a group in the US who arranged for children to escape the trauma of the conflict and experience a peaceful environment for a number of weeks. He was so pleased that his daughter was given the chance to have a holiday of a lifetime. Nothing would do but he had to arrange presents for Finbarr, Gerry and myself. We told him we didn't want anything and not to burden Bernadette. He insisted and said that if we wouldn't decide he would choose for us.

Joe prided himself on his dress code. He had an eye for fashion and had always turned out well. He had his mind set on a new leather jacket, which had to be three-quarter length, the right cut and colour. The US being a bigger market, Joe reckoned there was every chance his perfect coat could be found there. He wanted to know would it be too cheeky to ask Bernadette's American host family to check out the coats and as an act of charitable solidarity provide the necessary dollars. Naturally, we told him he had a brass neck and if the Yanks had any sense, they'd tell him where to stick his 'Fancy Dan' coat. Not that that would dissuade Joe.

"Fuair Robairt bas"

The tension in the wing grew as we received reports that Bobby's condition had deteriorated. Despite the world-wide publicity, which appeared to be largely favourable, and a number of interventions to seek a solution, which included the European Commission of Human Rights, and the Pope sending his envoy, Fr John Magee to see Bobby, Thatcher was not interested in a settlement. Their intentions were good, but they met a brick wall. Don Concannon, however, who visited Bobby during his last days, his intentions were despicable. On the North he spoke for the British Labour Party. This ghoul actually came into Bobby's cell, stood at the bedside to tell a dying man that the Labour Party agreed with Thatcher's stance in refusing political status.

Throughout the conflict Labour and the Tories had a bi-partisan approach to the North so if that was the reason for the visit it was superfluous. It was more like he came to gloat and get himself some publicity by singing the right tune for the gutter press.

Despite the high hopes generated by Bobby's election and the subsequent international interest, as he neared his final days, we realised that Thatcher was going to let him die.

In the early hours of May 5th Gino *scairted* across to our side of the wing the awful news, "Fuair Robairt bas."

The only sound to be heard was the pipes knocking as the message was passed from cell to cell. The mood was very sombre.

Alone with our thoughts I'm sure some prayed for his soul, and probably many thought of the times we shared together, the books he told, his belting out the *Curragh of Kildare* that gave us goose pimples, and the arguments over football. While I could feel the grief, I think anger was the more dominant emotion. What we were asking for was reasonable: opportunities for compromise did present themselves which could have avoided Bobby (and others) dying. The screws read the mood, the anger was bubbling, and they knew this was not the time for jibes about Bobby or the Blocks would have exploded. Sensibly, they remained low key.

The focus now changed to the three other lads and Joe. Not only had Thatcher withstood the pressure of Bobby's death but she never flinched and remained defiant. Therefore, we felt there was little hope for Frank, Raymie and Patsy. Reports coming from the hospital were that Frank was very weak, he had lost his eyesight and had only a few days to live.

Meanwhile, Joe, who had psyched himself up in readiness to replace Bobby, was becoming very anxious as word had not come through from the camp staff to join the strike as planned. He was concerned about his family too, as he had prepared them for what was to happen, and now they were left in a state of limbo and possibly even building false hopes that he wasn't going on *stailc* after all. The waiting game over the next few days was difficult for Joe and I witnessed this one morning when we were out together to wash.

Off-loading all his anger and frustration he told me *Taobh Amuigh* was against anybody else going on *stailc*. I had never seen him as angry as he questioned their right to interfere in "our hunger strike". He said that by limiting the *stailc* to the three lads they were throwing them to the wolves because Thatcher only had to ride out the storm of their expected deaths for another couple of weeks. But if there were more *stailceoirí* coming down the line, as planned, she would realise the pressure was not going to go away and she might more readily be prompted to act. It was clear the prevarication was taking its toll on him and I felt a bit useless because I hadn't the words that could assuage his anger and anxiety.

Joe joins the stailc ocrais

The uncertainty and waiting game ended later that day when Gino *scairted* across to Joe that it had just been announced on the news he was to join the *stailc*. Joe *scairted* to the OC and asked what was he to do, as there was no official word from the camp staff. Jake Emmanuel told him to go ahead as confirmation would undoubtedly follow. It was difficult to know exactly what Joe was going through, but the news appeared to relieve the pressure of the last few days and he was more like himself and up for whatever lay ahead. His thoughts were with his family that night. He hoped that, unlike his experience, *Taobh Amuigh* had given advance warning to them before it hit the news.

His conversation was animated as he couldn't conceal his excitement with the prospect of seeing his family again, who he had not seen since going on the protest in October 1977. I couldn't share his excitement or his relief with the news of the *stailc ocrais*. There couldn't be a good way to embark on a *stailc*, but Joe had the worst of starts and I couldn't help but feel annoyed for him. Not that I betrayed my feelings to him. We kept the conversation upbeat and slagged the life out of him that Goretti would sue for a divorce when she saw how fat he had become.

But it wasn't easy, keeping up the pretence that we were happy for him. He had longed for the 'Big Day' when he would see his family again, victorious, wearing his own clothes. But now the visit that he had dreamed about would take place with his life hanging in the balance and, for an hour, wearing the gear that he had so fought against. I think I almost felt crushed with the injustice of this. Joe and his family deserved more. They should have had their big day that he had often talked about. I couldn't see it any other way than tragic.

Bobby's death and Joe following him on the *stailc* was a turning point in my life. I had been convinced that justice always prevails and those who fight for what is right always win through. I never really doubted that we would win and that Joe would have his 'Big Day'. Now reality was hitting me and I realised that being right did not necessarily equate with gaining justice. I believe, like others, I suffered from the delusion that there were a set of imaginary scales at work in this world. Whatever wrongs or injustices were perpetrated on people the scales would swing back again and they would have redress and reward. Karma is probably a more popular way of describing this. The delusion that there were such scales was shattered forever by our experiences during that harrowing period.

The following morning when Joe refused breakfast he was moved into a cell on his own at the top of the wing. Regrettably, that was the end of our conversations at the windows. No longer would I enjoy the banter, the *scéal* and the little bits of LT (loose talk) that had kept myself and others entertained and helped us to escape our bleak, hostile surroundings. The void that he left was perceptible and a constant reminder of the character that only time would erode, but never extinguish. I did get to speak to him during Mass but between him running about scrounging *toitin* and reassuring everyone he was fine (as everybody wanted a bit of him), conversation was limited.

Death of Frank

Frank Hughes died the following week and was replaced by Brendan McLaughlin (Andy Capp).

In a new departure the Brits hijacked the hearse containing Frank's body as it was coming out of the morgue. Thousands had gathered in West Belfast to pay their respects, but the RUC invoked the Flags and Emblems Act to forcibly redirect the route of the funeral cortege and sent it through the loyalist estate of Belvoir Park. Bobby's funeral the previous week, with over 100,000 in attendance, had been of major embarrassment to the Thatcher government and once again exposed their propaganda before the world's media that we were merely 'a bunch of criminals' who were not supported by the nationalist community.

The following day, Julie Livingstone, the fourteen-year-old sister of Patrick and Martin who were on the blanket, was shot dead with a plastic bullet while going to the local sweet shop. The media, as usual, carried the story from the British Army's perspective, that the bullet was fired during a riot; but it was later proved there was no riot or disturbance of any kind. The *Belfast Telegraph*, as if to justify it, made reference to Julie's two brothers being on the blanket protest. My father was livid, wrote a letter of complaint, which was never printed, and never bought the paper again. Patrick, who was in the wing with me, was never one for showing his emotions, especially in front of screws, and I can only guess the heartbreak it brought both him and Martin, who had been my co-accused. Julie was only nine when they were last with her. I wrote a *teachtaireacht* to Martin expressing my deepest sympathy.

Deaths of Patsy and Raymond

Scatter O'Hara was permitted a couple of visits with his brother Patsy as he entered his final days. He told us how Patsy had described the heroic way Frank and Bobby faced their deaths. At times I asked myself, is this really happening? It seemed unreal and difficult to comprehend. Lads, who only weeks before were with us, healthy and buzzing with life, were now dead or dying. But it was real and sadly there was an inevitability about the deaths of Patsy and Raymond that followed after a further week. Both men died on the same day. Gino, our radio man, gave Scatter the sad news about his brother's death. The familiar sound of pipes rapping out the news was followed by reverential silence.

Joe had to go through the routine of going out to the Circle to have daily medical checks. This exposed him, like all the *stailceoirí*, to the taunts from screws. Screws, of course, who were safely behind locked grilles. Once Joe was within earshot they would exchange stories of alleged recent experiences of culinary delights. They would question if he would 'bottle it' and if not, when dead, would anyone, even 'Adams & Company', bother to turn up at his funeral. They would bet on how long a *stailceoirí* would last before dying and argue with each other about their predictions.

"I've a score on him to last sixty."

"No way, that bastard won't go more than fifty. Look at the shape of him!"

This callous and hate-filled drama would be played out before the target, Joe. While it would have been better to ignore them, Joe was never one for turning the other cheek and, as well as challenging them to come out from behind the grilles and repeat their taunts, he would have had plenty to say in return. At Mass one morning we had great difficulty restraining Joe when he spotted one of his main tormentors. The screw, alerted by the commotion, immediately locked the grille and wasted no time scurrying out of the wing.

Brendan McLaughlin, while only on *stailc* about a week, was taken out of the wing and brought to the hospital, very sick and in pain. Our newscaster, Gino, informed us that Brendan had a perforated ulcer and would die in a matter of days if he remained on *stailc*. Political pressure and publicity generates as a *stailc ocrais* builds, as the weeks move by, but Brendan dying within such a short period would not effectively build that pressure and publicity so the camp staff took the decision to order him off the *stailc*.

Joe leaves for the prison hospital

The events of Ascension Thursday will probably remain etched in my mind for the rest of my days. Being a Holy Day, we had Mass, so it was an opportunity to have a yarn with Joe. He wasn't himself that morning. The exuberant, indefatigable Joe had dimmed, lost his shine, and was replaced with an alien, subdued, taciturn character. I wondered if seeing his family again made him melancholy or, now that the four lads were dead and Brendan was off the *stailc*, was the pressure of being the *front* man on *stailc* weighing heavily. Whatever was wrong he didn't reveal. As he sat between Gino and me, I tried to cheer him up and knowing how much he went on about the leather coat, I told him that he would have no problem getting it now. He turned to me and with a deep sincerity that I can never forget, said "I'll never wear it." This shook me. I was left speechless. This was not the response I expected from the eternal optimist, the person who had been a tower of strength to all those around him and to me personally. I did try to retrieve the situation by telling him to wise up, he'd be fine, but the pause, which was only a few seconds but felt longer, appeared to make it insincere and only underlined the truth of Joe's statement.

Later that day I had my monthly visit with my parents. I was not looking forward to it as I had to tell them I was joining the *stailc*. To make matters worse, because I had been caught with a *bairt* some weeks before, it was to be a 'closed visit'. This meant I would be in a cubicle, separated from my visitors by a glass screen. The atmosphere was really bad. I could tell from the tension that my parents knew what was coming but I didn't broach the subject because the screw stood inside the cubicle hanging over the top of me. I kept the conversation to small talk hoping the screw would move. But he was like a leech and with the clock running down, 'the elephant in the room' had to be addressed. Trying to be cryptic I raised the matter. The reaction was much, much worse than I had anticipated. My mother broke down crying and pleaded with me not to go on hunger strike.

I was gutted, watching the misery I was causing her, and to compound this nightmare I was burning up, conscious that the screw was observing. He was invading our privacy in this most sensitive personal moment. I felt violated. I don't know which was the stronger emotion: anger or embarrassment. The instinct was to tell him to "Fuck Off" but that would have made my mother worse so I restrained myself. It was too much; I couldn't tolerate this nightmare any longer but there was only one way to end it. I told her what she wanted, I'd withdraw from the *stailc*. While this did settle my mother and ease the tension, it did not put my mind at rest. My conscience was eating me up.

Back in the block, as I made my way down the wing, I rapped Joe's cell door. His first question, which I knew it would be, was, "How did it go?" I didn't think it appropriate to tell him there and then as he had enough to contend with. I just told him it was a long story and I'd tell him when we were out again (meaning, at Mass). The screw who was escorting me back to my cell began shouting, telling me to move on. In a way this suited because if I'd have talked to Joe much longer, he would have gathered from my demeanour what had happened on the visit. I wasn't to know that was to be our last conversation.

A few hours later, during lock-up, we heard the bolt being shot in Joe's cell. He called out, "That's me away lads!" and he shouted out a few personal goodbyes to one or two others, including myself. Amid the crescendo of cheers and well-wishing that ensued, I bellowed, "All the best Joe!"

We were all gutted for him. He didn't get the send-off he deserved. The plan was to have a going-away concert in his honour, but the unexpected move put paid to that. After three weeks, the first *stailceoirí* had been moved to the prison hospital, but Joe was moved after twenty days. Joe, unlike Raymond, remained physically very strong, showing no signs of deterioration, so we had not anticipated the move. It was a day I just wanted to end. Apart from a feeling of emptiness, I had guilt gnawing at me.

Big Doc, Martin Hurson

The *stailc* intensified as each week another lad joined the strike. Among them was Big Doc (Kieran Doherty). I knew him from the IRA outside as our paths had crossed several times and he was someone whom I had looked up to. He had been with Sean McDermott in 1976 when Sean was shot dead escaping from a bombing mission. Mairead Farrell was captured on that same operation.

Martin Hurson, who was in H5, also joined the *stailc*. I spoke to him when we were together at Mass and because he was shortly due to be moved to the hospital, I asked him to take a *teacht* to Joe. I handed it to him and, as I turned to leave, he asked me when I was going on the *stailc*. I pretended not to hear him and walked away.

I'm quite sure because of the usual din in the canteen he would have thought I didn't hear him. I was too ashamed and embarrassed to reveal my decision to him, nor would it have been right to do so. But the guilt came crashing in on me because it was obvious Martin wanted to talk to me in particular about the *stailc* and no doubt this was because he felt I was, or was about to be, in the same boat as himself. He was moved to the hospital wing a few days later where I'm sure he was able to share and confide his thoughts and feelings with the comrades there. However, he didn't manage to get the *teacht* to Joe because the move was unexpected and he had left it with a comrade in the next cell. It was fortunate that he did. Foolishly, in the *teacht*, I had explained why I was not joining the *stailc*. Joe had enough to deal with without me offloading my guilt.

A couple of weeks later, I was delighted to receive a *teacht* from Joe. I had been worried and concerned because of our last conversation at Mass but reading his *teacht* was a real relief because the indefatigable Joe shone through again. He would have had me believe that he was living it up with plenty of smokes, a television, *craic* with the lads and great visits with the family. Of course, I didn't believe half of it. The only sour note was that David Steel, leader of the Liberal party, had visited his cell but had misquoted him to the press. I wanted to hang on to that *teacht*. I felt it could have been his last – but then I thought perhaps that was a bit morbid. In the end I decided to send it to the Lenadoon lads, Gilly, Gerry and Benny, in the Yippee wing. They had been worried about Joe and it would set their minds at ease to learn that he was holding up well.

Kieran Doherty becomes a TD

After the funerals of Bobby, Frank, Raymie and Patsy there was a bit of a hiatus in the exposure the *stailc ocrais* was receiving in the media. The decision to put prisoners forward as candidates in the Twenty-Six-County election in June 1981 changed that. Joe was selected for Sligo/Leitrim on the Anti-H-Block/Armagh ticket. Unfortunately, he missed being elected by just over three hundred votes. However, Big Doc was successful in Cavan/Monaghan and blanket man Paddy Agnew in Louth. The *stailc* placed Fianna Fáil and Fine Gael in a difficult position and in particular it exposed the rhetoric of Fianna Fáil as being the 'Republican Party'. Both parties were concerned about the rise in support for the Republican Movement and consequently they wanted the *stailc* ended but not in a victory for the IRA.

As Joe edged close to death there were two developments. Fr Faul began to put pressure on the families of the *stailceoirí* to sanction medical intervention when their loved one became unconscious. Joe's wife and family initially were the main target of this pressure. In particular, Faul singled out the women, the mothers and wives, played on their emotions and stated it was their Catholic duty to save their sons and husbands. This added to what was already an extremely difficult and traumatic time for the families. Naturally, none of the families wanted their loved ones to die but, difficult as it was, they respected their wishes to see the battle through. Fr. Faul's actions did sow some discord among the families and in several cases split them.

Another development was the intervention of the ICJP (the Irish Commission for Justice and Peace), a body made up of Catholic clergy and lay people (including a politician from the SDLP, a party opposed to the Republican Movement). Initially, we didn't hold out much hope with this group but as the days passed, days crucial to Joe, who at the stage was nearing sixty days on *stailc*, our expectations began to build. There was *scéal* that negotiations were taking place and there was some indication that the Brits had conceded some ground, particularly with clothing. *Stailceoirí* on the wings were brought to the prison hospital so that all were together for a meeting with the ICJP. Bik McFarlane, Blocks OC, was also transported back and forward to meetings. Perhaps most telling of all, Danny Morrison, who had been banned from the prison, was allowed into the hospital to meet with the *stailceoirí* and, separately, with Bik. Recognition of our structures both inside and outside the jail by the Brits (as clearance for Danny would have had to come from someone senior in the British government) suggested there was something in the air.

I should have learned from all the false dawns but I couldn't help but build my hopes up. I think many of the lads felt the same and there was a definite buzz in the air. I tried to convince myself that Joe could be saved as the Brits might give way, realising now that it wasn't just a case of riding out the death of four *stailceori*, there was a literal conveyor belt of *stailceoirí* coming and it wasn't brinkmanship. On a lighter note, I thought Joe was going to be hard to stick as he would claim that it was he who won us political status.

"Fuair Seosamh Ramhar bas"

But it wasn't to be. Early on July 8th Gino *scairted* across to me. "*Fuair Seosamh Ramhar bas.*" (Joe has died.) I'm not good with grief or emotion. I always try to brush it away and outwardly remain stoical. Yet I owed it to Joe to be broken and overwhelmed with grief and I almost wished this to be case. Yes, it did bite. I was hurt but deep down I felt it wasn't enough. I was annoyed with myself. I questioned myself and looking back I think the guilt that I felt for not being totally crushed was stronger than the actual grief I did feel. While this did torment me for quite a while, later I consoled myself with the fact that it just didn't seem real. I didn't see the body; I didn't attend the funeral or wake. There was no actual 'closure'. All I got was, "*Fuair Seosamh Ramhar bas.*"

There's no guilt anymore. I do miss him and I do feel it. Even as I pen these words, I feel the emotion welling up. I have found that when I speak about Joe at commemorations, I struggle to maintain my composure. If I'm out on a social night and the song *Joe McDonnell* is played, I battle my way through it, trying not to listen because I'm on the verge of tears. Not wishing to show disrespect but there have been occasions when I know the song is about to be played and I feel I may not be able to hold it together; I head for the toilets where I remain until it is over.

> My name is Joe McDonnell from
> Belfast town I came
> That city I will
> Never see again
> For in the town of Belfast

I spent many happy days
I love that town in oh so many ways
For it's there I spent my childhood and found
For me a wife
I then set out to make
For her a life
But all my young ambitions met with bitterness and hate
I soon found myself inside a prison gate

While I don't want to show anyone my emotion, I have an inner peace that his loss still hurts. I don't want that ever to be different because I owe so much to him. He died for me. He died for all the lads. All the *stailceoirí* died for the republican POWs. Yes, it was more than that. They were totally dedicated republicans and they died for the struggle. But I would argue there was a bond that grew between us during those years of protest, the depth of which others could never understand.

We were more than blanket men. We were brothers.

That bond sustained the ten lads through the *stailc*. They didn't want to let us down.

The Dark and Sean McKenna would bear witness to this. Both men were dedicated republicans and both were prepared to sacrifice everything for the cause. While I'm convinced the Dark was ready to die on the first *stailc*, he found it too difficult to stand by and watch someone else die when there was a possible solution. He said it himself, he felt responsible for all us.

But let's be absolutely clear. Moral responsibility for the ten prison deaths in 1981, and dozens of others on the outside, lies solely with the British government. We don't know if Sean's death or that of others at that point would have resulted in a resolution or a frustrated outcome. However, tragically for everyone, the British government interpreted the December 18th decision to end the *stailc* as weakness and a sign that no one was prepared to die, and this certainly misinformed their initial handling of the second strike. In my opinion, December 18th overshadowed the Dark's subsequent life, explained his gradual estrangement from old comrades, contributed to his poor mental and physical health, and expressed itself in criticism of the mainstream Republican Movement. The Dark died in 2008, at the age of fifty nine. Sean McKenna also believed that he himself had let us down, which was clearly untrue. Unable to live with this torment Sean took his own life.

A few years ago, I was invited to speak at a march in Clonmel, County Tipperary, commemorating the hunger strike. At the very back of the march holding an A4 size photograph of Sean was his brother, while leading the march were people carrying ten billboard-sized photographs of the ten hunger strikers. This was no fault of the organisers as they were unaware that Sean's brother was attending. His brother, wanting to remain discreet, deliberately chose to join the end of the march as it passed. No doubt he felt a duty to his brother, that he should not be forgotten. Lucky enough I was also at the back, otherwise, like the majority who were there, I would not have been aware of his presence. I was pleased and honoured to meet his brother. I walked along with him and we exchanged reminiscences about Sean.

When I stepped up to the platform, bedecked with hunger strikers' placards and I could see Sean's brother, still holding the photo and still trying to be unobtrusive at the back, I couldn't help but feel that history was dealing Sean an injustice. It angered me. I discarded the speech I had prepared, and I drew the crowd's attention to Sean's brother holding the photo. I told them that his photo should be at the platform and not hidden at the back. Relating some of my experiences with Sean I hope I did him some justice and the people left with some knowledge of and respect for the man, the republican and the leader that was Sean.

Death of Martin

Several days after Joe died Martin Hurson from Cappagh unexpectedly died after only forty-six days on *stailc ocrais*. The experience of losing another comrade was numbing. Martin had been the 'life and soul' of the party, always wanting to get the craic going and that full of *joie de vivre* that there were those who asked, "What's he on!"

When he first arrived in the Blocks he wanted to know his name in Irish. Typically, the lads taking advantage of the opportunity for a 'wind up' told him it was 'O'Haratach', which translated means 'monster'. Martin, none the wiser, was delighted it translated so well because there was a great ring to it. Nothing would do but he had to pass the news on to his father, who was equally delighted and adopted the name for himself. Months later, Seany McVeigh, in agreement with the wing, decided the joke had gone on long enough and decided to reveal the truth. He called Martin to the door, unsure how he would take it. The wing held its breath as the disclosure was made.

"Bastards!" came the scream from Martin. Silence fell for a few seconds followed by Martin's loud laughter and shouted, "What to fuck am I going to tell my Da?" Being the character he was, he continued to allow himself to be referred to as O'Haratach. I don't know if his dad was ever told the truth.

Fr Faul, from what I could gather at the time, took Martin's death badly. While he had been a friend of the prisoners throughout the protest, he opposed the *stailc ocrais*, and in the lead up to Joe's death he had pressed Joe's family to take him off. After Martin's death he appeared to pull out all the stops to pursue the *stailceoirí* families and in particular the mothers and used moral and emotional blackmail to force them to take their sons off the strike. This partially resulted in the focus shifting away from the British government and on to the mothers. Despite what must have been unbearable pressure, both Mrs Doherty and Mrs Lynch, who would have dearly loved their sons to live, respected their wishes and did not intervene.

Deaths of Kieran, then Kevin, then Thomas …

I didn't know Kevin Lynch. Our paths never crossed. He came from Dungiven and had been on the protest in H3. The sum of my knowledge of Kevin was he captained his county to victory in an All-Ireland Hurling Final at under-16 level, which was quite an accolade. He died on August 1st and the following day Kieran Doherty died.

Kieran Doherty, on the other hand, who we referred to as Big Doc, I knew quite well. He had quite a reputation and his exploits both inside and outside the jail had gained him respect and admiration. I believe even the screws had a grudging respect for him and they certainly were very wary of him. When it came to the forced washing, they hit his cell first, knowing what a formidable character he was, hoping to catch him off guard because they knew his resistance would be fierce. No doubt the four or five screws who were tasked to shadow him spent a sleepless time the night before. Kieran's bravery and commitment were renowned throughout the blanket Blocks and instilled a determination in us all and in particular in H4 where he was imprisoned.

Thomas McElwee, cousin of Francis Hughes, died on August 8th. The following Sunday, a very emotional Fr Toner shared with us Tom's final moments. He had been with Tom, who was sitting up in his cell chatting away when Fr Toner had to step out for a minute. But when he came back he was profoundly shocked to find Tom dead. He was glad he had spent those comforting minutes with him and was relieved that he had died peacefully. Despite having witnessed eight other *stailceoirí* die, the fact that a lucid, intelligent, conversant human being was gone within a snap of the fingers clearly shook him to the core.

While Fr Toner stuck rigidly to what he believed to be his pastoral duties, he was opposed to the Republican Movement. But he was deeply affected by the tragedy that surrounded us. We left Mass silently that Sunday morning and went back to our cells. We had run out of words. We admired the bravery of Tom and were deeply proud of him, but we were drained. Within a matter of just over a week three of the lads were dead. The price that was being exacted was beyond our comprehension. The life, laughter and the craic were sucked out of the wings because of our loss and bubbling away was resentment. Resentment because so-called nationalist politicians were either silent or, worse, rounded on the IRA and Sinn Féin.

The end of the strike

We could feel the momentum slipping away from us. Mothers pressed by emotional blackmail were beginning to take their sons off the *stailc ocrais*. Our camp staff were powerless to do anything about this.

On August 20th Micky Devine (Red Mick) became the tenth and last *stailceoir* to die. It was also the day of polling for the second Fermanagh and South Tyrone by-election, following Bobby's death, which Owen Carron, Bobby's election agent, now contested and won.

Some weeks later, on 3rd October, with men on the verge of death and dozens more ready to join the strike, the seven-month long *stailc* was called off. There were dissenting voices who argued that we shouldn't stop until we won our demands and we owed it to the ten lads to continue, otherwise their deaths would have been in vain. This was very much a minority view and I believe there was an overwhelming sense of relief that it was ended.

The lads' deaths were not in vain. Their action had highlighted not just the justification of our prison struggle but the overall unjust political context that gave rise to the re-emergence of the IRA in 1969. It gained the Republican Movement support throughout the world and left the 'criminalisation' policy in tatters. It propelled the Movement into electoral politics, mobilised the nationalist people who not only found their voice but became assertive, demanding their rights and equality. At the time, it was difficult to gauge the impact, but I did feel it was significant. Yet the gains made for the overall struggle for me personally at that time did not compensate for the loss of the ten men and the fact that we did not win all our demands. I was gutted because the outcome which I had hoped for and dreamed of, and was even sure would happen, hadn't happened.

We had no idea now that the *stailc ocrais* was over where we would go from here, but we were resolute there would be no giving in, we would continue the protest until we won our demands. Feelings were raw in the wing; we were hurting but, if anything, our losses steeled us to continue. Speaking for our wing, which I'm sure would have mirrored the rest of the protesting wings, had the order come to completely end the protest I doubt if too many would have complied.

XII
OUT OF THE CELLS

The one significant demand achieved was the right to wear our own clothes, thus ending the hallmark of the criminal, the prison uniform. This brought major change to our situation as the 'blanket' ended. It took a while for our clothes to be allowed in and there was a lot of pettiness as to what was and was not permitted. Much of this was due to screws who were livid with what they believed was a concession. We were allowed a limited time out of the cells for association, mealtimes and to exercise in the yard. I wouldn't totally agree with the adage, 'clothes maketh the man', but it was a great feeling to have clothes on my back again. I felt more secure and less vulnerable. Walking around the yard, lapping up the fresh air in a wide-open space, albeit confined, and awkwardly exercising limbs that for years had been restricted to a few steps, breathed new life into a body seized up with deprivation.

The prison administration, whether concerned about our poor health or perhaps hoping to entice us with what was on offer *if we conformed*, offered us some time in the gym to regain fitness. The unnerving sensation of legs buckling and falling to the floor as I tried to run, underlined the muscle wastage and lack of fitness. Unlike many others, however, I did not throw up.

No longer had I to eat sitting on a damp mattress with a plate on my lap. Dining at a table, together with friends and comrades, made the meals so much more enjoyable.

We had some access to the television in the canteen and this gave us a glimpse of the outside world. The music scene had an importance to us as a common saying was, "Once you stop watching *Top of the Pops,* you're over the hill!" While our youth was slipping away, nobody, almost to the point of desperation, wanted to be 'over the hill'! But with restricted access to the television it was a while before we saw *Top of the Pops* and so we had to make do with *Swap Shop* as a measuring stick that played pop hits. To my concern, the first hit I was exposed to was 'Happy Birthday' by Altered Images and I hated it. Was I over the hill? God forbid. Thankfully, reassurances came with music from Dire Straits, Meat Loaf and The Jam. There was still young blood running through my veins.

It really rankled me that a screw sat on a high chair, observing us while we were in the association area, the canteen. I doubt if any screw wanted to sit there as they were probably worried that scores were to be settled and with us now out of our cells the numbers game had dramatically changed. Even if they were left squirming in the chair, it didn't assuage my resentment their being in our space. While our demands had not yet been conceded and we continued to be on protest, I had a clear vision of the future – control of the wings with the screws' role reduced to opening and closing grilles, in the same way that republican POWs with political status, further down the camp, controlled their Cages while the screws patrolled externally.

Four of the lads were appointed orderlies. This meant they looked after the maintenance of the wing. We had always insisted we would maintain the wing and did not want anyone outside our ranks doing it. Initially, the screws tried to select the orderlies, but we met this with non-cooperation and they were forced to relent. They soon learned that if they wanted the wing to run smoothly they had to work with our OC.

Being an orderly meant entitlement to full privileges that included a weekly visit, a parcel, full association and access to the Tuck Shop, expenditure to which was limited to a couple of pounds. Our orderlies pooled their money together and bought tobacco for the smokers and chocolate for the non-smokers. More importantly, unlike the rest of us who continued to lose ten days' remission every month, it meant a return of fifty per cent remission with no further loss.

Lads who would benefit most from this – that is, those who were closest to their release dates – were selected for orderlies. This set in train a trickle of releases. Orderlies released were replaced by those next in line 'closest to the gate'. While it was great to see lads being released, because of the years spent together, it was sad to see them go. My own release date, about which I had no idea as I was still losing remission, was not something I thought about. It was too far away and I wanted to believe that something would come along before then. But I was no longer as optimistic as I once was because the struggle for political status and the *stailc ocrais* in particular brought a new reality to my outlook. However, I never abandoned hope. Like many of my comrades, hope was crucial in sustaining me through the years and more and more it began to crystallise in the form of an escape.

I ruled out the idea of escaping from the Blocks, as at the time they seemed insurmountable. Once again, my attention centred on the outside hospital. Once again, it was another hare-brained scheme that was never going to amount to anything. I had arranged a visit with a friend who was an active IRA member to check if she could get me a gun. She said it wouldn't be a problem but in retrospect she probably said to herself, "I'll say 'Yes', because it's never going to happen. His plan will never get off the ground." If those were her thoughts, she was spot on as there were so many unanswered questions to the plan that wasn't really a plan. Through one of the lads I made a tenuous contact with a nurse. I've no idea why but it seemed the right thing to do. There was no escape committee at the time, at least none of which I was aware, so I didn't seek clearance or reveal my motives to the IRA leadership. Firstly, I had to find a way to get out to reconnoitre the hospital. I felt impressive using that word 'reconnoitre' when discussing the matter with a small coterie of comrades. It sounded professional but was anything but. My ticket to the outside hospital did, however, sound very plausible. A few months before I was arrested, I had my jaw broken and a wire was inserted. The plan was I would complain that the wire was giving me a lot of pain in the hope that they would have to bring me to the outside hospital to have it removed. Or so I thought. The surgery was actually performed in the prison hospital, resulting in me being told by a comrade that my plan had been 'wired up'!

Football in the yard

We asked for a football but this was rejected so we made our own from socks. The lads were bursting with enthusiasm to kick a ball again, even one made from socks. Two teams were picked. There must have been fifteen or sixteen a side. Within minutes, thirty or so sets of feet, within the confines of a small yard, clambering to boot the ball, saw it morph into a shapeless lump devoid of bounce. Undeterred, we kept kicking it (and each other) until it fell to bits, socks scattering around the yard. Hastily putting it together again we continued with the onslaught until it was beyond repair or lodged in the barbed wire above the fence.

Eventually, they did give us a ball and we were in our glory. We were big into football and very competitive. Sometimes too competitive. It was the cause of many rows but they were always sorted out very quickly and there was no lasting ill feeling. It didn't do to kick a ball over the fence because that was the game over. There was little said to the culprit but that made the 'crime' worse. Even had it not been totally sincere, it would have been of some comfort to the offender to have heard, "Don't worry, it could have happened to anyone." But there wasn't a chance of that! Having hoofed the ball over the fence myself, I experienced first-hand the pressures and subtle opprobrium. There was an inescapable feeling of being in the 'dog house' until the ball was returned and sometimes, to add to the misery, depending on who the screws were on duty, that could take a day or two. The pressure remained even when the ball was returned because, fearful of repeating the offence, the culprit would feel compelled to rein in their enthusiasm and, against all instinct, treat the ball gently, almost as if it was a precious egg. Many a time I wanted to blast that ball for the goal of the century but had to bite the bullet and instead give the pass. We continually petitioned for extra footballs so as games would not end when one was kicked over the fence. Eventually, after a couple of months they did concede an extra ball. At this time, I had made attempts to write a diary but gave up after realising the problems keeping it hidden from the screws. The following is an extract from what survived:

It was Marty who knocked the ball over in the first half. We still had a second ball so were able to play on. At half-time as we sprawled along the catwalk (fence) grabbing a much needed breather Schofield, an English screw, dandered up the cat walk to our group, leaned on the fence in a casual manner that was reminiscent of my corner boy days and tried to join in the conversation as if he was one of the lads. I can't stand screws being friendly because I can't bring myself to return their friendliness and for some reason or other it troubles my conscience. Schofield's forever trying to be friendly although he's a terrible bore with it. As he leaned against that fence, he couldn't seem to realise that there was more than just a fence between us. I felt rotten for not conversing with him. In the second half, Tommy's shot at goal ricocheted off the keeper and went over the fence so we were left with no ball. John, the referee, asked Schofield how long was left to play and we were surprised to hear him say, "Eight minutes and fifty six seconds," not because we thought the time would've been either more or less but because it was so precise. Schofield must've taken his time keeping very serious. Unknown to me there was a third ball in Bleep Mailey's cell and Schofield fetched it, threw it into the yard, and then timed the last eight minutes not forgetting the fifty-six seconds. I'll bet he shouted, "Time up," dead on time. We won 8 – 6 and that put us second place in the league, one point behind Barney Fox.

A five-a-side football tournament was organised with the prize of a couple of packets of biscuits. Biscuits, supplied by the orderlies, were a luxury item and with my sweet tooth there could not have been a better incentive to win. And win my team did, but I'll not put that all down to me. Well, not entirely. My cellmate Gerry was one of those players who are known as 'match winners' and I was fortunate to have him on my team. We were duly presented with a packet of Golden Crunch biscuits which we set aside to eat later that night, away from the begging stare of the losers. However, on that day of our victory, the screws hit the wing for a search. Afterwards, when returning to my cell, I was apoplectic upon discovering the Golden Crunch gone! Gerry's amusement with my tantrum didn't help. The screws, with obvious delight, informed me they had confiscated them because given that I was 'on protest' I had no access to parcels or the tuck shop, therefore biscuits, 'being a privilege', were denied to me. McConville later quipped, "That really took the biscuit!"

A pair of trainers

With playing on the tarmac surface, especially in the manner we played, we went through footwear like there was no tomorrow. Trainers which normally had a lifespan of six months-to-a-year, if taking care, lasted about six weeks. The burden of continually supplying trainers fell to our families.

One day, during a visit, my parents informed me they had left a pair of trainers in for me – *again*. But this pair was a present from Joe McDonnell's daughter, Bernadette. I was choking with emotion. Joe, persistent and true to his word, insisting that I receive a present, arranged this when Bernadette was in America. It was, in the true sense, his parting gift. I had to treasure this tangible link to and reminder of Joe as it would have been sacrilegious to have destroyed them playing football. While my intentions were good, football is an addiction, and I caved in – maybe a little too quickly. My conscience was eased with the promise that I would tread very carefully but it was a promise that went against the grain and proved very difficult to keep. While the trainers were to last longer than the typical H-Block life span, they eventually met the same fate. I'm sure Joe would have understood, but I'm equally sure, being the raker, he wouldn't have let up slagging me: "And after all the trouble Bernadette went through to get them for you. Tttt."

Bye to 'Maggie Taggart'

Given that we had access to the news via the orderlies' radios and limited access to the television, Gino, who had looked after the 'Maggie Taggart', decided he no longer wanted the hassle. He offered it to me and I willingly accepted because, even then, I knew it was part of history. It was how we learned of the heart-breaking news of the deaths of our ten comrades and the many deaths of others during that traumatic period. It kept us in touch with political developments that both raised our hopes and caused despair. It brought us that iconic moment when Bobby was elected and the political landscape was changed forever. There was no way I could part with it. Assiduously, I guarded it for the next couple of months, keeping it safe from the ongoing searches. Each night after lock-up, I attached it to the window grille and covered it with a towel that hung over the window like a curtain. Should a screw look through the spyhole, the only part that was exposed was the ear piece and its wire leading to the 'Maggie Taggart'. The lads still shouted if there was a screw in the wing so I had plenty of time to take the ear piece out and allow it to hang from the radio behind the towel. However, one night there was no shout and, on hearing footsteps outside the cell, I instinctively leapt up causing the ear piece to be pulled out of my ear and like a pendulum it swung and hit the wall and smashed. Thankfully, the screw was not alerted to anything and I was able to replace the broken piece by cutting the top of a biro and using its threads to screw into the main body of the earpiece. However, this was a wakeup call. Gino was correct. There was no need to have the 'Maggie Taggart' anymore and it would have been criminal to have allowed it to fall into the screws' hands. So I decided to smuggle it out.

On that final night as I listened to it bringing news that Thatcher had sent a Task Force to the Malvinas, I had hoped the Argies would give them a bloody nose. I wrote out instructions on toilet paper how to use it and together with the radio safely smuggled them out.

Former blanket man Seando Moore years later used it in the H-Block exhibition that toured Ireland. Seando died in 2010 but his wife Patricia still has the 'Maggie Taggart' displayed in a glass case on her living room wall. Patricia's brother Jim's wife, mother of three, Nora McCabe, was killed yards from her front door by the RUC on the morning that Joe McDonnell died, one of many, including children that the RUC and British Army killed during the hunger strike.

We change strategy

Imprisonment never weighed that heavily on me and I believe that it was the same for the vast majority of political prisoners. The comradeship and the pride and honour of being part of a historical struggle was the oxygen that helped us not just survive but to flourish. That's not to say, that either for us or our families, there were no bad days. Family occasions such as weddings, births, deaths and Christmases, did make the separation that much more acute. An odd time a dark cloud would descend and bring the unwelcome thought that I'd be well over the hill, maybe even in my forties, before I was released. Being in my early twenties, 'forty' was like your life was over. No wife, no children, no football or hurling and just to throw in, no interest in *Top of the Pops*! That summer, in 1982, the Rolling Stones, my favourite group, came to Ireland to play at Slane. All my friends on the outside were there enjoying the concert on a lovely summer's day. I should have been there with them. Imprisonment did weigh heavily that day.

There was a realisation, around the spring of 1982, that the protest was going nowhere. The prison administration was content because it made its job of controlling the wings easier. It meant we were prolonging our imprisonment and were under impossible odds to escape or to develop our politics. We had played all our cards and had nothing left to give, or rather that's what I thought. While our wing held firm, there was a trickle of men leaving the protest. However, our stance was more a case of not giving in rather than making progress with our demands. Submitting to prison work was just unthinkable. Our camp staff asked all protesting wings to review the situation: were we in favour of continuing the protest, or should we consider alternatives. Our wing could not countenance ending the protest and I was very much behind that. It wasn't long before we learned that the camp staff was not prepared to continue with a protest that had run its course and there was going to be a strategic change.

Men were selected from our ranks to come off the protest, declare themselves 'available for prison work', and enter the conforming wings with a subversive mission – to drive the loyalists into their cells and create the conditions for segregation. Borrowing the term the media used for the British fleet sent to the Malvinas, these Volunteers were described as the 'Task Force'. I was asked to join but, wrongly, I refused. Psychologically, I was locked into the protest and could not bring myself to be 'available' for prison work. Some of us felt strongly that to do 'prison work' would be a betrayal of our ten comrades. Nor was I convinced that it wasn't just a sop to get us off the protest and avoid a split. I was wrong to doubt and wrong not to have gone with the Task Force.

The Task Force did a brilliant job. While they were outnumbered, their campaign of intimidation, violence and firebombing within the conforming wings, successfully managed to put the loyalists on the back foot. The loyalists locked themselves in their cells and effectively went on protest demanding segregation, which was our goal. All of this was carried out under-the-radar, so to speak. Neither *Taobh Amuigh* nor we POWs demanded segregation or engaged in a publicity campaign, as we knew this would only stiffen the British government's opposition. Instead, the Task Force manipulated loyalist prisoners, through fear of violence, to put pressure on unionist politicians to demand segregation. The unionists did campaign on their behalf (and, unwittingly, for us too) and the government, their natural allies, unofficially and quietly conceded.

The protest comes to an end

We had achieved another one of our demands and the camp staff felt the time was now ripe to definitively end the protest. We weren't prepared to conform and never would be. We were prepared to tolerate their system only to change it.

On November 1st 1982, the administration was informed of our decision. My feelings were mixed. Five years of protesting and ten men dead and it had not produced the outright victory that I believed could be the only conclusion. From time to time the thought that we had let the ten lads down niggled me. It was definitely the final nail in my naivety and the belief that justice always prevails. As someone once said, the graveyards are filled with the oppressed. I ended the protest reluctantly, with no sense of jubilation and tried to console myself with the belief that only the scene had changed, not the battle.

We wanted to remain together in the wing, but the administration would not accept this. Within a short period of time we were split up into batches and sent to different Blocks. It was heart-breaking. Years of protesting had bonded us so tightly, the strength of which I was never to experience again. We had looked after and comforted one another, shared our ups and downs and made light of the harshest of onslaughts that the regime had thrown at us. I had hoped that at the very least they would move us by cell and I'd remain with Gerry. But that didn't happen and I was left wondering where I would ever get an easy-going cellmate like him again.

To H7

Cormac Mac Airt and I were moved to H7. The wing was a mixture of former blanket men, some of whom had been on the Task Force; recently sentenced prisoners, who also had been involved in the Task Force fighting for segregation, and some republican POWs who had either left the protest at some stage or hadn't joined the blanket protest. There was no animosity shown towards the latter but initially I think some of them were worried that they would be treated as second-class citizens. They soon realised their fears were unfounded and that they were accepted as full and equal members of the wing. But their environment did change as we set about creating our own structures and ethos. In the conforming wings the screws had treated them as *individuals*. There were perks, particularly if chosen to be an orderly, such as extra money in the tuck shop, extra food and milk, permission to stay out in canteen during lock-ups and a degree of freedom to move about the wings. The screws had used these to exercise some control and create rivalry. Once again, our OC informed the screws that we would choose who was to be an orderly. Screws, worried about repercussions from the blanket days and having witnessed our strength during the segregation battle, were not prepared to challenge this.

The weekly money we received from the prison was pooled and after necessities were purchased from the tuck shop, the money was divided equally, leaving each prisoner to decide what they wished to purchase. Likewise, all food was distributed on an equal basis. Sharing, and a collective mentality, was ingrained in the blanket men. *Toitín*, that had always been scarce, was stretched to ensure

176

no smoker was left out. Initially, this mentality did not sit well with some who had been in the conforming Blocks but anxious not to go against the flow they soon accepted our sub-cultural ways.

Official resistance to movement about the block and access to the canteen during lock-ups was gradually broken down and relaxed. But our block staff, anxious to create and maintain conditions conducive to an escape (about which I knew nothing), exercised some control over the movement.

Dropping stitches

The moment came that I had dreaded – and during the years of protest never imagined would happen. I was assigned to a workshop. I think I felt close to humiliation as I walked out into the Circle along with six or seven others to board the transport. For some reason it brought back the memory of just under six years earlier when I walked into the Circle in H2 for the first time and had to strip. But that was a different humiliation. I was proud and determined with my stance then, but not now. I knew there were plans to wreck the workshops but that did not assuage my anger, resentment and humiliation with having to go to work.

We were taken to a Nissen hut, an old cage (or 'compound', the Brits' nomenclature) which contained twenty or more sewing machines, all on desks in rows just like school. We were asked, yes, asked ever so politely, to sit at a machine. The instructor, who smelt of alcohol and tobacco, came around us one by one explaining how to sew. When it came my turn, he disregarded the fact that I was lounged back in the chair with my legs outstretched, and head tilted looking up to the ceiling. He conducted himself as if he had my attention and, unfazed, launched into a demonstration of the machine. While he could read my body language, it was obvious he ignored it because he was afraid. This made me feel a bit guilty, as if I was the class bully, so I felt I had to alter my stance to make it less obvious but still enough to register I wasn't interested. I didn't want to humiliate him and I understood why he kept to his script. He moved to the next machine leaving me to play with my new toy.

177

I had the idea that I could burn out the machine by going at it full blast. Pressing the pedal down fully and keeping it there I made stitches up and down, criss-crossing, circling, until the material was just a mass of higgledy-piggledy stitching. My exuberance attracted the attention of others who I suspect, much to my embarrassment, believed that I was really into this prison work. That put paid to that. I sat at the machine for another ten minutes before getting up and grabbing a seat beside one of my comrades.

The two of us were joined by others and we simply ignored all work and chatted and there was no attempt to force us to do otherwise. Emboldened by the screw's response, or lack of it, the next day I didn't even sit at the machine. In fact, I never sat at it ever again. The workshop was beneficial in that I met lads from other Blocks. We would gather together in an adjoining hut and catch up on each other's news. There were one or two non-political prisoners and one 'Born Again Christian' ex-loyalist in the workshop, and between them and the instructor, who worked like a Trojan, they managed to produce some output and maybe justified their position (and by default ours, not that we cared). Although I suspect that justification probably was not required as the administration were more concerned about the appearance of us 'being at work' rather than the reality. Fortunately, for me, my time in the workshop was very short as I became the beneficiary of an incident in the wing.

Becoming an orderly

Most of the sadistic screws from the blanket, who we named '*fir donna*' (the bad men), disappeared off the wings once we ended the protest, but several, whether through bravado or foolishness, remained, and we had one in our wing. He was warned to remove himself, but this was ignored. A couple of the lads were selected to give him a battering and several others were on standby to ensure no screw interfered. There was no shortage of volunteers prepared to give him a touch of his own medicine. He was duly battered and left the wing unceremoniously, feet first. There were, of course, repercussions.

Four or five of the lads were trailed out and taken to the boards. The OC warned the PO that if they were beaten further action would follow. While they were not ill-treated, after some time on the boards they were sent to different Blocks. Some of them were not even involved in the incident. One was an orderly and this left an opening which I was asked to fulfil. All those rosaries and *Hail Marys* paid off after all! I know I shouldn't have been, but I couldn't help myself being cock-a-hoop. That cloud most certainly did have a silver lining – well, for me anyway. Being an orderly meant that I did not do 'prison work'. I helped maintain the wing but this was always acceptable and never classed as prison work.

There was some discussion both before and after the screw was battered. It wasn't just revenge, the screw in question was petty to the point where it was harassment. We had to send a message out to the administration and prison staff: just do your job and you'll not be a target. This screw had distinguished himself by his actions. Despite all that had happened in the past, our staff showed maturity and decided that there was to be no revenge. We had a higher moral code than our jailers. Violence would only be used when necessary to further our aims and would be a last resort. Our decision not to bar 'blanket screws' from working on our wings paid dividends. In general, blanket screws were easier to work with and manipulate because they knew their past singled them out, so they felt they had to prove themselves by trying to please us, as far as possible, without giving us the keys.

Activities on the wing

Having partially vegetated for years, there was a real thirst for education among the blanket men and most of the newly sentenced prisoners. There was a big demand for learning the Irish language. *Ranganna* (classes) were organised to cater for the different levels from basics to the *Fáinne Óir* (a badge indicating basic fluency). The camp staff encouraged us to push the prison authorities for education courses. Within our own structures we tentatively rolled out some of our own programmes, but it took some years to provide consistency and continuity. There were competing ideas and, while this could make for good debate, unfortunately there were a few who withdrew when their ideas were eclipsed. We recognised the need to politicise and we knew this would make us more effective in achieving our aims. We had received a massive boost by the results of the new northern Assembly when five members of Sinn Féin were elected and we won ten per cent of the vote.

We knew the struggle had taken on a new dimension and we took some pride in this because the election of Bobby had kick-started our entry to elections and the heroism of the ten lads had undoubtedly boosted our support throughout the country and beyond.

Our success with electoral politics precipitated lively debates. Should we take our seats in Stormont and Leinster House? Should we form a Pan-Nationalist Front? Should the war be wound down? How do we maximise our support? How do we reach out to the Protestant working class? Are we just nationalists with a socialist tinge? Should the Socialist/Marxist agenda be pushed more?

These debates varied from the same two or three individuals exchanging views, with the rest (at best) listening, to full animated, heated debates where almost all expressed a view. Books about national liberation struggles throughout the world were read to discover how we could learn from them. While the majority of the lads, to different degrees, engaged with the politicisation, there were those who opted out. Some were cynical of the process; some had lost interest and a few were opposed to the direction our politics took.

The hobbies room was very popular, where there was access to tools, such as hammers, chisels, saws etc., to make harps, crosses and other crafts. Some of the lads were very talented in making handicrafts and they would have been tortured by others who lacked those skills and needed help. Seany McVeigh was an exceptionally talented artist and he had such a kind nature that, even although he was swamped with work, he could never say no to the requests for Celtic drawings in particular and artwork in general. That was one of those times that I was grateful for my lack of talent.

Christmas was on its way and Dermy Finucane thought it would be a good idea to smuggle drink in. I was definitely up for it, as were Rab McCallum and Bobby Storey. The four of us arranged to have the right people visit in that final week before Christmas, as not all visitors had the nerve to smuggle anything bigger than a *teachtaireacht*. We weren't interested in having oranges syringed with vodka and sent in with a parcel, hopefully undetected. We wanted the pure stuff and the method was to put it in a balloon. All three of the lads successfully smuggled the drink in but a couple of days before Christmas, Dermy and Bobby were hit with a cell search and their drink was caught. I had a visit the following day and so it was down to me to ensure we didn't have a completely dry Christmas.

I had three visitors and I was shocked and unprepared when I discovered all three each had a balloon filled with vodka. Dermy had arranged this but conveniently didn't tell me. I had been expecting one balloon. One was just about manageable, providing it was a reasonable size. But three, and each one filled to about the size of a pear. I could have killed him. I couldn't very well tell my visitors I would chance one balloon only because they had gone to the trouble of smuggling for me and, furthermore, I didn't want to come across as a wimp. Stuffing the balloons down the front of my trousers, I tried to act naturally as if it was no big deal, that I did this all the time, but I was filled with dread. If I was called for a strip search, I was goosed! Strip searches were on a random basis. More than any other category, republican POWs were more likely to be selected. I said my goodbyes to my visitors, took a deep breath and crossed my fingers as the screw led me and another prisoner, who I believe was a loyalist, along the exit corridor of the visits. My heart missed a beat when I saw a screw standing outside the strip search box awaiting his next victim. I made no eye contact but I knew he had me in his sights.

"Strip search, McCann!" he shouted. I played stupid, ignored him and kept walking. I'd nothing to lose. I was finished if I stopped for the search and would spend Christmas on the boards. The screw, perhaps unsure whether it was defiance or deafness, shouted again much louder. I didn't falter, I kept walking at the same pace, neither quicker nor slower, heading for the end of the corridor that took a right angle and led to the exit door about twenty feet away where a screw was positioned to rub down prisoners before they boarded the transport back to the Blocks. The prisoner beside me looked at me in consternation. I think he was about to say the screw wants me for a search, but my look confirmed the obvious, I wasn't deaf and I wasn't for stopping.

As I turned at the right angle, just about to go out of sight of the exasperated screw, he screamed, "Strip search!"

There was no escaping the tension. The two screws on the exit door sensing something was going wrong looked up anxiously and turned their gaze on me. The screw who was the escort stopped dead in his tracks. The prisoner whose step had faltered from the second shout, knowing there was about to be a confrontation and wanting to distance himself from me, either stopped or slowed almost to a stop. I didn't know which because I didn't look back and, trying to be ever so casual, I kept walking. I heard the sound of boots breaking into a run behind me and I thought, this is it. But relief of relief I then heard the screw speak the words, "Ah you'll do." I didn't dare push my luck to look around to see the prisoner taken away for a strip search but continued faking an air of detachment as if I was engrossed with thoughts about the visit and oblivious to the commotion.

Tension over, the two screws on the door relaxed. Now I was to face a body search. I could only hope that it wouldn't be thorough and having evaded the strip search in such dramatic fashion, I felt it was going to be my day. The fact that the balloons were down the front of my trousers I hoped that the screw whether through laziness or, which was rare, a little sensitive about frisking the private area would not detect the obvious bulge. It was my day. The body search was just a quick frisk.

As I boarded the transport, I felt like letting a roar out of me of joy and to release the tension but held it until I was safely back in the wing. I had a few words with Dermy but it was more a case of friendly scolding as I was that chuffed with myself. I'd got one over the system and had something to brag about which I did, time and time again until no one else would listen.

It was one of the better Christmases I had in jail. We were permitted Christmas parcels for the first time and they contained a lot of luxury items such as chocolate and cakes. Our group also managed to obtain a little more alcohol. The day did not disappoint. *Top of the Pops*, good food, good company and a few drinks. We shared the drink equally and once we finished our allocation there was a little left but not enough to share between the four of us. We decided to play darts for it. Bobby and Rab were eliminated in the first round so it came down to Dermy and me. Dart for dart we fought it out and disputed some of the throws arguing about feet over the line. In the end I won (although Dermy will dispute this) and when I went to drink my winnings, it was gone! Engrossed in the dart duel, we did not see Bobby sneaking along and drinking the prize 'money'.

Losing our way, befriending screws

The good spirits at Christmas did not reflect my true form. The victory for segregation, the plans to burn the workshops and the push to control the wings, reducing the screws' role to opening and closing grilles, had helped my morale that was low after the protest ended, because we were still carrying on the fight that ten men had died for.

However, as 1983 moved along, we appeared to be losing our way, becoming complacent and accepting the status quo. There was no more talk of burning the workshops. I'm not sure if it was said directly or intimated that they facilitated strategic movement and communication with other Blocks but I wasn't satisfied with that.

While I was okay as an orderly, it annoyed me to hear the shout for the workshops each morning and watch the lads trundle off. To me, it was a cardinal sin. We had endured so much for years to ensure this would never happen. Even worse was the chummy attitude of some of the lads to the screws. As an orderly, I had access to the Circle because now and again I would require items from the store room. Tony McAllister, my cellmate, was a Circle orderly and he tended to stay in the store room. I didn't like the fact that republican POWs were Circle orderlies because this meant looking after screws. Wing orderlies were fine because we were looking after our own. If I required something from the store I'd nip in and out without delay and most definitely there would be no conversations with screws.

One day Tony invited me to sit down and have a cup of tea as he was making one for Ronnie. Ronnie? He was now on first name terms with a screw? Resisting the urge to tell him where to stick his tea, Ronnie joined Tony and almost urged me to sit down and have a cuppa.

"Here's the paper," said Ronnie. "Have a read at it while you're having your tea."

No way was I going to accept his hospitality but, because he was so pleasant, I almost felt bad for refusing. I did not accept, and Ronnie came to accept that I didn't want to engage. Difficult as it was to stand Tony's attitude, I found it impossible to tolerate the behaviour of some senior republicans.

Bik McFarlane and Cormac Mc Airt, both of whom I had a lot of respect, were two notable offenders. Like Tony, they were on first name terms with screws. Best buddies, if you don't mind – and I did. They were making tea for the screws, helping them with crosswords, brushing their offices – and I actually spotted them several times sitting down with them, having a laugh like they were one of them. All that was missing were the uniforms and keys. And they were two solid republicans. It was as if they had been tamed. The war was over.

Apparently, Eddie Wylie, who was the block SO and always one for boasting, did put it around that he had the Provies where he wanted them – model, conforming prisoners. Everything was just wonderful in his block, no problems, and full acceptance of the regime. The days of protest were gone. I found it almost humiliating. What had happened that dogged spirit that both men had exemplified during the blanket? Where had their republican principles gone? There was no let up as the situation continued to deteriorate and I was dumbfounded when the OC told me and a couple of other orderlies that we had to restrict our movement, particularly to the Circle. Was the staff now acquiescing to the screws demand for controlled movement? The whole climate was depressing me.

XIII
THE BIG ESCAPE

But then, a few months later, with a few magical, fantastic, unbelievable words my whole world was completely and sensationally transformed. I was taken to one side and informed there was an escape on and asked if I wanted to be included. I couldn't believe it. I had to ask him to repeat his words in case my ears were deceiving me. I then questioned if it was a 'wind up' because the lads were always playing pranks. I was in heaven, ecstatic and overflowing with restored pride to be a republican POW.

Everything began to fall into place. I was wrong to have doubted my comrades. Bik, Cormac, Tony and others had been carefully *conditioning* the screws into believing they presented no danger and were fully compliant. The escape was dependent on unquestionable access to the Circle and H7's external gate. They, and several others, had created those conditions. Rather than being tamed, they *tamed* the screws. The staff were concerned in case too much movement into the Circle and wings would panic the screws and they would stop it. Apparently, there were mutterings from screws in other Blocks that the Provies in H7 were getting the run of the place. So, our staff restricted the movement in order that it remained at a comfortable level for the screws but still gave individuals access to all areas.

I found it difficult to contain my excitement and joy. I wanted to share it with others and celebrate but I couldn't because it had to remain secret. Apart from some of the key players, I didn't even know who was going on the escape and their roles. I checked people out in the wing, looking for tell-tale signs like a bounce in their step and, like me, an eternal grin. Those unknown others were probably doing the same but not a word was spoken.

As the great day approached, I was drip-fed information, just enough to fulfil my role and I didn't cease to be amazed as the scale of the plan gradually unfolded. It was kept very tight – on a need-to-know basis – and, apart from a core group, the majority of the escapees were not told until after their visit on that final week. I was told in advance of that only because my visit was on the Saturday, the day before the escape, and it was felt that that would have been leaving it too late to acclimatise me to my specific role. I could understand the thinking behind that because when I was first told about the escape my head was buzzing and incapable of taking anything else in. However, I wished that I had only been told the day before because the days leading to the escape dragged and I had great difficulty sleeping as I went through all the possibilities of what might and might not happen.

While the majority of the wing, not being aware of the plans, were oblivious to the tension, I was not. It was thick in the air and was almost palpable. Those involved guarded their every step and observed the block routine with an intense alertness because the escape was predicated on routine and a change could make it unfeasible. As nerves became frayed, trivial incidents at times became magnified. There was so much at stake and there was so much that could go wrong. For example, the RUC had been called in a couple of weeks before as the screws went on strike, with the result that we were placed on a 24-hour lock-up. A block search could take place and one or all of the weapons discovered. A *teachtaireacht* could be caught revealing or even hinting about the plan. *Teachtaireachts* were going in and out on a regular basis as the escape committee and the IRA on the outside made preparations.

Bobby Storey, who was in charge of the escape, had several of us in the wing acting as couriers and our visits were spread out to ensure, as far as possible, that communications between Monday and Saturday were covered. Not being privy to the plans until the last week, I had no idea of the significance of the *teachts*. A few weeks earlier I reported to Bobby that my visitor had to swallow a *teacht*. He was urgent and adamant: get word out to her immediately to retrieve it when it passes through her body. There was no way I was going to tell a girl to do that and I told him where to stick his *teacht*, realising the irony as soon as it left my mouth.

My visit was to be on the Saturday, the last contact with the outside, and I was up to high doh. Smuggling, that had become natural to me, was nerve-wracking now that I knew the significance.

The thought of being caught, which wouldn't leave my mind, and alerting the prison administration to the escape worried me to death.

Kieran Fleming breaks his arm

On the Thursday, football was called. There was always a big demand for that but in a block of approximately one hundred and sixty men only twenty-two could go. To ensure fairness, a rota was operated, but since a lot were out at the workshops during the week the orderlies got more than their fair share. A lot of the orderlies were involved in the escape and in particular the squad who were to seize the Circle. Anxious in case there were any injuries (and the games were *very* competitive), there was a reluctance on the part of some to go to the football. Knowing how fanatical we were, if we failed to field twenty-two players, it would have been a first, and the screws would have undoubtedly suspected something wasn't right. The OC had to order men to go and we were warned that there was to be no madness and to tackle with care. Most of us didn't need the warning. It was played at a gentle pace and in a very sporting manner. I'm sure the screws wondered if we had been sedated. It was not a display characteristic of our games. However, once a goal was scored the competitive edge surfaced with a few, common sense no longer prevailed, and it was hell-for-leather until Kieran ('Hush Hush') Fleming was tackled to the ground and ended up with a broken arm. Words were exchanged, the lads came to their senses and the game returned to the pedestrian pace. Hush Hush was taken to the prison hospital, but he downplayed his injury so as he could remain in the wing – with a broken arm. While he was still permitted to go on the escape, he could no longer have a role.[8]

Saturday afternoon, as planned, I had a visit. I had nothing to smuggle out and I was warned to be careful if any *teachts* were to be smuggled back. I didn't need that warning. I was on red alert. Family were up to see me. First, I asked had they any *teachts*. I was

---

[8] Kieran did escape three days later, but in 1984 during a gun battle with the SAS he drowned in the River Bannagh, in Fermanagh, attempting to make his getaway. Two others died in the battle: IRA Volunteer Antoine Mac Giolla Bhrighde and SAS soldier Alistair Slater.

really relieved when the answer was negative because not only was no news good news but importantly, I could relax, nothing to smuggle back – meaning no anxiety about being caught and the whole escape up in the air. Nonetheless, I wasn't myself, relaxing wasn't to be had. The adrenaline was pumping as I could feel the clock ticking down to the escape. I kept the conversation to the usual small talk, but my mind wasn't really tuned in to it because racing through my mind was the escape and the possibilities it presented – good and bad.

My Dad, a teacher and big into education, wanted to know what I was going to do with my time. Would I apply for the Open University and other academic correspondence courses? I simply did not want to get into a conversation about this but couldn't very well explain to him that I had no intention of doing any, as plans were afoot. He was disappointed and even annoyed with my lack of engagement on the subject. My Mum, sensing this, took control of the conversation and the small talk continued while my Dad side-lined himself. I desperately wanted the visit to end on good terms because I couldn't be sure what the news would bring them twenty-four hours later. The visit ended, we said our goodbyes, but I could read my Dad's mood, he was annoyed. I grabbed my Mum and said to her that everything was going to be alright and please explain to my Dad I was sorry, and I knew his intentions were good but this was not the day to discuss my intentions for the future. I knew those words would have more significance the next day and they were insurance in case anything did go wrong, there would be no guilt, as my Dad would realise that I did understand he had my best interests at heart and it was appreciated.

Eve of escape

That night some of us who were aware of the escape gathered in two or three cells to comfort and reassure each other and while away the hours with some craic. We moved between those cells to make sure we spent a bit of time with all concerned and wished each other well. The conversations in the main were either directly or indirectly related to the escape but would change immediately if anyone who was not aware of the escape joined. If that person stayed, there was a slow drift out to one of the other two cells where they could resume speculating what the future would bring. While there were some doubts, the confidence was there that we would succeed. A big question was who would be on duty in the control room as it was the nerve centre of the block and in direct communication with the Central Control Room. There was one screw in particular we had concern about and hoped he would not be on duty. He was a bit lacking in common sense, danger didn't always register and unwittingly could do something stupid.

There was a subdued party atmosphere as tuck shops were opened up (revealing some of the lads as hoarders!) as there was no point in leaving it behind for the screws. Despite my sweet tooth, my stomach, which was in knots, wouldn't let me indulge. Others had no such problems and one notable *Big Effort* had, within a few hours, put away a month's supply and was ready for more, but ironically didn't want to appear greedy. I asked Rab McCallum for his new shoes because they were light whereas mine, with soles an inch and a half thick, were heavy. When he asked what the big deal with the shoes was, I explained that I just knew I'd be running. Nobody wanted to hear this. There was a chorus of, "Your feet won't even touch the ground."

The plan was that tomorrow's hijacked food lorry, having cleared all checkpoints and gates would, under armed escort from the South Armagh Brigade of the IRA, take us the whole way across the border and to refuge in the South. But I just had a very strong premonition that I would have to run. I suppose it was more of a dread because running was a weakness of mine. When running around the yard with others I always struggled. The group would be chatting away as they put in the laps while I, gasping for air, unable to speak, would cut corners to stay with them. (Years later I discovered I suffered from pernicious anaemia).

My request to Rab for his shoes was quickly dismissed and I was basically told to wise up.

That night I tossed and turned in my bed, a bit like a kid on Christmas Eve awaiting Santa. Only difference was the next day's Santa was for real.

Eventually, the morning arrived and the tension could be felt in the wing. It was stressed to all involved in the *ealu* (escape), "Everything has to be as normal." But how could it be! The day held such unbelievable promise and was now within touching distance. As IRA volunteers we were so proud to be back on active service and privileged to be part of an audacious, daring operation that would shake the British government and enter the history books. It would send shock waves through the whole prison system from the ordinary screw right up to the NIO and British government and would be a sorry reminder to them who they were dealing with and just what they were up against. We were never going to lie down; we were never going to stop pushing for our demands as political prisoners and our commitment to our republican ideals would never waver. I was on a high. This was to be the day that we talked about, longed for and fought for while on the blanket but never came. Now it was here, the day of victory. It was going to be a hard job acting normal.

Mass was late that day. As we walked in groups around the yard in the customary anti-clockwise fashion, nerves already on edge were further tested as we wondered why it had not been called. As stated, the smallest of matters became magnified. The tension dropped when the call eventually did come and departing from the norm, faces that hadn't been seen at Mass for God knows how long marched in from the two Wings, C and D, on our side of the block. Not only would the attendance have broken the Guinness H-Block Book of Records (if leaving aside the blanket era), miraculously the dozens queuing for Holy Communion were joined by the Prodigal Sons. A blind man would have noticed there was something up. The furtive glances and winks as the D Wing lads left, Mass being in our wing, was further evidence we were anything but normal.

The Mass had run late and left little time for dinner before the lock-up was called at 12.30. As an orderly one of my responsibilities was to serve out the food held in the containers sent from the kitchens, load the empty containers onto a trolley and push it out to the Circle before the lock-up. I was scurrying about like a man possessed trying to have everything complete before the call. Ardoyne republican Frank Maguire, another orderly, was doing likewise and, in his haste, he filled the boiler before everyone had the chance to grab a cup of tea. The lads liked to bring a cup of tea back to their cells when locking up so, being the Good Samaritan and to save the whinging, I took their mugs and was about to make my way to D Wing to use their boiler when Bik stopped me, wanting to know where I was going. Of course, with six mugs in my hands and heading out of the canteen, he knew damn well. I was tempted to tell him that I was heading into the Circle to make tea for the screws, but his expression told me this was not the time for humour. He was sharp, to the point where it was almost nasty, when telling me I wasn't to go to D Wing as movement was restricted. It was not in Bik's character to be nasty and I should have known that this normally pleasant, mild-mannered-man-turned-Hitler was not of a mind to be reasoned with. Obviously, the impending escape had frayed nerves and caused the momentary transition. But trying to reason with him I did: the lads need their tea, it's normal for me to go to D Wing, what's the big deal? This only agitated him further.

Meanwhile, Frank Maguire was loading the containers onto the trolley and making such a din that it was obvious he wasn't a happy bunny doing it on his own. I took the not-so-subtle hint and told Bik I had to help Frank load the trolley and wheel it out. I was at a complete loss when Bik snapped, "Leave it where it is!" It was not normal to leave the trolley in the canteen over lock-up so checking if I had heard the words correctly, wondering if he had taken leave of his senses, and with a look that suggested my disbelief, I repeated back to him, "Leave it where it is?" He said nothing but his pained expression seemed to suggest that his patience was teetering and the instruction which was clear even to the simplest of minds didn't need clarification.

Wasn't everything to be normal, stay in routine, were the thoughts going through my head, but the words didn't come out in time before Bik took to his heels. I did feel I should chase after him and confront him to double-check his words but I reluctantly let it go.

I re-joined Frank, who with a long face was still loading the trolley with enough noise to awaken the dead. I knew he wasn't too pleased with me because lock-up was imminent and I showed no sense of urgency to get the trolley out.

"Leave the trolley where it is," I told him.

"What?" he shrieked, letting go of the container with a bang and springing upright. "But everything was to be as normal," he said emphatically, as if challenging me to tell him he was wrong, knowing full well he wasn't.

"I know," I said, with a shrug of resignation, not at all liking the position I had somehow been manoeuvred into defending, and added, "But Bik wants the trolley left here." With that, his challenging attitude immediately changed to unquestioning compliance. Wiping his hands Pontius Pilate fashion, he shrugged his shoulders and calmly said, "Okay, if *you* say so," and departed for lock-up that had just been called, with an air that suggested his conscience was clear, he had made his protest about the trolley and could not be held responsible for the impending disastrous consequences – but I would!

Frank's response unnerved me. His parting words, "If *you* say so!" clearly put me in the frame of responsibility rather than Bik. I could feel panic setting in and I tried to calm down by telling myself I was only following his instruction. Yes, it was all Bik's fault and I consoled myself with the thought that I attempted to question him but he was beyond reason. But then another voice broke into my consciousness, berating me, suggesting I should have been more forthright and challenged him and left him, the way Frank left me, under no doubt that it was *his* responsibility. Mentally, this debate stalked me for the next hour and a half and for some reason guilt began to seep in.

There were four of us left in the canteen over the lock-up – Joe Simpson, Gerry ('Blute') McDonnell, Paul Kane and me. We tried to kill time by playing snooker and listening to the *Jimmy Saville Golden Hour* but my mind was elsewhere. I simply could not get that trolley out of my head. For some reason, possibly connected with the canteen empty of the men, every time I looked around, it appeared to take on a much larger appearance and doubly emphasised the incongruity of its presence. It was like a magnet: with increasing frequency I stared at it and the more I did the more I convinced myself that it should not be there. I gave up the pretence of being calm and began to pace the floor. I was sick with worry. I could see it all before me. The kitchen would miss the trolley; the food lorry would be sent at un-lock (two o'clock) to the block to collect it; but to save the lorry having to do a second journey the kitchen would load that afternoon's tea (a salad) and the lorry would arrive an hour early, instead of the usual time, three o'clock. It would be catastrophic to our timing because in order to commandeer the lorry, the block had to be commandeered first. And we couldn't do that until after two when everyone was unlocked and in position. In short, the escape would not happen – and all because of a missing trolley.

I really got myself worked up. How could Bik McFarlane make a mistake of such magnitude? He knew everything was to be normal but he departed from that directive and consequently, I feared, *he* had blown the plan apart. Then it struck me: he might deny that he had told me to leave the trolley. Given that he was clearly very tense, he might genuinely forget. This would leave me the villain of the piece, the man responsible for scuttling what would have been one of the most historic events in republican history. The blood drained from me. How would I ever endure the indignity of that? I cursed McFarlane up and down. He was putting me through hell.

A bit of madness must have set in because as the agony persisted, I began to seriously question if he had definitely told me to leave it. Was it possible he was actually referring to something else, like the boiler? But the anger would swell up in me and I'd say to myself with some conviction that there was no mistake, it had been the trolley he was referring to. The doubts ebbed and flowed and by the time un-lock came, a bloody eternity, I was drowning. I had worked myself up into such a state I was no longer certain what Bik had said.

As soon as the canteen grille was unlocked, I was out like a whippet, heart thumping, racing down the wing to confront him and saying into myself over and over again, "Please, God, make everything okay." I spotted Bik, took a big deep breath and doing my best to sound casual, not betraying the riot within me, I calmly said, "Bik, I left that trolley in the canteen for you." I tensed myself, awaiting the reaction.

"You did what?" he barked, in an agitated tone which I interpreted as, "Tell me I'm not hearing this, you didn't leave the trolley in the canteen!" I let out a gasp. The nightmare had arrived. I put my hand against the wall to steady myself as I could feel my legs going.

I closed my eyes and tried to wish the whole thing away. In the nearest I have come to what I imagine would be a dying breath, I muttered, pleadingly, "Ah Bik, you told me to leave the trolley." Slouched against the wall I could actually feel myself slipping down. My world was collapsing but then to my utter and unbelievable relief, in a matter of fact tone, he said, "Oh yes, the trolley, thanks. Sound job," and carried on walking up the wing without so much as batting an eyelid. I was flabbergasted. All that torture for an hour and a half because of him and there he was nonchalantly dandering away as if nothing had happened.

By now, all the cells had been unlocked. When I went into my cell Gilly shoved what looked like a prayer in a plastic cover before me and in his own rough and well-intentioned way, he said, "Here, take that." When I asked what it was, he told me it was a prayer to Padre Pio. Thanks, but no thanks, I had to say to him. I didn't go into the story about the last time I had been with Raymond McCreesh, he had a large scapular of Padre Pio hanging around his neck, supposedly protecting him. If he didn't do it for a devout Catholic like Raymond, then I'd no chance. So, holding a bit of a grudge with the Padre, I passed.

The main responsibility for taking the block rested with those IRA Volunteers acting as Circle orderlies: Brendy ('Meader') Mead, Tony McAllister, Gerry Kelly, Bobby Storey and Bik McFarlane and all, apart from Gerry, were from our wing. With four of our number in the Circle it was left to Dermy Finucane, Joe Simpson, Paul Kane, Blute McDonnell, Robert ('Goose') Russell and myself to take our wing, in concert with the other three wings. We had to ensure that all alarms were guarded and no screw (or anyone else for that matter) would get near to set them off. There were three alarms – one in the canteen, one at the top of the wing and one at the bottom. Dermy was to guard the alarm at the top, Joe and Paul the one in the canteen and, because we were stretched, we had to ask a couple of lads from the 'Rear Guard' to look after the bottom alarm. The Rear Guard would not escape but would hold the block after we had left. We were unsure how many screws would be on the wing but we planned for the norm which tended to be three but were ready should there be more.

Joe and Paul were to take the screw in the canteen. They would work it out between themselves as to who would put him down and who guarded the alarm. Goose and Blute were to take the screw on the canteen grille and I was to take the third on C Wing grille. I was very chuffed that the staff had such faith in me to do it on my own – but then, bringing me down to earth, I was informed that a member of the Rear Guard would be watching near at hand if I encountered problems. The screws would be at the top of the wing and also in the canteen so the Rear Guard at the bottom alarm would have been safe enough. Had any screw attempted to make it down the wing we would have stopped him, but it was just an extra precaution to place men at the bottom.

At 2.20pm the six of us moved near to our positions (depending on what the situation allowed). There were three screws as expected but one left for a break, making our job easier but more difficult for the lads in the Circle. Screws in other wings, skiving, as they do, headed out to the Circle for a break too, leaving the five Circle orderlies with much more than was bargained for. A prison officer called Williams was on the canteen grille and another, Goldstraw, stood at the razor box, adjacent to C Wing grille. Joe and Paul, blocking the path to the canteen alarm, placed an ironing board in front of it and began ironing. Blute and Goose tidied up the newspapers that were on a shelf four or five feet from the canteen grille where Williams was positioned. Dermy stood at C Wing inner grille, guarding the alarm, and he looked across to his equal number Seamus ('Cleaky') Clarke, doing a similar job at D Wing inner grille. The same scenario was playing out in the other wings of H7.

The bumper is called for

I moved to the ablutions where I took up my position at a sink and began to wash a shirt. While there was still too much ground between Goldstraw and myself, it enabled me to keep an eye on him as he hovered about the razor box. Once the shout came from the Circle to bring the bumper out, that was the cue to be, "On your marks", I would move closer to my screw. Bobby was at the sink next to me, likewise washing a shirt, bracing himself in readiness for the call. I wasn't that nervous. I think all the nervousness and anxiety had been flushed out of me after the gruelling time over the lock-up. We began some small talk but there was only one thing on our minds and naturally the conversation strayed on to the escape. The minutes passed and as half two came I began to regret not having brought more shirts to wash. Goldstraw had thrown Bobby and me a few furtive glances. He could well have thought it odd, as we did, that we were both still washing the same shirts and possibly he could sense that there was some tension in the air and something was afoot.

Concerned that we might be giving him tell-tale signs, Bobby asked me if it was noticeable that the pistol in his waistband was showing. I was too quick to tell him that his bulky cardigan covered it well – and missed the opportunity to tell him that with his belly he'd get away with a rocket launcher. In turn, I asked him if the hammer down my waistband showed and he assured me that it was fine. I wasn't comfortable with a hammer. There was something barbaric about it and I hoped I wouldn't have to use it.

As I watched Goldstraw, I wondered what sort of resistance he would offer. He was stockily built and had the look of a fighter about him. Or at least so he appeared to me at the time, but rising tension and some nerves probably saw me make a prize fighter where none existed. With the clock ticking down and too much time to think, the awful thought descended, what if I failed to restrain him and he managed to hit the alarm. This fear worked on me for a while until I looked over to Goldstraw, gave him a long hard stare and thought to myself, there is my bar to freedom, no way was I going to allow him to block my path. This filled me with determination and I became very confident I would take him.

Still washing the same shirt, I thought that this is getting beyond a joke, it's a wonder it didn't disintegrate, why were we waiting so long? I turned again to Bobby, looking for reassurance, but I could tell he was concerned too. He said the call was supposed to come by 2.30pm. Sensing there must be a problem in the Circle, I asked him if the lads would be able to take the Circle okay. In a confident tone, he replied, "With six guns, it won't be a problem."

His confidence boosted mine but the concern about the delay grew.

At about 2.40pm Bobby said, with a definite air of despair, "If the call doesn't come now, the game is up." We both fell silent. There was nothing else to say. My spirits began to flag. I willed hard for that shout to come and I'm sure Bobby did the same.

"Send the bumper out!" shouted Bik.

Relief of reliefs! The magic words came.

Bobby was jarred into action and the adrenaline pumped into my veins. He discarded the shirt in the sink, stood erect, checked his waistband and asked again did the pistol show. Not the time for jokes about big bellies, I told him he was fine and wished him good luck. He strolled into the canteen, collected the bumper and pushing it out the grilles looked every bit the man on a mission.

Making my way closer to my prey, I moved to the upper canteen grille (there were two canteen grilles) and pretended to be interested in what was on the TV. Ironically, the Formula 1 Grand Prix was on the grid, just like us, ready for the green light. I had one eye on the television and the other on Goldstraw, who was leaning with his back to me on the razor box. Williams stood beside me, watching the Grand Prix and we exchanged a few words. I had become an eleventh hour convert to the value of talking to screws.

"GO!" was shouted.

I leaped across the two paces to Goldstraw, locked my arm around his neck and screamed at him to get down on the floor. I barely had the words out of my mouth than he was face down on the floor offering no resistance. As I sat on top of him holding him down, I was so pleased that my aggression had worked. But my ego trip ended with the thought that it was quite possible that Goldstraw saw Rab Kerr pull a gun on the C/D grille screw, as he was facing that way and perhaps assumed I was armed too. He was terrified, pleaded with me he would cause no problem and would do exactly as I said. I was not interested in humiliating the man or adding to his fears. I did my best to calm him down and reassure him that he would not be harmed.

I talked him through the parts of 'my brief', I'd memorised, in a calm voice. I pulled out the pillowcase hidden under my jumper and to avoid panic explained that I was going to place it over his head. Next, I informed him I was going to take his keys. He relaxed, his breathing returned to normal and I don't mind saying, I felt triumphant. I had carried out my brief to the letter with no mishaps. I had to laugh a couple of years later when I read his statement. He alleged he was in the canteen (where he should have been) when *several* men jumped him, punched and kicked him and dragged him out (some twenty or thirty feet) on to the wing.

Blute and Goose had Williams secured on the floor facing down the wing, a couple of metres in front of me. We gave each other the thumbs up and stayed in our positions to await the next command.

Dermy shouted out to the Circle, "C Wing secure!"

"D Wing secure!" came from the other side of the Circle.

Out of earshot, A and B Wings confirmed the success of the takeover.

The Circle was secure, so we now had complete control of H-Block 7, apart from the external gate.

Then, suddenly, there were two loud bangs in the Circle.

What had happened? Within seconds word went out that John Adams in the control room had been shot when he tried to close the door. Some had predicted that he would do something stupid.

The wing went deadly silent. No one spoke, as we anxiously awaited to carry out the next part of our briefs. The lads in the canteen, uninvolved in the escape and most having no knowledge of it, were told to remain where they were.

Breaking the silence, a door swung open at the bottom of the wing and we immediately turned our heads to this unaccounted-for sound. Out came Paul Duffy, whistling, with a spring in his step, swinging his arms with his blue mug in hand heading for a cuppa, so happy, without a care in the world, and so wrapped up in his thoughts, oblivious to the scene at the top of the wing where men with hammers and chisels were on top of and surrounding two floored screws with pillowcases over their heads. It was comical to watch him as it slowly dawned that something was not right. He just seemed to fizzle out; the whistle trailed off; the arc of the swinging arms diminished until they hung limp; the stride faltered until coming to a halt, the glowing smiling face changed to puzzlement and then shock. He froze about fifteen feet in front of us and Joe walked over to him, put his arm on his shoulder to assure him everything was alright, and told him to return to his cell. All those in the canteen who were not involved in the escape were also told to return their cells.

The order then came to move the screws into the big cell, Cell 26, where we told the screws to remove their uniforms. We placed the uniforms in brown bags on which we wrote their details. For example – "Williams, 5' 11", medium build." This meant that the lads who had to don uniforms to later secure the Tally Lodge, at the far end of the prison camp, would look at the tags and know which uniforms best fitted. We draped ponchos made from blankets over the screws heads to preserve their dignity. We would not do to them what they did to us. Their hands were then tied behind their backs.

After that I left to prepare the C/D classroom for the arrival of the captured screws. The door was locked. I walked over to the Circle and gave Bobby a shout for the keys. I stayed at C/D Circle grille. Bobby behaved in a regimental fashion. Replicating the routine of a PO he shouted the command to the control room – "A/B classroom keys! C/D classroom keys!"

When they were handed to him, he marched over to A/B Circle grille, shouted out, "A/B classroom keys!" and mimicking the PO to the letter, flung the keys along the floor sending them skidding along the full length of the corridor and hitting the back wall of A/B. He marched over to C/D Circle grille, where I stood. I held my hand out to collect the keys but as if I didn't exist, he performed the same action at my side of the block. "C/D classroom keys!" he roared and flung them along the floor. They went flying past me and hit the back wall. So, I had to walk back up the corridor to retrieve the keys and walk back again to open the classroom. I didn't know whether to be impressed or laugh.

Exiting H7

Once the wings and Circle had been secured it only remained for the external gate to be taken to have total control of the block. For weeks Bik had been conditioning the screws to accept his presence at the gate under the pretence that the area had to be brushed. Bik, following this routine, made his way as per normal with brush in hand, but as was not normal, a pistol in his waistband. The screw obligingly opened the gate to allow him into the external air-lock and Bik pulled out the gun, arrested him and escorted him into the block. One of our team, now in prison officer's uniform, took the screw's position and operated the external gate. He would be replaced by one of the rear guard, in uniform, when we left and would continue to operate the gates after we had departed in order to buy us time.

Over the next half hour, the captured screws were filtered into the classroom in military fashion, beginning with A Wing, followed by B and then C and D. We sat them down and tied them in pairs. I took their names in the order they were seated. This was in case a phone call came through for a particular screw: I could look at my list and know exactly where he was seated. We would know precisely what to do if a call did come. One or two of the screws had difficulty giving me their names. This was not due to resistance but nerves that were that bad they could barely speak. With so many screws in the classroom, it became very warm. For the screws this was exacerbated by the pillowcases over their heads. With their nerves settling and knowing our objective was to escape and not as some may have thought, retribution for the blanket, one or two voices spoke up asking for the pillowcases to be removed so they could get some air. The lads obliged them as best they could, lifting the cases slightly and fanning them with table-tennis bats. They were given water.

The food lorry arrived at the front gate which was now manned by us. The lorry, driven by a screw with his helper, a young orderly, drove up to the front door. There, they were put under arrest and offered no resistance. Our lads emptied the lorry of its food containers. Bobby gave the driver instructions, which he had to follow to the letter: he was to drive the van through all the security gates as was routine, was to act normal, was to stop at the Tally Lodge for clearance and then proceed along the perimeter wall and out past the security checkpoint to the main road. The driver was shown the wounded John Adams. The driver said he understood and would do as he was told. He was put in the van, his foot was tied to the clutch, a (dummy) grenade was placed under his seat and Gerry

Kelly, lying low in the cab, pointed a gun at him. It was made clear: only if he followed instructions would he come to no harm.

The word came to move out about 3.40pm. We secured the classroom and handed the keys over to the Rear Guard. I said my goodbyes to my friends and comrades and left the wing. Bobby was in the Circle with clipboard in hand and looking very official. I was going to say something to him but he was poker-faced and didn't give me the least sign of recognition. It was obvious he was totally consumed with his role as he looked up, without making eye contact, ticked his clipboard and never uttered a word. Made me wonder if he missed his vocation in life.

I was one of the last to make my way out and board the food lorry which was backed up against the block's front doors. Joe Simpson, who had taken photographs of the escape, handed me the camera. It was entrusted to me because of my experience on the blanket but there were quite a few others who would have been more than qualified and, had the right person been chosen, those photographs would have hit the newspapers and made very interesting viewing.

Bobby was the last to jump into the lorry. He pulled the shutter down, gave a quick pep talk and emphasised that silence was now demanded. He didn't have to tell us twice.

As the lorry made its way through the block gates and then the phase gates, we held our breath. Luckily the screws on the gates whether complacent or lazy did not do checks on the lorry and waved us through. Had they done so, the plan was to arrest them and put them in the lorry with us. There were volunteers in uniform on stand-by ready to replace them at the gates. Just before the Tally Lodge, the lorry pulled in and Bobby and the lads in uniform jumped out. Armed, they were to take over the Tally and operate the gates. The lorry went through the first set of gates and came to a stop at the air-lock to await clearance before the main Tally gate was opened.

The plan was that our lads would arrest those manning the Tally, take up their positions, open the main prison gate and allow us to make our way to the final camp gate guarded by the British Army. Shortly after we were gone, they would then follow in screws cars that they would take from the car park, using keys taken from screws.

As I sat in silence in the lorry with my heart pounding, I knew something was wrong as I could hear shouts and scuffling. We did not break our silence but it was nerve-wracking listening to the commotion and not knowing exactly what was happening although I knew it did not augur well. My hopes were raised some minutes later when the shutter went up and Bobby jumped back into the lorry and the command was given to drive on.

But it didn't move! Bik, who was outside the lorry, then banged the shutter. It was pulled up again and he told Bobby there were problems. Bobby jumped back out and told us to do the same. I was devastated. I thought that was it, we were finished and about to surrender. I think most people in the lorry felt the same and that was probably why there appeared to be no hurry to disembark. The tail board was up which meant only one person at a time could climb out and this also accounted for the slow emptying process.

Being at the back of the lorry, beside the shutter, I was one of the first out. It became clear that Bobby needed help in the Tally Lodge as the lads were in danger of being overrun. We followed behind him but when I saw the reception committee that awaited us, I hesitated on entering. The screws had gathered in the hallway, highly excited and some appeared primed for action. Punches were exchanged as they tried to grab us. Initially, there were only a few of us to confront them – Meader, Bobby, Goose, Dermy and myself and one or two others who I don't recall. I think the screws believed we were cornered and that our numbers were limited to what was before their eyes which made it manageable. They thought they outnumbered us. In the ensuing struggle I ended up pinned against the doorway, half in and half out of the Tally Lodge. Meader, in a similar position, came very close to being dragged into the middle of them. They were like a pack of wild dogs.

Bobby stepped in and in an attempt to deceive them said, "You win! We lose!" But it made matters worse. They were baying for blood. He then pulled out his pistol and rammed it under the jaw of the screw who appeared to be leading the charge. But it made no difference, he kept struggling. I discovered later that some of the screws had come on duty quite drunk.

Bobby turned to the SO and asked that he cool his men down. He asked for Bobby's gun which, of course, was never going to be handed over.

While all this was going on, the lads had spilled out of the back of the lorry. Looks of astonishment appeared on the screws faces when they saw just how large were our numbers. The fight went out of them.

The shout came, "Head for the gate!" and I turned immediately and ran out.

Outside the gate there were more screws with batons drawn confronting us. Spotting a red car in the screws' car park I, followed by others, ran through the baton-wielders and made straight for it. I grabbed the door handle but the door wouldn't open. The car started up and accelerated away with me still hanging on to the handle. I had to let go. I wasn't sure what to do next. Some were making for the fields but I had no intention of following them because I felt sure the Brits in the watchtowers overlooking the Tally Lodge would shoot them. The screws, in hysterics and seething with rage, kept shouting to the Brits, "Shoot them!" Then I saw a yellow car – but it meant running back through the screws. It was my only chance, so I ran and dived in through the driver's door over the top of Meader, who was sitting in the driver's seat, and scrambled over to the front passenger seat. Kevin Barry Artt, Jimmy Donnelly and Paul Kane were in the back seat and then Jimmy Burns came charging and dived into the back and lay on top of them.

The screws surrounded the car, opened the driver's door and tried to pull Meader out. They managed to snatch the keys and whether they were thrown away or fell, I'm not sure, but Meader jumped out and with fists flying got them back. But he could not start the car. I kept saying to myself over and over again, 'Please, please start.' Harry Murray appeared at my window. He looked in at me with pleading eyes as I struggled to open the door. It wouldn't open! More and more screws were swarming around the car so Harry had to make a run for it. Minutes later Harry was shot by the Brit in the watch tower. The car still wouldn't start and the screws were banging on the windows trying to get in. They had encircled the car, taken out

H Blocks, Long Kesh Escape Route

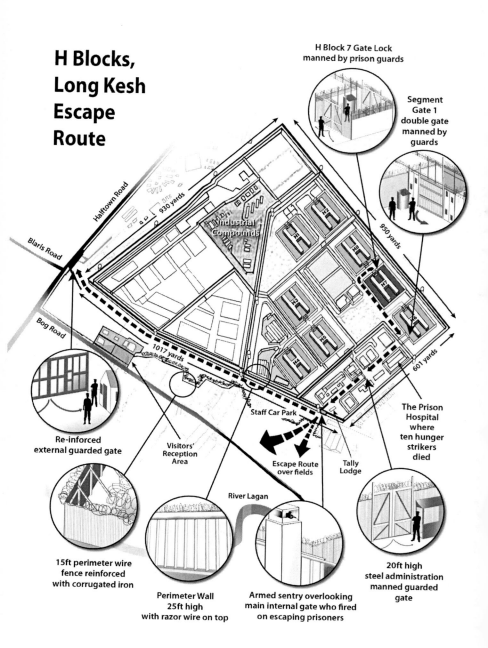

H Block 7 Gate Lock manned by prison guards

Segment Gate 1 double gate manned by guards

Halftown Road

930 yards

Blaris Road

Industrial Compounds

Bog Road

1017 yards

950 yards

601 yards

Re-inforced external guarded gate

Visitors' Reception Area

Staff Car Park

Escape Route over fields

Tally Lodge

The Prison Hospital where ten hunger strikers died

River Lagan

15ft perimeter wire fence reinforced with corrugated iron

Perimeter Wall 25ft high with razor wire on top

Armed sentry overlooking main internal gate who fired on escaping prisoners

20ft high steel administration manned guarded gate

Long Kesh
External Gate

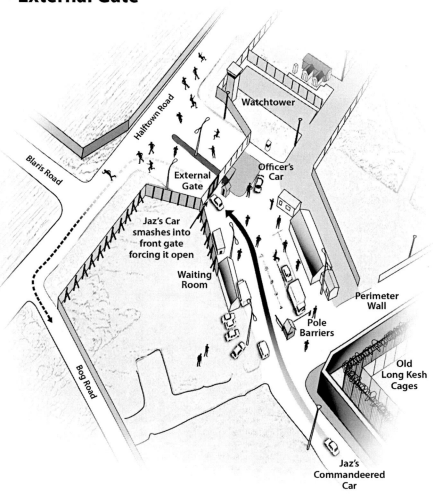

Blaris Road

Halftown Road

Watchtower

External Gate

Officer's Car

Jaz's Car smashes into front gate forcing it open

Waiting Room

Bog Road

Perimeter Wall

Pole Barriers

Old Long Kesh Cages

Jaz's Commandeered Car

their batons and were smashing the windows. One stood in front of the car and had a gun pointing at us. I think he tried to fire it but it jammed so he used the gun to join those using batons to batter the front windscreen. The window caved in showering Meader and I with glass and I was probably close to panic as we were seconds away from being mauled, when suddenly the car started. The screws leaped out of the way and the one with the gun, in a desperate bid to put Meader off his driving, flung the gun at him in through the smashed screen. What a relief it was to drive off and leave that frenzy behind us. The danger was not over but at least we were still *escaping* and I felt that it was all on us in the car to escape because I wrote off those who took to the fields. I was convinced they would be shot, entangled in the barbed wire and cut off by the Brits.

My next concern was the Brit watchtowers. As we drove around the perimeter wall, I could see a Brit staring down at us. Scared out of my wits, I awaited the inevitable shooting to begin. We had no cover. I was sure the Brits would blow us to pieces. It was nerve-wracking waiting on the shots and not able to do a thing about it. I didn't doubt that they would fire. We were escaping prisoners and it was their duty to stop us. What I didn't realise at the time was they didn't know what was happening. This was one of the most secure prisons in the world. It was escape proof so, lucky for us, they were more inclined to the possibility that the whole melee was screws fighting amongst themselves. As we passed one tower after another, with no shots being fired, I suspected that they must be leading us into an ambush.

I noticed the red car, the one I had tried to take, was chasing us. I told Meader to put the boot down and he told me to, "Fuck Up!" Not the time for arguments, nothing I could do, he was behind the wheel so, no choice, I had to suck it up. His thinking, I learned, was if he drove easy the Brits might be unsure if we were escapers but if he put the boot down, it would remove any doubt and they would shoot.

As we reached the end of the perimeter wall and were about to swing left to the external gate, the pursuing car overtook us. The driver began to blare his horn to alert the security on the gate. The barriers were up but in response the Brit and screws on the gate hurriedly began closing it. I thought that was the end. Our path was now blocked but Meader then put his boot to the board and the car accelerated to the gate. The Brit dived to shut it. I thought for sure we would be mangled. As we hurtled towards the gate, I climbed slightly up on the seat, hoping to protect my legs from the impending crash. This can't be happening, I said to myself, and as I braced myself for the impact I remember saying in sheer desperation, "Jesus Christ!"

There was a loud bang as we smashed into the gate. I was thrown forward and then whipped back again. I couldn't believe it. I was unscathed. Survival instinct took over. I still anticipated the shooting starting and with the car now stationary, an even easier target, was not the place to be. I clambered out through the smashed window of my door. My ears were ringing. The collision had succeeded in wedging the gate open. Kudos to Meader.

As I made my escape out of the camp it was one of the strangest sensations I have ever experienced. I felt that everything around me had stopped moving. It was like a freeze frame in a movie except that I was the only character moving and I felt that I was moving in slow motion. The sensation wore off as I moved further away from the car. I broke into a run. It was a fantastic feeling to be out, to be free, to have beaten the system. Even if I was to be caught somewhere down the line, I felt that every step I took was a victory. I turned around to see if Meader and the lads had made it out of the car but it was surrounded by a Brit and screws. A Brit and two screws came running after me. I had already written off the lads escaping over the fields and now all in the car had been captured so I was of the opinion, it was all on me. I alone have escaped.

I turned left and ran down the Halftown Road, keeping left because the sentry box could see the right-hand side and prevented me from taking the preferred route, turning right onto Blaris Road towards Belfast. The Brit who had overtaken the screws and was about twenty yards away, screamed, "Stop or I'll shoot!" I don't know exactly why but listening to the excitement in his voice, I sensed that he didn't want to shoot and it was as if he was saying, "Wise up. Don't make me do this." Knowing the bullets were about to come my way, in a desperate attempt to make myself less of a sitting duck, I began zig-zagging. I heard the crack of gunfire. He was either a bad shot or fired over my head as a warning but I suspected it was the latter, although I was sure the next one wouldn't be a warning. Lots of thoughts were going through my head. Didn't I tell the lads I was going to be running! Why did I have to be right when I so wanted to be wrong! Is Padre Pio going to have me shot because I rejected him? Is my Dad going to feel really bad, given how we left each other, if this doesn't turn out okay? There was a second crack. Much closer, it sent my ears ringing. My hair stood on end as I knew my luck wouldn't hold out for the next one but I had to keep going.

I saw a turn off to the left. What a godsend. It gave me hope and something to run for. I ran my heart out to make it and I did. I was elated. Safe, my life no longer in danger. But the elation didn't last long. I was on the Bog Road which ran parallel to the camp. The prison visiting areas was only a hundred metres away. The road was straight. No cover. I had to get off the road so I made to get into a field but it was completely ploughed. There weren't even furrows to run between. I thought about it for a few seconds but I knew it would be like trying to make my way through quicksand. So, deflated, I got back onto the road. Out of danger I could feel my exhaustion. Gasping for a breath and with nowhere to hide my energy was sapped. The Brit, having closed the gap and made it around to the Bog Road, was close and screaming for me to stop. I couldn't stop but neither had I a breath left to run.

The debate raged within me. There's no point running to be shot, you've nowhere to go. You are heading back towards the prison. But I couldn't give in, I had to keep going. Yet, walking was a form of stopping and I suppose it was a way of coming to terms with the inevitable. This all took place within seconds and within seconds the Brit was in on top of me, gun to my head. I was shattered. Numbed. The escape planned with such precision and daring, I thought, ended with me, the only one who made it out the gate but now caught.

The Brit was very excited and shaking. Still looking for an opening, and in desperation I weighed him up and considered the chances of taking him. One well aimed punch or kick might do the job but the gun remained levelled at my head. He was on high alert and, as if reading my thoughts, he told me to turn around and walk in front of him. Meanwhile, I noticed a car had stopped where I had turned from the Halftown Road on to the Bog Road. A screw, who had been chasing me, got out of the car and ran towards us. As soon as he reached me, catching me off-guard because I didn't for one minute believe he would have the audacity, he tried to throw his arm around my neck and put my arm up my back. I exploded. There was no way a screw was going to frogmarch me back to the prison. There was a scuffle and I threw him off. I could have killed him. The indignity of it. I was going back with a gun to my head – not as a screw's captive.

The screw, Jones, appealed to the Brit to help him subdue me. The Brit, obviously with a bit more wit, told Jones to stand aside as he was in the line of fire. My adrenaline was already at bursting point but he really rattled me: as much as being caught. Perhaps that's an exaggeration but this idiot knew his intervention was neither asked for nor needed. Clearly, for the glory and his ego, he wanted to claim my capture. God knows the story this Walter Mitty was going to live on.

As the Brit took me back at gunpoint with Jones walking alongside, with the anger in me, I couldn't help myself but have a go at the idiot. I said to him, "No way, would you have caught me." But his response, "I know, kid," was disarming. It was certainly not what I had expected and put paid to any further comments. The message was clear and accepted – no screw caught me! Well, so I thought.

A couple of years later I learned from his statement, which he repeated in court, that he actually did claim that he subdued me, put my arm up my back and frogmarched me back to the prison. Of course, the idiot forgot that the Brit was there and he too would make a statement and appear in court. The Brit told exactly how it was, apart from one detail. Jones wasn't alone in his exaggerations and lies. Many of his fellow screws did likewise, some to the point of ridiculousness. This became apparent during our trial and actually helped us because the judge knew the screws were, to put it mildly, unreliable. Had they told the truth, our sentences would have been much heavier.

The one detail the Brit omitted was that he fired two shots. He claimed one. I could not understand why he would lie. It just didn't make sense. Sometime later I read in a local paper, kept from that period, that an eyewitness described to a reporter how 'shots' were fired at a fleeing prisoner. Other papers, obviously quoting the NIO line, reported one shot. Jones, in his statement, stated the Brit fired two shots.[9]

I was taken back to the external Tally where we had crashed through the front gate. It was close to pandemonium. Brits and screws scrambling about and Landrovers speeding out through the camp in chase of my comrades. I was handed over to the screws, one of whom had a dog, which he set on me. The screw gave it just enough lead for the dog to repeatedly leap up snapping just inches from my face. Normally, I'd have been scared out of my wits but I was that pumped up I didn't give a damn. I gave my best Clint Eastwood stare at the dog handler, didn't flinch and, realising he wasn't going to make sport of me, he stopped.

I was taken into the gate house, strip-searched and received the customary kicking. Again, I didn't feel it. My pain was all consumed with being caught.

I was placed in a holding room where I was shocked to find only Jimmy Donnelly there. He had been knocked unconscious from the impact of the car crashing into the gate. When he had regained consciousness, he overheard the screws saying that Meader, Paul Kane, Jimmy Burns, and Barry Artt, who ran to the right, hadn't been recaptured, whereas I was chased to the left! While I cursed my luck, it was great to know that they had made it, but I was devastated I wasn't with them. Transport arrived to take us to the boards and

---

[9] Years later, some light was shed on this while I was canvassing during election time for Sinn Féin. I called at a door in South Belfast and the occupant wanted to know why, as a civil servant, he had been classed as a target by the IRA. During our conversation he revealed he was no ordinary civil servant but a senior NIO official in the prison service, as I suspected. He had quite a bit to say about prison officers being shot and then, as if to emphasise how unfair things were, he said with some anger that, "The soldiers were not allowed to fire on the escaping prisoners." I sensed that he was annoyed we hadn't all been shot. I asked him if this was true why then was Harry Murray shot. He pointed out that Harry was only shot after he had produced a gun and shot a prison officer. I didn't reveal that I was an escapee, but it left me wondering if this was true it made sense that the Brit would be told to say he only fired one warning shot.

a governor, very excited, appeared. He told the driver we were not to be taken via the main Tally Lodge but would enter the camp at the political status Cages end. He boarded the minibus with us to ensure this would happen. I must be in his debt because I was later to discover that the screws at the Tally Lodge had lost all discipline and, if not in a mutiny were close to it, tried to get into the armoury, ready to tear us apart. The lads that didn't make it out of the Tally did receive very bad beatings, some being kicked unconscious, but it could have been much worse had the screws got their hands on weapons.[10]

To the boards

I expected a welcome committee on the boards but thankfully, and possibly down to the governor, who I did hear instruct screws that I was not to be touched, there wasn't too much hassle. Others were not so lucky. A steady stream of escapees were trailed into the boards. The yells, thuds, smacks were unbearable to listen to. A reminder of the bad old days *Ar an Pluid*. The screws were like a pack of wild dogs. Some of the lads, naked, with hands handcuffed behind their backs, were trailed out of the transport by the feet, heads bouncing off the foot rest on to the ground, dragged across the yard, skin ripping off their backs, pulled down the wing of the boards, banging into grilles and kicked all the way. After each victim there was silence and real fear and concern that someone might be killed. I was glad my door was shut and wanted it to remain that way as it was never far from my mind that they might call in on me.

The silence was broken by Bobby Storey's voice. He wanted to do a roll call and find out everyone's condition. At that stage there

---

[10] Paul Kane and Meader made it as far as Castlewellan where they were caught the next day. Jimmy B, in screw's uniform, flagged down a car just outside the camp and pleaded with the driver to take him to the Royal Maternity Hospital where he alleged his wife was about to have their baby. The car was stopped at a road block just outside Twinbrook and Jimmy, despite the protests of the deceived driver that he was on 'a mission of mercy', was arrested. Barry Artt managed to commandeer a bicycle, bluffed his way through a number of road-blocks and made his way to a safe house in Andersonstown. Shortly afterwards he travelled to California where he remains to this day.

was about a dozen of us and it was then that I found out the lads who took to the fields actually *did* make it. So the escape was a big success! Bobby began organising. He wanted us to demand water, bedding and those with injuries to have medical attention. I had to admire his leadership as he was their Number One enemy and they had just kicked the shit out of him, but he would not lie down. My respect grew for him that day. He took responsibility, had all our backs and I think I'd have been prepared to follow him to hell and back from that day forward.[11]

Personally, while I was thirsty and had no bedding, I just wanted to batten down the hatches and hope by the morning things may have cooled. The last thing I wanted was screws at the door, especially screws on the warpath baying for blood. However, I did call the screws – we all did – and made our demands. Bedding and water did follow later, much later. I went to sleep that night exhausted, thinking about what might have been. From that day I don't know how many times I relived being in that car or running down that road but each and every time I make my escape.

The camera

I expected to be on the boards for months but we only remained for a few days. My clothes were taken, for forensics they alleged, so effectively I ended up on the blanket as did the others. I still had the camera inside my back passage but the cling film which protected it, keeping it dry, was degrading fast and, expecting to be in for the long haul, I decided, as a temporary measure until I could get more cling film, and in an attempt to extend its lifespan, to hide it behind a small grille in the wall over lock-up periods when it was safe. Or so I thought. With no warning the door suddenly opened one day and I was told I was moving. I thought I was just going to another cell, but the door was shut behind me and I was escorted out of the building to make my way to H7. So the camera was gone. There was

[11] Bobby Storey served over twenty years in prison. After his release he became northern chair-person of Sinn Féin. He died on 21st June, 2020, aged sixty-four, following complications during lung transplant surgery.

never another word about it. I don't know if it is still there behind that grille or more than likely the screws got it and, realising how embarrassing the photographs were, simply destroyed them.

All the recaptured POWs were moved to an isolation wing back in H7. The prison's attempt at poetic justice was lost on us. It became an interrogation centre and over the next couple of days RUC detectives questioned us several times. The screws kept their petty harassment up, banging doors with their batons throughout the night. It was the blanket all over again, locked up 24/7, no visits, and we communicated out the doors and windows. It replicated those days so closely that I actually had a momentary lapse when at the window one day calling Joe Simpson in the adjacent cell,

I shouted, "Fat Joe", calling to Joe McDonnell, Joe who had died two years earlier. I realised my mistake as soon as the words left my mouth. Old habits die hard I suppose. Joe Simpson said it was an honour to be called after Joe. "You better believe it," I said. Funny enough they were both similar insofar as they were great rakers in an endearing way.

We were only prepared to put up with prison reprisals for so long. We began to assert ourselves and demanded to speak to a governor and our solicitors.

Pat Finucane, acting on our behalf, took out a *habeas corpus* order in an attempt to end our isolation and we demanded the governor allow us to receive clothes. All our possessions had been destroyed. The governor told me that if he had his way the only clothes we would wear would be a prison uniform adorned with a big yellow stripe. I said, you tried that for years, but if you want, bring it on. Of course, it was the last thing I wanted but we both knew he was talking nonsense. Prison uniform would not prevent escape, but I couldn't miss the opportunity to put him in his place and rub it in that we *won*.[12]

---

[12] Human Rights lawyer Pat Finucane was assassinated at his home in 1989 by loyalist para-militaries working for British Intelligence. The British Government admitted that there was collusion in his killing but have refused to carry out a public inquiry despite calls by international bodies and the Irish Government.

Win we did. Not only was the escape a fantastic victory and morale boost for the POWs, the Republican Movement and our supporters, but the one outstanding demand that had not been achieved, an end to prison work, was abandoned by the authorities because we had subverted its meaning and used tools and communication from those very workshops to escape. Our full demands from hunger strike and blanket protest were now met. Granted, the prison, stung by the escape, tightened their regime but like everything else they flung at us we would eventually grind it down.

All escapees were now categorised as Red Book prisoners, which entailed frequent moving from block to block, with stays lasting anything from a week to three weeks. We were subjected to 'closed visits', restricted movement and half-hour checks throughout the night. The action was more punitive than security-related. We were an organisation, an army. Closed visits would achieve nothing unless all POWs were subject to them. Singling POWs out did not impair our functioning. The continual shifts from block to block were personally disruptive and unsettling but it had its benefits. It was great to get around and see old friends and meet people who, if I had had to stay in one block for my entire sentence, I probably would never have met.

The differences between the wings became apparent, some being more progressive than others, and we were in a position where we could communicate this to our camp staff, learn from best practice and change regimes.

XIV
THE AFTERMATH

The commune that I had been used to in H7 was either non-existent or at best partial in most wings. Although appointing orderlies became redundant, as prison work was abolished, everyone was expected to do their bit to maintain the wings. Some held on to the role and with it the privileges. This was counter to our ethos. A levelling process took place throughout the Blocks. We were all equal, we had equal rights and equal opportunities and equally we were expected to contribute to the daily routine of maintaining the wings. No one was told or ordered to do so: it was expected. It was, after all, our home, so we knew we were collectively responsible to maintain its upkeep. It took a while for this to be accepted, and there was some opposition, but the fact that it was in the interest of all rather than the few meant it was always going to succeed.

I, and my fellow recaptured comrades, had to put up with petty harassment for months afterwards. It did lessen as time went by and after a while came down to screws who weren't regulars on the wings and whose duties involved either the visits or parcels or were drafted in to do nights. The most common form of harassment was the half-hour checks at night when the spyhole flap would be banged down or even a baton used on the door. This was regular for the first few weeks but thankfully faded out, although there was always the odd screw who could not let the opportunity go by. It faded for two reasons. The lads in the wing would give the petty harasser sustained abuse. The message was clear: you do it to one of us, you do it to us all, and so it was best for the screw to desist rather than go about the wing in fear. Secondly, in general, the screws were too lazy to do the checks every half hour. If they checked at all it would only be when they had to come into the wing to hit the security button.

The closed visits, in my view, were the worst aspect of the Red Book. I could never get used to sitting in a box with a Perspex screen and a screw hovering behind me. I preferred not to take them at all but for the sake of family I bore with it. I wasn't at all sorry when our staff took the decision to boycott them. It was some time before the prison relented and agreed to us having normal visits.

Escape fever

The escape ignited the possibility of escapes within the minds of many POWs. Most prisoners dream about escapes and some actively scheme to do so but September 25th made it a reality. It wasn't so much that we had demolished the myth that the H-Blocks were escape-proof, but that the nature of the escape opened minds to wider possibilities. No longer was the scheming limited to the traditional digging of tunnels or cutting wire and throwing a hook over a wall.

There was of course a core of schemers, notably Larry Marley, who were innovative and had always thought big. Now all the schemers and the recent upsurge of converts were no longer limiting their schemes to traditional ways.

There were structures in place to pass on ideas and information and the point of contact had always been our intelligence officers. What I didn't know, but I suppose should have, was that there was an actual *Ealu* (escape) Committee. This was revealed to me by Larry Marley when I was shifted into his wing. Meader was moved with me, and Larry had long talks with the two of us. I was blown away with what he had to disclose and the confidence he exuded. He put us both in the picture because he wanted us to be part of the Ealu Committee. I felt very proud and valued to be asked and was overawed to learn how professional and sophisticated our organisation was and that I was going to be part of that, albeit on the periphery.[13]

Provided with an alias and codes to use when communicating, I fed information into the structure and received instruction on what was required of me. I had no idea of the size of the committee but I'm quite sure dozens were involved and within that, unlike the majority of us, only a small core would see all the pieces of the jigsaw.

[13] Larry was released from prison in 1985. Two years after his release he was assassinated in front of his wife Kate and children at his Ardoyne home. Although the killing was claimed by the loyalist Ulster Volunteer Force it is widely believed that British Intelligence planned and coordinated the attack.

This role was very important as it gave me a sense of purpose and made me feel like an active volunteer again, still engaged in the war. I had lost that feeling when the protest ended, it had been the lowest point of my imprisonment, but now this meaningful role would help sustain me in the years ahead. There were periods of inactivity in the role but there were times when activity was intense and we came unbelievably close to making history.

The scale of the plan Larry was working on was revealed to Meader and myself when he asked us to think about how the metal grille on the Emergency Control Room (ECR), that controlled the whole camp, could be overcome. I really wanted to come up with some realistic proposals so I could be considered as someone who would make a worthwhile contribution and my involvement secured as I felt I was on probation. However, neither Meader nor I had any idea how to overcome that grille and it worried me in case Larry thought he was wasting his time and cut me loose. He didn't, and thankfully he continued to throw out ideas and problems for us to mull over. Larry had ruled out himself for escape as he had only a couple of years left on his sentence and would be of much more value to the IRA as a free man rather than an 'on the run'.

I never met anyone as security-conscious. For example, when he wrote *teachts* containing sensitive information, he would get me to stick the skins together, so as he left no DNA, to wipe the skins down, leaving no fingerprints; and wrap them up. It made no odds to me as, intent on escaping, my sentence was only a number and I was only a small fish, unlike Larry who the Brits would target as a senior republican. Having had a glimpse of the effectiveness of the Ealu Committee I was reasonably confident the opportunity for escape would come around again.

Billy Gorman

One life which was transformed by the escape was Billy Gorman from Belfast's New Lodge. He had been captured after being caught up in the barbed wire around the perimeter of the jail.

Billy was serving an indeterminate sentence, detained under what is known as the Secretary of State's Pleasure. In the mid-1970s Billy had been arrested and beaten. In Castlereagh Interrogation Centre he signed a confession that when he was fourteen he was involved in the killing of an RUC officer. Billy was completely innocent, although it would be twenty years before the Special Branch was exposed as having concocted his confession and Billy had his conviction overturned.

After we were moved out of the isolation and interrogation wing in H7, we were dispersed throughout the Blocks and Billy and I ended up in the same wing. Escape was still very much running through our veins and for days our conversations amounted to post-mortems – "What if I'd done this or that?" I've no doubt we all had our 'What if' moments but it appeared to be consuming Billy.

I had been in the wing with him before the escape and while he was an easy-going, very likable character, I regarded his behaviour as a bit odd. He was the only prisoner I ever knew who stayed indoors and never, ever, went to the yard. Prisoners love to be out in the fresh air stretching their legs, but not Billy. He treaded the same path every day from his cell to the canteen, where he sat watching TV and played snooker. I was amazed at his prodigious appetite. I recall shortages been sent up from the kitchens, dixies of cabbage, for example, containing five or six portions which in the end no one would eat – except Billy. Now he was questioning that lifestyle as he relived the fact that while his comrades raced over the fields, leaping over the coils of barbed wire, he, unfit, trundling behind, became entangled in the wire and was captured. He confided in me that he would change, and he would never be left behind again. Starting from the next day, he declared there was going to be a new Billy and he would begin with a run in the yard. I wouldn't take him seriously. It was a big enough change for him to enter the yard, never mind run. My dismissal angered him. I just could not envisage Billy having his 'road to Damascus'. Yet he had a look of conviction about him that I never witnessed before and he stomped away with a parting comment, "Watch this space."

What a sight greeted me the next morning! Billy in shorts and trainers and a black bin bag covering his top, to intensify sweating.

He cut a comical figure. All that was missing was a hanky knotted at the four corners and placed on his head. Going against everything I knew about this character, he made his way out to the yard, did a few laps and came in with the sweat dripping and a sense of achievement. He never looked back after that. Every day, our very own Forest Gump was biting at the yard gate waiting on the screw opening up so he could go for his daily run. The yards were not opened if the weather was bad, but Billy would not accept this as he needed his fix. I recall heavy snow covering the yard and Billy at the grille screaming to get out for his run.

And it didn't end there. He became very conscious about his diet. I ended up in a cell with him several times during our escape trial. I couldn't put food to my mouth without lectures on healthy eating and calorie counts. He would remonstrate with me about my posture. "Sit like this. That's bad for your back." If I crossed my legs I would hear, "That's bad for your circulation." A complete fanatic. After we were released, I met him a couple of times – me driving, him running. I've no idea how many marathons he completed.

Christmas move

Five or six days before Christmas 1983 I was moved to another block which suited me, because, with the shifts averaging two weeks, I could settle down safe in the knowledge I'd be there over the Christmas period. Christmas parcels were always something to look forward to because we were allowed a cake, chocolate and biscuits. Two days after I arrived in the block I was expecting my parcel which my parents had left in. Plenty of parcels came into the wing, but not mine. I asked the screws to check but there was no word. The next day when enquiring again they discovered it had gone to another block. I received it later that night and it was in quite a state. They must have kicked it from one end of the prison to the other. Packets ripped open, cake squashed and mixed in with broken biscuits and chocolate. I was able to salvage some of it and it didn't matter that much because we shared everything, so I didn't go without. I didn't let their vindictiveness annoy me too much but the next day, Christmas Eve, I was taken aback when told I was moving and that did get to me. I had let my guard down, bedded in with the wing plans to celebrate Christmas and had got into the festive mood.

While I knew I was moving to a block where I had friends, as was the case with all our wings, that move was particularly unsettling. My feet had barely touched the ground in the new block when the OC called me aside. He wanted me to speak to a prisoner whom he suspected of having explosives and I was to get them off him. He was that matter-of-fact about the whole thing, and I thought he didn't really believe it himself. I took the suspect into a cell and questioned him but he was quite adamant that he had nothing. I believed him and told the OC he was clean. Christmas morning, the OC informed me that our suspect would be giving me a parcel and I had to dispose of it. I was both raging and embarrassed. Embarrassed because the OC had got the prisoner to confess, something which I had failed to do, and livid because the culprit had taken me for a fool. When he came to me, basically with cap in hand, and handed over the *bairt*, I was that angry I couldn't look him square in the eye as I was sure my eyes were blazing and I didn't want him to know that he had fired me up by making a fool out of me. I could understand how anyone wanting to escape would want to keep it quiet if they were not aware of the structure in place for escapes but the fact that I had been acting officially, as the IRA, when I questioned him, should have been enough for him as a volunteer to adhere to the rules. He had put himself before the movement and it was only when the OC threatened him with what he was prepared to do to get the *bairt* that he gave way. There were no words exchanged when he handed it to me. None were needed. He knew I was disgusted with him and over the next few days I know he felt awkward, but I made no attempt to make him feel otherwise. We were in the wing together several times after that but I had no time for him. Had there been an apology my attitude would have been different.

His *bairt* contained bell wire rather than explosives. Others had the explosives which were disposed of after they had to hand them over. I spent hours over Christmas stripping the bell wire down and flushing it down the toilet.

Off the Red Book/Disaffection

While it was good to move around the wings and see old friends and comrades and make new ones, living out of a brown paper bag (my suitcase) was tiresome and unsettling. I was very relieved when the day did come and I was taken off the Red Book. Others were not so lucky and remained on it until the day of their release. We campaigned to have the Red Book removed and while we succeeded in removing some of the harsher aspects, it was never abolished. Yes, all POWs were eventually moved from block to block but between times you could be in the same wing for years.

I did miss aspects of the Red Book. Every wing I entered I was treated almost like a celebrity and killed with kindness. The lads could never do enough, making me feel at home, providing chocolate, biscuits, books, and newspapers, and offering to smuggle *teachts* in and out. I witnessed how Blocks, learning from each other grew stronger and stronger, unified and committed. However, I did come across small pockets of disaffection. Regrettably, attempts to reconcile them were not always successful.

I first came across this disaffection when after the escape I landed in H1 and was very surprised when confronted by a republican for whom I had the greatest respect. Along with his followers, he basically ambushed me. His line was, why was H7 chosen above H1 for the escape? Weren't the men in H1 a better bunch of more committed volunteers? Granted they were not exactly his words but that was what it amounted to. He ran some of the escapees down and, sweeping his hand over his followers, like they were his prized possessions, asked if I thought I was more worthy than them, obviously wanting to massage their egos and keep them in his pocket. I had no pretensions about myself, I was just lucky to be in the right place at the right time and told him I was just as worthy. But given the performance and commitment *some* (not all) of his circle showed in the years that followed, if asked today I wouldn't have a problem giving him an answer that he wouldn't be too pleased with.

I was really taken aback, in particular by two or three who I had always regarded (and still do) as some of the Movement's finest. In retrospect, I think an initial lack of communication, parochialism, personal disappointment, and the sheer drive to escape combined to colour their judgement for a short period. Today, they remain part of the backbone of the Republican Movement continuing to devote their lives to the cause of freedom.

Unknown to me at the time, my disaffected, respected republican and several others in H1 had put an escape together, an unsophisticated plan, which amounted to cutting wire and slinging a hook over the wall. But it coincided, compromised and endangered the much bigger escape planned for H7. The camp staff had to tell them to abandon their plans because had they proceeded the inevitable clampdown that would have followed would have undone the months of conditioning in H7, making the escape impossible, as it was premised on the free and unchallenged movement of orderlies.

I never faulted them for their obsession with escapes. I, and many others, were the same. I could understand how deflated they were when clearance for their escape was refused. I can understand their jealousy that they had no opportunity of being on the big one. While the POWs throughout the camp were delighted and proud of the escape, it appeared to open a wound with my erstwhile comrade and some of his followers. They were no longer happy with the camp leadership. They dressed up their disaffection with a myriad of complaints and, as each one was dealt with, they would raise another. They became a thorn in the side of the staff and sought opportunities to undermine them. The reality was they wanted to be in charge of the structures in order to serve their own interests and not to benefit the camp. They were stung by not being on the big escape and, never wanting that to happen again, they sought control to ensure their places would be secure for the next escape that came along.

I had quite a few run-ins with them and was accused of being a 'lackey' and a sheep. Like the overwhelming majority, I had every confidence in the staff, whom I regarded as progressive, committed and acting in the interests of all republican POWs, rather than the few. That's not to say I didn't have some differences with them. I did but they were few and what was important was that I, like others, was allowed to express those differences.

I remember once in my role as OC being very angry and frustrated with the staff because, wrongly in my view, they told me to order a *non-political* off the wings. I wrote to the Camp IO as follows –

A chara,

There is a feeling of anger and disgust in the wing tonight due to BH being told to leave. I have been placed in the unenviable position of having to defend the IRA line even though my heart is with BH. Given that you are aware of the circumstances of both his offence and his entry to these wings, I find it difficult to believe that you would put him through the ordeal of leaving the wing simply because no formal clearance has been received. I doubt if we've reached that stage of bureaucracy or heartlessness which leads me to suspect that there could be something questionable about his case. But knowing the man as I do, I find this equally difficult to believe. His character suggests that the details he gave to the IO are a true record of what happened. He strongly feels that an injustice is being done (as do most of the lads) because he was invited onto these wings by Jimmy Doran and E. Moore. I've tried not to personalise the issue too much and view it in its wider context, with regard to the difficult task of implementing procedures to ensure security. However, it is possible that I am not aware of all the facts that are before you, therefore I reserve my criticism for now. But I must inform you that even though I have attempted to quell it (and will continue to do so), criticism in the wing is very loud and could well spread. BH was an asset to the wing and he'll be sorely missed.

Slan – Jaz, H6, 10-7-88

A second group who dissented from the Army line was led by Tommy McKearney, and their opposition was due to ideological reasons and the way the war was prosecuted. Tommy's view, as I understood it, was that republicans should be active uniting workers, infiltrating unions and taking up popular causes. He was opposed to the camp education programme as it wasn't Marxist enough for him. He had all the theory but in the view of many lacked reality. It was good to have opposing views but Tommy's limited following, somewhat similar to my other disgruntled comrade in H1, was less to do with ideology and more to do with parochialism. Both groups failed to appeal to any real support and ended up leaving the republican wings and going to Maghaberry Prison. For some it was a flag of convenience to go against Army orders and to enter the 'Lifer Review' process (which we were discussing with *Taobh Amuigh* but had not yet finalised a position). Others, after a while, realised their mistake and requested a move back to our wings and the camp as a whole were delighted to have them back with us again. (In 1989 we were to change our policy and lifers subsequently entered the review process on an organised basis which led to more favourable conditions being secured around the release schemes.)

In fairness to Tommy, he wasn't alone in lacking reality. In my view, and I include myself in this, having spent long years in the rarefied environment of the H-Blocks, reality escaped many of us. This is not to rubbish our education process. I gained a lot from it and it helped to make me what I am today – but a few months on the outside soon put it into perspective.

Education

Now off the Red Book, the long stays enabled me to take on responsibility in the wings, previously not possible. The camp staff actively promoted and encouraged POWs (and others who were not part of our movement) to participate in both the formal prison education, from remedial courses to GCSEs, right up to Open University, and our own informal but structured education programmes.

Our programmes were wide ranging and included Irish republican history, liberation movements and their struggles, competing ideologies from Conservatism to Marxism, and some of this overlapped with and drew on Open University modules. 'Training for Transformation', one of the initial programmes, commonly referred to as TFT, was derogatorily named the 'Tufty Club' by some of those comrades who had no interest in political education or tended to hold conservative views. They were a very small minority and some of them hid behind the label, "I'm just a military man." Others had formed a negative attitude to education, probably as a result of a bad experience from school, and baulked at the idea of going down a previously travelled road where their value and worth were measured and graded. The camp staff gave up on no one and, through persuasion and encouragement, the negativity gradually disappeared and, in general, once lads dipped their toes into the education process there was no turning back.

There were even those, like Billy Gorman with the running, who were completely transformed, found a love for education and their lives were never the same again. The catalyst for the education and politicisation was our republicanism. We wanted to make our contribution to the Republican Movement more effective and in doing so help build a stronger, bigger, more effective movement that would one day succeed in winning our objectives. The dominant ethos was: use your time wisely, educate and politicise for personal development and for the betterment of the Movement and the struggle.

The political education sessions were *facilitated*, rather than *dictated*, by those who were well-versed on the topics to encourage active participation rather than passive listening, although there were occasions when it leaned towards conventional lecturing. Discussions could be heated but the emphasis was on respect and no one was to be ridiculed or put down. There were one or two 'intellectual bullies' who would have tried it on and dismissed lads (in particular the less-politicised) if they said something contrary to their view. Thankfully, there were only one or two and they were usually tackled and exposed by others. It was important that political education was a positive experience.

Bap McGreevy

There was a lighter side to life in the wings and with so many characters the craic was ongoing. Video nights in particular were occasions when the slagging and banter went into full swing. There were always at least one or two characters in the films that bore some resemblance to some of the lads and they were tortured with hoots, laughter and sarcastic comments throughout. Connections, however tenuous, had to be made!

I had the good fortune to end up in the wing for several months with a notorious character in the Blocks, Bap McGreevy. Everybody, even the screws, loved Bap. There was an air of innocence and naivety about him and what you saw was what you got. From day one he talked to screws, even when it was scorned, because it was in his nature to be friendly with everyone. He loved his magazines and radio and I believe he would have been happy to have served out his sentence locked in his cell 24/7 with those two beloved items. We did not want him to drift, staying with the group was important for that sense of belonging and even mental well-being. We looked for roles that gave him responsibility and a sense of worth. Firstly, we put him in charge of the tuck shop. This meant he took the orders from the wing, collected the shop from the screws and distributed it. There were some mishaps and the final straw came with the batteries. A lot of the lads were up in arms when they received the wrong order. They had put an order in for Ever Ready HP11, which most radios used, but they received HP2s. As prisoners, locked up most of the day, radios played an important part in their life, so it wouldn't do to go without.

Bap was called for and when questioned he was quite indignant; he had followed their tuck shop orders to the letter. To settle matters, he fetched the orders that he kept in case there were disputes (which were not uncommon since he assumed the role) and with unabashed triumph stabbed with his index finger the line that stated 'HP11 batteries', and stated, "There, what does that say!"

We were flummoxed because it was as if he was saying, "I rest my case. I'm right. You all must be stupid." But the evidence was to the contrary. Someone said, "But Bap, you have given us HP2s." Again, with a look that suggested our stupidity was wearing his patience thin, he emphatically stabbed the line HP11 and asserted, "What does that say? 1 and 1. And what does that make – two!" We were lost for words.

Next, we put him in charge of the weekly visits. The visits had to be spread out from Monday to Saturday in order that they would not be top heavy on one or two days. Saturdays were much sought after for visitors who worked during the week and for children and, to achieve fairness, whoever was in charge would ensure we were permitted one or, if lucky, two Saturdays a month. There was uproar in the wing one week when for some unknown reason no one received a Saturday or Friday visit. Bap was asked to explain. Even by Bap standards he surpassed himself by suggesting there was no Friday and Saturday of that week. We were intrigued. He produced his calendar which was opened on that particular month, May, and almost in lecturing tone, said, "Look, Sunday 27th, Monday 28th, Tuesday 29th, Wednesday 30th, Thursday 31st and there is no Friday or Saturday that week, they are blank." We looked at each other in amazement, before we told him to turn the page to June where he would find Friday and Saturday.

Bap was extremely 'cell proud.' He cleaned his cell daily with an energy and enthusiasm that I never witnessed before or after. Had there been prizes for best kept cell, he would have cleaned the boards (so to speak). It was for this very reason he was the ideal candidate for a prank.

On Fridays we always had fish for dinner so it was decided we would take one of the fish and using Sellotape stick it underneath Bap's cell chair. Later that night, Bap was up at his door asking if anyone had noticed a bad smell in the wing. Of course, no one had. Next day, trying to get as much mileage as possible out of the prank, the lads made sure they commented, not mincing their words, about the 'stink' as they passed his cell. Bap, possibly slightly embarrassed, wasted no time in gathering cleaning materials together and scrubbed his den with added vigour. The following day, with the smell getting stronger, the lads kept him going, "Bap, did something die in there?" He emptied the contents of his cell, lashed disinfectant around the floor and walls and scrubbed the place from top to bottom, left it to dry out, came back, breathed in the air, was satisfied and put the contents back in again.

We had to suppress our laughter as we could hear him that night moaning about the smell. Next morning as soon as unlock came, a distraught Bap marched up to the screws and insisted they move him as there was something wrong with his cell. He was moved to an empty cell to the bottom of the wing which he set about cleaning with his characteristic commitment. Following that he removed all of the contents of his old cell (including the chair) and brought them to his new cell. That night, we could hear the groans again. He couldn't believe it; the smell was worse! This continued and was that bad I believe his eyes were watering until eventually a couple of nights later we heard the roar, "You bastards!" The fish had rotted and fallen to the floor.[14]

I was moved to another wing where I became the OC. At this stage, the administration was still smarting from the escape and trying to exercise controlled movement but the screws on the wings, worn down by the hassle and pressure we exerted, were losing the will to implement the policy. How well a block was run would depend on the PO and how he interpreted and applied the rules. A PO with a bit of savvy and initiative, both in the interest of his staff and the smooth running of the block, would be in regular communication with the IRA OC to arrange workable compromises. For example, controlled movement would be relaxed – provided we played ball and allowed the screws to immediately implement it if a governor walked into the wing. We did go along with this for a while but once we established it with the screws, the governors had to accept it too. No more pretence, and we'd move on to the next battle to improve and relax our conditions.

Our block PO Barlow thankfully possessed a lot of common sense and we had a reasonable working relationship. He was big into rugby, I wasn't, but to build a relationship I'd throw in my tuppence worth. One of his ambitions was for him and his son to play on the same team one day. Noting his passion, I'm sure he would have gone beyond his sell-by-date to ensure he had that proud and memorable day. However, his SO, my 'friend' Jones, was a complete ass. Being thick as he was, initiative was beyond him and he robotically followed the rule book. It didn't matter that the rules were more to do with the

---

[14] After his release Bap settled down for a quiet life only to be killed by a thug high on drugs and alcohol who broke into his flat in West Belfast and seriously assaulted him. Bap died three days later.

theory of how the jail should work rather than the practice. Left on his own he upset that fine balance between the smooth running of a wing and breakdown. I sometimes wondered if Barlow used Jones to tie us up and deflect our demands. I continually told him that he needed to rein Jones in or the situation would get out of hand. I nearly choked one day when on the same subject he said I had it in for Jones because he caught me. I put Barlow right on that one but after that I really did have it in for that Walter Mitty. I wanted to punch the head of him. I made up my mind this was going to happen, not just because of me personally but he was creating too much hassle. Camp staff wouldn't allow any action. I knew they believed I was motivated because it was Jones (they knew the story, I told everyone) and so to take it away from the personal, in a bid to get the go-ahead, I said I wouldn't be involved, but they weren't for changing. That really annoyed me because it was impossible to work with Jones, he just had to be taken off the wing. But if the staff believed the driving force was my personal animosity would they now suspect that I was getting others to do my dirty work? That thought bugged me for a long, long time. In the end, one of the lads did smack Jones but his independent, spontaneous reaction did not help the situation. I knew someone would eventually take the matter into their own hands and that is why I had wanted to take control and make sure it was organised properly. Shortly after the incident I was moved to another block.

XV
THE ESCAPE TRIAL

Those of us recaptured were charged with a wide range of offences, about forty charges each, ranging from escape, kidnap, and possession of guns, hijacking and murder. The murder charge was later changed to manslaughter. A prison officer, Jimmy Ferris, had been stabbed during the escape but his subsequent death was caused by a heart attack brought on by a pre-existing condition.

I was philosophical about the charges and was optimistic that our return to Crumlin Road Jail as remand prisoners would offer other escape possibilities.

The preliminary enquiry was scheduled for late 1984. We pushed for a full enquiry, that would last for weeks rather than a few days, as it would buy us time to suss out the security in the Crum.

Back in the Crum

We were transferred to the jail under very tight and impressive security that included armoured vehicles, British Army and RUC personnel and a helicopter to monitor the convoy's journey. It was almost presidential as outriders on motorbikes raced ahead, closing off roads to ensure the cavalcade had a straight run with no stoppages. Sitting in what was commonly known as the 'Horse Box', handcuffed in a locked, claustrophobic cubicle, floor space less than a square metre, I didn't feel that presidential. Only saving grace was a tiny little window to which I was glued, watching as the 'free' world flew past, looking out for familiar landmarks and trying to work out the circuitous route. I would tense up each time on numerous journeys our path took us over one of the bridges at the River Lagan because the Horse Box swung from side to side, and with so much rocking there was that feeling of helplessness that comes from being handcuffed and locked up, the possibility of the van toppling into the river and us drowning.

With sirens blaring we sped through Belfast. I could see shoppers pausing for a moment as we went by. It was dark, the Christmas lights were on and I caught a glimpse of the Christmas tree at the City Hall. Confronted with this scene, out of the cocoon of the Blocks, I did have a sore heart. I should have been out there free, but here I was on my way possibly to face another lengthy sentence to go on top of my original sentence of twenty-five years. While the melancholy never lingered, there was something about Christmas that could bring it out in me, but I was upbeat about the potential with the Crum.

We were taken to D-Wing and placed in a part of that wing that was closed off from the rest. A prison within a prison. We were soon to learn that not only did they intend to isolate us from the rest of the prisoners, but they weren't even prepared to let us out of the cells. Our banging of doors and ringing of the bells to be allowed access to the toilet were ignored. The screws were obviously prepared for this because, unusually, there wasn't the slightest reaction. While there was only the standard chamber pot in the cells, there were those prisoners who followed a long jail custom of doing their 'number twos' on a newspaper, wrapping it up and throwing it out the window. These packages, the ironic 'mystery parcels', were collected each morning by an unfortunate orderly who was escorted around the prison. The screws may have thought this custom was good enough for us and were content to keep our doors shut but we were determined. However, they were soon to learn. Aware that the screws were listening, Bobby Storey called us up to the doors for a meeting. He said that if the screws do not let us out to the toilet we will be forced to spread it on the cell walls and the following day in court highlight the conditions under which we were held. Within a matter of minutes, the cell doors were opened. No harm to Bobby, while I was prepared to do whatever was necessary, I never ever wanted to return to those conditions. Whether we needed the toilet or not we got on those bells to get out. It was in our DNA to break their systems down and, furthermore, 'escape' was very much on our minds and being permanently locked up made that impossible.

Strangely, while we had no books, newspapers or radios in the cells, later, Meader got up to the door and in excited tones informed us that a screw had just left a radio into his cell. We had mixed feelings about this. While anything to break the boredom of being locked up was to be welcomed, did this mean they were planning to keep us long term in isolation and realised they had to grant us some comforts? This was not good because if there was a chance of escape, we needed to get out of isolation and into the wings proper. With the hours passing without any further compromises, we realised the radio was a one off. Meader knew the screw, Punchy F, who gave him the radio. Punchy F, along with other screws, had given Meader a bad beating during the blanket protest. Punchy was clearly hoping to buy his forgiveness.

In the early hours of the morning I was awakened with the familiar sound, but unwelcome at that time, of the cell door lock being shot. Two screws came bursting in and shouted to get up, that it was a 'cell search'. My body had acclimatised over the years to searches and doors being banged with batons in the wee small hours, so I quickly went into full alert without precious seconds wasted wiping away sleep. My hand instinctively grabbed the *bairt* under my pillow and, pretending to be half asleep, under the cover of the blankets, I was able to conceal it on my person before getting up. All my fellow escapees experienced the same unwelcome intrusion at the exact same time. One of our very light sleepers had observed the screws tip-toeing into the wing, wearing plimsolls rather than the customary boots, lining up outside our cells and, on the command of a PO, in synchronisation, opened the doors. Warning was signalled down the pipes but either it didn't reach me in time, or I didn't hear it. No matter, the screws left empty-handed as nothing was discovered. Better still, it wasn't long before we were moved into the remand wings. I don't know if this was due to our persistence not to accept their 'isolation regime' or if they had only intended to hold us there for a limited time.

It had been almost eight years since I was in A Wing. Nothing had changed. It was as if time stood still. Stood still for me that is because friends on the outside had married, had children and were no longer going to our favourite haunts to while the nights away. However, I was with the best of friends and comrades on the inside because for the first-time we escapees were all together again. I could almost taste the freedom in the Crum. Unlike Long Kesh, where we were ensconced in the middle of a camp surrounded by multiple walls and layers of fences and barbed wire, freedom here was less than one hundred metres away. I could see the city and hear the noise from my cell. The walls seemed to resonate 'escape' and in that respect things had changed for me from eight years earlier.

Each morning after breakfast, as was to become the ritual for the next couple of weeks, we were handcuffed in twos and taken through the damp Victorian tunnel that joined the prison to the High Court, across the Crumlin Road. Apparently, the RUC/Brits wanted us to remain cuffed throughout the hearing, but this was overruled by the judge. We were held in a room under the Number One court from which one of the doors opened to a staircase that led to the dock. As expected, there was a heavy security presence. Our families and friends were seated behind us, our legal teams in front, journalists to the right and left and the RUC dotted the court. We sat passively listening to the proceedings, hoping that it could be dragged out as long as possible, to buy us time to put together an escape. I was neither party nor privy to the planning, but I was confident it was going on at a more senior level. The very fact that Bobby wanted a full preliminary enquiry was enough to know, without it being said, that something was going on 'behind the scenes.'

We didn't get to stay in the Crum every weekend. Those in charge of our security, anxious about a possible escape, did not want to establish a pattern, and so the moves were unpredictable. We were returned to the Blocks when the preliminary enquiry ended, with an increased expectation, certainly on my behalf and a few others (without any sign from Bobby), that the walls could be, and were crying out to be, breached.

Ironic as it may sound, I was glad to be back in the Blocks. Just like going away for a holiday can be good, so too is being back home and the Blocks were home. The lads were glad to see us too and of course they wanted to hear all the *scéal* about the Crum.

To H6

While I was well used to moving blocks, it came as a real shock to the system to be told I was moving to a wing in H6. We suspected that this particular wing was set up by the administration for prisoners who were less resistant and more compliant to their regime. The question that was going through my mind was, how the hell do I fit in there? I was devastated. I could not understand how I could possibly be perceived as being in that category. I had always prided myself in being one hundred per cent republican, a thorn in the side of the administration and an agitator, just like the vast majority of my comrades, but here I was being singled out. Bobby Storey was in the wing with me and I went to him looking some solace. I wanted to hear that they had made a mistake, "There is no way you could be classed as 'watery'."

Bobby, as ever, was more concerned with finding out what was happening in the H6 wing and getting it organised rather than in my ego. He was glad I was going to the wing. I was not to resist the move and I was to tie in with him, take charge and organise. He wasn't that interested in second-guessing what the administration was at, his priority was to have that wing tied in and functioning like the rest of the republican wings, whereas, with my ego dented, I was totally absorbed with the possible thinking behind it and in particular my presence. I suspected, whether through coercion or incentive, the admin was nipping away at our edges and trying to draw numbers away from the Army control. But that placed me on the 'edges' which was not something I could countenance. It really troubled me and made me question myself.

The wing was a mixture of IRA and INLA prisoners, republican sympathisers (not actually in the IRA but possibly minding guns, or falsely imprisoned) and there were a few non-politicals (ODCs). The atmosphere of comradeship and collectivism that I was used to was lacking. There was a core of republican POWs who coalesced and, while they were still very much committed republicans, they lacked purpose and direction. They were probably in a similar vein of mind as me, feeling a bit depressed, suspecting their presence here relegated them to second-class republicans. They were glad to see me, and I them, but there were a few others who were not overjoyed with my presence. The latter might have had concerns that I was going to upset the apple cart.

They were right to be concerned – that was my exact plan.

No sooner had I unpacked when Barlow, the block PO, appeared at the top of the wing. I suspected that he had selected me for H6. Given our previous history he would have been confident that I'd have been the OC and the person he would deal with. What concerned me was did he think he could work me rather me him. Was I a soft touch? I don't believe I could ever be described as a soft touch, but it did niggle. I wanted to believe that he just wanted someone to work with rather than deal with thirty or forty individuals. We struck up a cordial conversation. I proceeded as if this was just another republican wing, no different from any other. I told him I was the OC, which he had already assumed, and that I didn't expect any hassle from him or a surrogate as, for example, the likes of Jones. Barlow didn't come across like someone who was on a mission and I sensed he didn't have the heart for it. If the intention was to pilot a strict regime, I couldn't work out why he would be given the task as there were quite a few infamous POs who would revel in the task.

I called a meeting for all republican POWs in the wing and I was heartened. A majority of them crammed into the big cell to hear me. To help explain my mission I had a target drawn out with a bullseye in the middle and three or four concentric circles moving out from the centre. I told them the model represented the Movement. The closer to the core (bullseye) the more the commitment and likewise the further away the less the commitment. I didn't suggest nor ask where the lads positioned themselves on the model, but I did say that those in the outer circles would be perceived as the weakest and likely targets if there was to be a move against us.

The message was clear, we would pull together as a unit, be assertive in our demands and the prison would be under no illusions – we were at the centre. I felt sure the lads left the meeting feeling a lot better, but I was confronted by one irate individual who wanted to know if I had suggested he was on the margins. I reminded him I didn't make any judgements and it was up to him where he placed himself. He wasn't happy with my response and pressed me for an answer, but I didn't reveal my true feelings, which he no doubt suspected with good cause, that he was very much on the margins and moving further and further out. While he didn't say it, I know why he challenged me. He was more or less putting me on notice that he had nothing to prove so wouldn't be involved in any campaign of overt or contrived militancy with the screws. True to form, he had nothing to do with our coordinated response, as did a couple of others. Of course, we weren't militant. I believe we found the right balance to let the screws know they were still dealing with an army rather than a collection of individuals. As a result, the morale of the wing rose and after a month or so I was moved out, to be followed shortly afterwards by others. The experiment was over. However, the person who challenged me never returned to the republican wings.

Two years passed from the preliminary enquiry before we received a date for the trial. In between times, I was overjoyed when I was approached to draw a sketch of that side of the Crum that backed onto my old St Malachy's.

The plan was that the wall at that end of the Crum would be blown by comrades on the outside and we would make our escape through the school. At that stage Bobby, as always operating on a need-to-know basis, did not reveal how we reached that wall. That there was a plan at all was only disclosed to me because, being a past pupil, I knew the layout of the school. I drew the map out for him and chartered a path through Lincoln Avenue which I explained offered a quicker exit rather than going through the main school building. I didn't destroy the map because I knew Bobby, in consultation with the IRA outside, would have more questions. Understandably, he was a stickler for detail.

The following day a wing search was called. Normally I'm at the ready for searches with *teachts* and the small watch in my possession had to be wrapped up into a *bairt*. But because we had been using the map I hid it in my cell, ready to be used again but out of sight and safe enough while I was in the canteen for twenty minutes. When the search was called, I rushed to my cell to retrieve the map. Could I remember where I put it! The door slammed behind me as the search team entered the wing. Utter panic set in as I began ripping the cell apart to find it. I upturned the mattress, pulled all my clothes out of the locker, shook them and tossed them to the side. It was like déjà vu from the time with the trolley before the big escape only this time my fate was firmly in my own sweating hands. Terrible and fearful thoughts gripped me as hope of finding it faded. Already I could hear the screws just one cell away – and I was next. If they discovered the map the escape was finished, and me with it. My name would be muck. I'd be hated and ridiculed. I wouldn't be able to face anybody. I'd have to leave the wings and maybe even emigrate when released. I pulled books from the shelf, flicking through the pages and flinging them in frustration to the floor. I couldn't calm myself to think straight but I knew under no circumstances could I allow them to find the map. I'd have to barricade myself in, possibly smack a screw and keep searching until I found it. I reached for the Bible, making all sorts of promises for atonement as I flicked through the pages and suddenly, as if my prayers were answered, there it was, resting among the Gospels. A miracle. With alacrity, I wrapped the map up with the *bairt* and secreted it safely, just in time as I heard the keys in the lock. The screws thought a bomb had hit the cell. Little did they know how explosive it could have been. I didn't breathe a word of this to Bobby as I knew he never would have trusted me again.

We were flown by helicopter to the Crum. In batches, they took us, handcuffed, in the prison van to the British Army camp, which was situated at the far end of Long Kesh. The chopper, with blades turning, awaited our arrival and encircling it were about a dozen Brits lying in the grass in the firing position. I have to confess, it made me feel ever so important, like a VIP. Probably bored, one of the Brits jumped up and raised his rifle as if he was going to fire. I didn't flinch and robbed him of his sport. I'd never been in a helicopter before and, despite the circumstances, I really enjoyed it and to top it all off we skirted along the Black and Divis Mountains so I had an aerial view of West Belfast. On one of the flights (of which there were a number) we actually flew over my house.

The choppers worked out to our advantage because the landing base was Girdwood Army Barracks adjacent to the jail. This enabled us to have a good glimpse of the back wall, the focus of our plans. We were split up between the remand Wings A and C, which I wasn't happy about because, while I still was not fully aware of the plan, I knew it would be difficult to synchronise the two positions.

The first day of the trial was very boring as the charges were read out one by one and each time, in alphabetical order, we had to answer 'guilty' or 'not guilty'. There were about forty charges and twenty-one of us in the dock. Naturally, we pleaded not guilty to each charge. Bobby, who sat beside me, asked me to plead not guilty on his behalf. He had a slight stutter and while he was fine when in full flow, he struggled, or rather stuttered, to get started, so being limited to two words each time was challenging. A packed court, a large percentage being the enemy (cops and screws), added to his anxiety. I didn't mind answering on his behalf as it wasn't as if I had any respect for the court.

Each time it came to 'Storey', I answered, changing my voice slightly. I was tempted to use a high-pitched squeaky tone to give the lads a laugh and get my own back on Bobby, who was a powerful mixer himself, but this would have drawn attention to that fact that I was answering for him. The scheme went undetected until the end when Bobby, Jimmy Donnelly, Jimmy B and I had four separate charges from the rest, for hi-jacking a car and possession of a pistol. Up until that point the alphabetical order ensured that after I answered each charge another six or seven of the lads had to answer before I had to step in for Bobby. But now, I had to answer directly after I had given my own plea. I think almost everyone in the courtroom, except the judge, caught on once I answered twice in a row, despite my attempt at changing the tone. I could see the RUC and screws shifting about in their seats in annoyance, probably feeling we were making a mockery of the proceedings. When the four of us were about to answer the second charge I could feel the mood of the courtroom had changed from boredom to interest and the focus was on me. Was I about to answer twice again and of course I was and no sooner had I uttered it for Bobby when everyone's attention was drawn to a little bald, bespectacled clerk scurrying up to the judge and obsequiously having a word in his ear. I'll bet during his school days he was the class tout. No one could hear what he had to say but we all knew. The judge lifted his head and stared into the dock. There was anticipation in the courtroom as all awaited what was next.

"Storey," he said. "How do you plead?"

There was a pause, an agonizing pause that seemed more like minutes than the actual few seconds. All below us, legal teams, clerks, reporters and RUC personnel were zeroed in on Bobby. I said nothing. Bobby was on his own. Breaking the silence, he yelled out, "N…N…NOT FUCKING GUILTY!" There was a collective gasp from the court. However, nothing more was said and that ended the charges. Bobby had to put 'fucking' in to lengthen the sentence thus making it easier to pronounce. If nothing else, it gave us all a laugh. Well, all except Bobby.

The trial, which went on for weeks, was more often than not entertaining as screws were caught out time and time again lying. Some had not been at their posts so they made up stories. Walter Mitty-type characters made themselves heroes and at times it left their colleagues and the cops cringing, while the judge was left with looks of incredulity.

The hostile environment on the remand wings in the Crum was reminiscent of the early days on the blanket and it made me realise the progress we had made in the Blocks in creating a more workable humane regime.

A few weeks into the trial, the IRA suffered its heaviest loss when eight volunteers were shot dead in an SAS ambush at Loughgall. The screws had the front-page banner headlines of newspapers on display at every grille, goading and outwardly celebrating. Most of us knew some of the lads who had been killed; two, Padraig McKearney and Gerard O'Callaghan, were former blanket men, and Padraig had been among those who had got away from H7 in the big escape.

The lads on remand were happy to see us and bled us dry about life in the Kesh. Given our background in the escape and protests, they looked up to us, watched us closely and took their lead from us. This put a bit of pressure on me because I had to get it right when confronting screws and, at the very least, show I had the measure of them.

One day, having been called for a solicitor's visit, standing beside three or four remand POWs, ready to exit the wing, a screw told me the visit was cancelled. I asked why. While I was used to questioning screws, from his reaction it was clear he wasn't used to prisoners questioning him. He did answer that he didn't know but I could tell he was at pains to do so. There was a clear ratchetting up of the tension when I wouldn't let go and asked to speak to the SO. The screw became quite agitated, said that the SO wasn't available. The remands were totally cued in to what was now a stand-off, probably pleased that I was taking on the screw. But for me it was no different from what I was used to and was only confrontational because of his attitude. Ignoring the screw, I walked over to the class office where I hoped to speak to an SO or someone more senior. On opening the door, I can only describe what followed as a screaming match. It was as if I had caught them in a compromising position. They were shocked. One of them jumped up to slam the door but, as I was already half-way in, I put my foot against it to stop being pinned against the frame. A screw screamed, "Get out! Get out!" Either he or one of the other screws opened the door fully to allow them all to confront me. Surrounded by three or four screws, the screamer, still highly excited and hyperventilating, could barely speak for breathlessness. Initially, I couldn't understand their reaction. It was as if the class office was sacred ground and I had broken its sanctity. I soon realised that is how they viewed it. The SO arrived, claimed he didn't know why the visit was cancelled, but by that stage the issue had moved on. I was escorted back to my cell and ten minutes later the door opened. I was told I was being charged and I was taken to the boards.

The boards – again

The boards were in B Wing and, to further emphasise its isolation, was behind a wire cage. On a trumped-up charge, I was sentenced to three days solitary to begin on the Friday so as it would not be broken by appearance in court. B Wing held short-term, non-political prisoners, and from my cell I could hear how the screws belittled and humiliated them. The FA Cup Final was played that Saturday and I could only guess the score from the cheers.

Back in the wing on Monday I found out I guessed wrong and that it was one of the better finals.

We didn't stay every weekend in the Crum. Helicopters were sometimes arranged to bring us back to the Blocks. Each time I came back to the Crum I hoped and prayed I would be placed in A Wing because I knew with the escape in the pipeline that was the place to be.

My prayers were not answered. When we arrived I was told I was going to C Wing. I felt sick. Fifty-fifty chance, and I lost. If it wasn't for bad luck, I'd have no luck. I felt really hard done by. After all the planning and expectation, I was going to miss out – again. Escape out of C Wing wasn't out of the question but it presented a much bigger problem because access to the yard differed from A Wing. Prisoners in the Crum operated an agreed programme of segregation. One day republicans would be in the yard, the next day it would be the turn of loyalists. The problem was when republicans in A Wing were in the yard, the loyalists in C Wing were out in their yard. Without revealing the plan, I told C Wing O/C he had to find a way to get us into the yard. In the end it made no difference because the escape was compromised. All my hopes and anxious nights came to nothing.

As can be imagined there was an air of despondency when we got together again at the court. Not everyone had been aware that an escape had been planned so there was no open discussion, only some cryptic exchanges. I'm sure, although they were not informed, they saw tell-tale signs and suspected something was going down and had expectations. Despite the disappointment I didn't abandon hope. While I was desperately clinging to straws, in retrospect I know it helped to sustain me through imprisonment. With only a couple of days left of the trial, already my mind was turning to the possibilities that an appeal would present.

Trial over, with the judgement awaited, we were returned to the Blocks where, after the Crum, I could appreciate all the more the somewhat relaxed atmosphere that we had created through hard struggle. Not that we were ever content or stopped struggling. We could appreciate how far we had come but there was *never* an endgame regarding jail conditions. We would always travel but never arrive. The prison administration had a fixed mindset, 'security', which they overplayed and blocked, even for some of the most minor concessions. Apart from one or two more liberal governors, the rationale that security should be external and a humane regime internal, was lost on them.

The verdict

In April 1988, we were returned to the Crum for the verdict. Given how the lies of the screws were exposed during the trial our legal teams were quietly confident that we would not be found guilty of the more serious charges. While awaiting sentence in the cell under the court, the possibility that Gerry Kelly (both he and Bik had successfully escaped until their arrest in Amsterdam in 1986 and their subsequent extradition from Holland) could go free was not ruled out and there was some deliberation as to what he should say to the press. There were others who weren't that optimistic and reminded us that Diplock Courts were not renowned for serving up justice. Gerry didn't walk out. Like the rest of us he received five years, apart from Harry Murray who was sentenced to eight years for shooting a screw. While we entered an appeal, this was simply to keep the opportunity to escape open and had nothing to do with beating the charges or receiving reduced sentences, because we knew there was no chance of that. However, a month or two later we were told to withdraw the appeal, so ending that saga. I suspect the plan wasn't totally abandoned because a few years later, in perhaps a modified version of our plans, Semtex explosives were found in the Crum.

All that remained from the 1983 escape was the case we took against the prison for the brutality we were subjected to when caught. The legal teams settled this out of court, so we didn't get another appearance or an opportunity to listen again to screws tying themselves in knots to avoid the truth. No doubt the prison service didn't want details of the brutality further aired. We received compensation ranging from £1,000 to £8,000. It made me wonder, had we taken a case during the blanket when brutality was a daily occurrence, and if justice had been allowed to take its course, what vast sums of money would have been awarded? Not that money was ever an objective. We wanted our ill-treatment highlighted and exposed and stopped.

XVI
THE HONOUR OF HAVING SERVED

With the trial over, little further opportunity for escaping, and with another five years added to my twenty-five year sentence, I wouldn't say I settled down to do the sentence, but for the first time ever I could see myself serving it.

I had almost completed twelve years and with the early release date I'd be out in over five years. Long release date without remission was 2006, early release date was 1994.

I was privileged to remain a small cog in the *Ealu* department, gathering information which, I hoped and believed, would have some value to the struggle both inside and outside the jail.

The jail population had changed. Most of my fellow blanket men and comrades had been released, although a few like my Lenadoon comrade Paddy McCotter were back in again. It left me surrounded by younger POWs where my status was morphing into that of a veteran. That didn't sit easy with me. I was always in denial of my age (and remain so today). In the main, all that remained from that era were the lifers, but their situation was also changing.

As stated, it had been policy not to co-operate with the Life Review Panel but the only possible way of release was *through* that panel. Some of the lifers in the Cages (where there was still political status) had spent fifteen and sixteen years in jail, while some of the lifers in the Blocks had spent up to twelve years. Originally, the thinking had been that lifers would not be released until the war was over, or they escaped. But by the 1980s it was clear that it was going to be a long war and as the years slipped by and the issue was continually debated, the logic of entering the review system gained momentum until eventually in 1989 it was agreed the policy had to change. We had learned that in the Cages the issue had proved divisive because it was not adequately addressed. Guidelines were drawn up on how to respond to sensitive questions which would be put to prisoners in the reviews such as 'guilt', 'remorse' and 'IRA membership'.

We would need to give broad answers that did not concede or compromise republican principles.

So, lifers now applied for review and began presenting themselves to the Review Panel – but without renouncing their political convictions and revolutionary actions.

Conditions

Alongside the changes taking place with the lifers the camp staff organised a concerted, non-violent campaign to improve and reform jail conditions. It touched just about every aspect of jail life such as food, parcels, censorship, lock-ups and paroles. It wasn't just a case of improving conditions, we wanted to change the philosophy of the NIO and the prison administration. We argued, debated and petitioned them that conditions were Victorian, security should be external to our environment and not be the ubiquitous block to all requests.

Our biggest battle was with the lock-ups. While we wanted them completely abolished, we started with the two lock-ups from 12.30pm to 2pm and 4.30pm to 5.30pm. Four orderlies were allowed to stay out in the canteen during those two lock-ups but if we wished we were able to get more men out by claiming food shortages. Extra food was sent for from the kitchen, the men were allowed to stay in the canteen to await its arrival and eat (if they so wished) and they then remained out throughout the lock-up. The screws turned a blind eye to this practice. We told the governors and the screws we had had enough of the pretence and we organised men to stay out on a rota basis without using the excuse of food shortages. Refusing the lock-up we emphasised that it was a peaceful protest. Refusal in earlier years had met with the riot squad entering and dishing out their customary brutality. Times were changing, the riot squads were not called but charges for refusing to lock-up did follow.

Our cause was given more weight when the last of the Cages men with political status voluntarily moved to a wing in H1 where they were not subjected to lock-ups. If that regime could work there then it could work throughout the prison. Further, the European Court ruled that prisoners should have access to toilets 24/7 and, since there were no toilets in the cells, this would necessitate leaving doors unlocked in order that the ablutions could be accessed. Progress was at a snail's pace and years later, helped by political progress on the outside, lock-ups were abolished – but by then I was released.

Progress, albeit after years of petitioning, did come with less controversial issues such as the quality of food, the right to make handicrafts and censorship of books and magazines. Kitchen staff met with our camp staff to discuss menus. Handicrafts that were withdrawn after the escape were gradually re-introduced, although there were restrictions placed on what tools were permissible. Censorship had been a real bugbear, with the overarching and over-interpreted term 'subversive' used ridiculously to ban books and newspapers that really were innocuous. That was eased somewhat. Previously, literature connected with some conflicts and in particular republican history were banned. Even a local West Belfast newspaper, the *Andersonstown News*, at one stage was on the list.

Most significant of all, in 1989 a sign that the regime was beginning to liberalise came with the introduction of parole for lifers who had spent over thirteen years in jail. Lifers, who only a few years earlier believed they would never see the outside until the war was over, were now entitled to two periods of parole annually, four days in summer and at Christmas. There was obvious joy with this development and their families were elated. However, given the history of the regime and how it tried to use imprisonment as a breakers yard, some were suspicious of the underlying motives and at best gave it a guarded welcome.

Vindictively, lifers on the Red Book, despite meeting the thirteen-year tariff, were excluded. Chris (Greek) Moran and I, who had both served over thirteen years but were not lifers, did not qualify either. We were well used to whatever the prison served up and were not too affected by the exclusion, but our families were devastated. Yet I'll not deny experiencing little pangs of jealously as friends and comrades said their goodbyes and walked out the gate on the morning of their parole.

Some of them, as promised, called in to see my parents and assured them I was fine. When they came back, we bled them dry for *scéal*, about women, clubs, music, style, meals and local gossip.

The following days and weeks I watched how well they settled back into routine. I was concerned that their spell of freedom would make their time in jail more difficult. In a way it is better not to know what is being missed but they no longer had that shield. However, there were no outward signs that they had been adversely affected and from private conversations with one or two I read a cautious optimism for the future. There was growing confidence that releases for lifers would eventually follow the paroles. But not losing the run of themselves there was a realisation that it would not be for a few years yet. But a few years was within their grasp and they had the comfort of knowing – assuming things would continue – that they would never spend another Christmas apart from their families.

My family, frustrated that I could not avail of the parole, felt that the decision should be contested. The camp staff similarly took the view that regardless of Red Book status or determinate sentence such exclusions amounted to victimisation. Those who were affected were told to write a letter to the governor asking for an explanation. The response to my letter was simple – the Lifer parole does not extend to determinate sentences but I would be entitled to parole in my final nine months of imprisonment. I believe the Red Book response was the usual 'security' reasons. My father, refusing to relent, wrote to the NIO and it came as no surprise when he received a negative response. The letter stated:

> Your son, as a determinate sentence prisoner, was eligible to 50% remission of this sentence, but as a result of breaches of prison discipline and his participation in various protest actions he forfeited 1,768 days of remission; 819 days of these have been restored to him. His current earliest date of release is therefore 9 January 1994 when he will have served nearly 17 years of his 30 year sentence. Your son would have been released last December but for his attempted escape and the breaches of prison discipline which led to the large amount of loss of remission.

The letter continued to state that an exception would not be made for me to be included in the recent parole scheme and as a determinate prisoner I would be eligible for parole in my last year.

Personally, I was chuffed and full of pride with the above paragraph quoted from the letter. If there was such a thing as a Republican CV, I would want this high recommendation included. Actually, they had under-calculated my sentence, commencing from when sentenced, February 4th 1977, rather than when imprisoned, June 5th 1976.

Christmas present

Undeterred, when I was again refused parole for the Christmas period, my father appealed the decision through the courts. It came as a complete surprise to me when I read from a newspaper just a few days before Christmas that my case was before the High Court. It never crossed my mind that I could be out for Christmas given that courts take weeks, months even, to deliberate, and even when the result was reached, I had no expectations it would be favourable. On December 23rd I said my goodbyes to the lifers going out for their second parole and settled down in the wing to celebrate Christmas with my fellow prisoners.

Christmas Eve morning, I rose as usual, readied myself for the doors to open and then headed up to the ablutions to wash and shave. I would go for a run three days a week; not like some who, Billy Gorman for example, ran every day. Many a morning I prayed for snow or torrential rain so that the yards would remain shut and there'd be no run. My conscience would be clear as the postponement wasn't of my doing. Running being such a pain, I would always want it over as soon as possible, and the minute the yard opened I was out.

Christmas Eve fell on one of the three days for the run. I looked out the window with fingers crossed but while it was raining it wasn't enough to close the yards. I hoped they would open the yard early so I could get it out of the way and then settle down to indulge in TV and some craic with the lads. While washing, the PO came into the wing smiling, walked over to me and said: "You may hurry up. You're getting out this morning for parole." Not for one minute did I believe him. My immediate thought was the lads must have involved him in a 'wind up' so I wasn't going to take the bait. I gave him a look of indifference and said, "Dead on." His demeanour changed, realising that I didn't believe him. "I'm serious," he said. "You really are getting out this morning. The courts sat late last night and decided."

I was stunned. I was lost for words. I was trying to gather my thoughts when he added, "And I'm really happy for you." His tone and expression left me in no doubt that he meant every word of it. Two knockout blows in quick succession. I was reeling. I was going to spend Christmas with my family and to top it off I had just witnessed an openly unashamed expression of humanity from a quarter I never expected. In truth he had always gone against the grain by acquitting himself with fairness and there wasn't a bitter bone in his body, but it was quite a revelation not only to hear those words but to be expressed in front of his fellow screws. This would have been unheard of a few years earlier. Humanity was beginning to seep into the H-Blocks.

Thinking of the lads around me, I held my emotions in and refrained from any overt celebrations. In double-quick time I finished washing and headed down to see John (Pickles) Pickering who I was to run with that morning. He was still lying in bed.

"John Henry, I'm not going for a run this morning." He turned his head to face me and asked, "What's the problem?"

"I'm going out on parole."

"Aye, dead on," he said, sounding exasperated and pulled the duvet back up over his shoulders and rolled on his side to face the wall, body language telling me, Sorry, I've no time for these stupid mixes. I equally had no time to begin persuading and said, "Okay, I'm away."

I went to my cell to change. Within a minute Pickles was in on top of me. Word had spread throughout the wing and like the rest of the lads, he realised it was true. He wished me all the best and I told him I would call in to see his Mum. I said my goodbyes to the lads and on a high, headed out to reception where I met Greek Moran whom, like me, had served over thirteen years of his determinate sentence and again, like myself, had only been told twenty minutes earlier about parole. He was still trying to take in that he was out for Christmas.

We were processed through the reception and escorted out the front gate where I had an emotional reunion with my parents and girlfriend. There was no one there for Greek. His family were obviously unaware that the court case had been successful. We drove him home and watched as the door opened, revealing in total disbelief what was I'm sure their best Christmas present ever – the return of a son and brother.

Friends, neighbours and ex-prisoners came to greet me and slipped me a few pounds to help see me through the next few days, although I didn't need money, as I wasn't allowed to spend a penny throughout.

Christmas dinner with the family was special. We were really happy that we were together, and it seemed to signal that the worst days were over; there was reason to be sanguine about the future.

In a way, I'd half-expected to pick up where I left off over thirteen years earlier but on paroles it would gradually dawn on me that this was not to be. So much had changed. The game changer was that my friends and I were no longer in our youth, we were men and unlike me, they were men with responsibilities. Jail had cushioned me from this. I was in a time warp but being on the outside it fairly hit me. I suspect my comrades on parole felt this too and it was another good reason why we tended to seek out each other's company. During paroles we would have at least one big night out together. That first parole we all met up with our families at a local West Belfast club on Boxing Night and it was one of my best nights ever.

Back to prison

Parole over, back in the Blocks, I settled quickly into the routine. It was now the 1990s, the third decade of my imprisonment, but it was the last. The finishing line was now in sight but I didn't allow it to affect me too much. I never succumbed to 'gate fever' and I think this was largely due to a sense that my time was never wasted.

During the protest years I felt proud and worthy that I was still part of the struggle. In the 1980s my role in escapes, albeit peripheral, also gave me that sense of worth that I remained an active IRA volunteer still contributing to operations that had the potential of undermining the British presence and boosting republican morale. I was active in delivering and promoting the camp education programme and in so doing, hopefully, contributed to the growth of Sinn Féin. Education had been (and remains) one of my priorities.

I completed an Open University degree and encouraged others to engage in the formal education process. I took responsibilities in the wings and played an ongoing role in protesting, petitioning and negotiating for improved conditions. Combined, these factors (and one or two more) added up to a busy, worthy, life-fulfilling time spent in jail. In the 1990s, serving out the last few years, while thankfully the protesting years were over and my role in escapes did not have the same prominence, I remained a busy participant and promoter in all other aspects. I still had a role with the *ealu* committee, but this had changed to more of an intelligence brief, passing on important information that had been gleaned in a number of ways.

Occasionally, visitors came into the Blocks that included clergy and politicians, and the Red Cross made a couple of appearances. Some would enter the wings and engage with us and others less so – they'd go no further than the grilles at the top of the wings. Cardinal Tomás Ó Fiaich made several visits, in particular during the height of the protest era, and despite the vitriol he faced from the British press and establishment, he remained supportive. Bishop Cahal Daly and Bishop Edward Daly visited the Blocks, but neither could ever be accused by the press or establishment as showing any solidarity towards us. Indeed, Bishop Cahal Daly was very much in tune with the British narrative on the conflict which, given the nexus between establishments religious and political, may well explain in part him succeeding Tomás Ó Fiaich as Cardinal after Ó Fiaich's sudden death in 1990. Nevertheless, Daly did come into the Blocks and in fairness he did engage with us in political discussions. He was actually mellower and more conciliatory than in his public persona. When we confronted him with some of his outrageous misrepresentations, he would claim that he had been quoted out of context.

Among the few politicians who visited was Peter Bottomley who at the time was a junior minister assigned to the NIO. We invited him into the big cell where we had a brief discussion with him about a united Ireland. He didn't have a great deal to say, other than the expected not in his lifetime, and I felt he was somewhat dismissive without offering a counter argument. No doubt, like his fellow British MPs he probably didn't give a damn about politics here and hated being exiled to the North of Ireland. As he was about to take his leave, I couldn't help myself but had to ask him how he felt about his wife, Virginia, being a member of the cabinet while he was just a junior minister. I know it was sexist of me, but this was the start of the 90s and my politicisation had still some way to go and, more to the point, I wanted to get a dig in. He laughed, a bit forced I thought, but he had no words, turned on his heels and left with I hope the proverbial tail between his legs.

Seany Bateson

That summer we were shocked to hear the awful news that Seany Bateson, who was in H2, dropped dead from a heart attack. Seany had kept the wing stocked up with *toitin* for a few months when he was in the cell next to me during the blanket and he was one of the Blocks' characters. He had been one of Larry Marley's sidekicks and played an important role in the 1983 escape. He was so looking forward to his first parole and being with his family. It was another one of those occasions where I felt life could be really unjust. All those years separated from his loved ones, the thought of being reunited with them keeping him going through the worst of times and just when he is on the verge of this happening, this is tragically denied.

Political climate

As we moved through the 1990s I could sense the political climate was gradually changing. The emergence of Sinn Féin was opening new doors and had the potential of bringing real and fundamental change. Within the jail there was talk of 'ceasefires' and the IRA stopping its campaign. The majority of POWs were very much opposed to this and strongly believed the IRA was the 'cutting edge', while Sinn Féin was its junior partner in the struggle. However, the debate had started and members were now beginning to look beyond the military campaign. Adding and giving momentum to this climate of change lifers were now going through the review process and were released in some numbers.

Lifers who were imprisoned around the same time as myself were either released or in the process of being released while I still had at least a couple of years to serve. The camp staff told me to petition the NIO for the return of remission lost during the blanket protest, as a precedent had already been set with two republican prisoners, one in the Blocks, the other in Armagh Jail, having had their remission returned.

In the letter I pointed out that the protest had taken place over a decade ago, it had been peaceful and the demands, apart from full restoration of remission, were now in place. I was right not to place any hope in a positive outcome. The petition was refused. Many years later, when we were able to access documents and correspondence about ourselves, I discovered the governor of the prison told the NIO that he had no reason to recommend the application for remission because, "McCann is a surly, arrogant individual who continually challenges the prison administration. He is regarded as a dedicated PIRA member in the segregated wings."

I'll put the 'surly, arrogant' down to being a thorn in their side. I wouldn't have had it any other way.

The graduate

I finished the Open University and went to the graduation ceremony in Coleraine University during a parole, along with my family and girlfriend. I ended up sitting beside a Mrs Bach, whose husband John Bach was on the Board of Visitors at the prison. Unlike her husband I found her to be quite pleasant and we struck up a conversation during which, beaming with pride, she informed me she was the first woman to become a Methodist minister. I congratulated her but didn't reveal that I was a POW.

I was taken unawares at the end of the ceremony when we were asked to stand up for the British national anthem, 'God Save The Queen'. No-one had warned me. I had no hesitation walking out and, being in the second row, it was quite a long walk. As I made way down the aisle, with my own head held high, I noticed the contrast in the audience. Some stood with their chests puffed out and sang, I felt, all the louder as I went by; while others' heads sank into chests, staring at the floor and I sensed, perhaps, a little ashamed and embarrassed.

When the strawberries and cream were being served, I was told that word circulated that the man who walked out may have been a prisoner. I'm sure Mrs Bach put one and one together. I asked Joe Watson, a fellow prisoner, also out on parole to graduate on that same day why he had not walked. I wasn't pleased when he told me that he knew they would play 'the Queen' and that he had left beforehand. I didn't want to cause a scene; I was caught out, but there was no way I was standing. However, it worked out well because I was told from a reliable source that that was the last time they played 'the Queen' at graduation in Coleraine. I'm claiming the credit.

Birth of my daughter

During the paroles my girlfriend became pregnant. I was absolutely delighted. I wasn't sure that I would ever have a family and often felt that life would pass me by in that respect. The prison had become quite flexible regarding paroles and I was allowed out to coincide with the birth.

On May 5th 1993 my daughter Naoise was born. I was elated. I savoured every moment. I don't quite know how to put it into words but I had this strong sense of being free, that I had overcome imprisonment and that not only was I going to have a life but I was going to share it with my loved ones. It was fulfilment, it was ecstasy. There had been special moments like Bobby's election, the escape, that first Christmas parole, but this capped them all.

This for me was the true meaning of life, watching my child being born and then bonding with her Mum. My heart swelled as the precious bundle was passed to me to take her in my arms and nurse. Mum needing rest, the proud father had the unforgettable privilege and honour of giving Naoise her first bottle (albeit it was nerve-wracking). Notably, Naoise was born on the anniversary of Bobby's death during those dark days, dark years ago. Bobby's quote, 'Our revenge will be the laughter of our children', resonated that day.

My last six months

During my last six months I put a lot of effort into making handicrafts as I wanted all those who had stood by me throughout my time in jail to receive some form of memento. With the help of our craftsmen the production line went to work on harps, jewellery boxes and paintings. We were only allowed thin plywood and veneer but to add to our supplies we set about cannibalising wood within the wings. Bed boards, prescribed by the doctor for lads who pretended they had bad backs, were sawn up, as were picture boards. We had a 'cottage industry' of our own, making quaint white-washed cottages, a la *The Quiet Man*. We used brush hairs for the thatch and, as can be imagined, we went through quite a lot of brushes. The screws didn't mind as they were happy to see us occupied and probably – wrongly – thought it would keep us quiet.

Half-way into my project I realised I was not going to produce the handicrafts I had first imagined and while I did receive help, I soon wore out those around me whose goodwill, while stretching to weeks, wasn't prepared to go into months. The pressure mounted as the 'gate' approached because I had my list and it just wouldn't have done to leave someone out. Harps and jewellery boxes were too time-consuming so, as the clock wound down, I went for artefacts that could be produced quickly – cottages and paintings – hoping that something was better than nothing. The handicrafts were therapeutic in a way as the days went in quickly and kept my mind busy rather than occupied with the 'gate'. I can't deny I did feel some stress as the big day neared. I recall more than once walking up the wing to do something and by the time I reached the top I had forgotten what it was. So much for being cool and believing I could take everything in my stride.

Departure

Before I knew it, it was my last night in the H-Blocks of Long Kesh, a dark hell for five, long years, with ineradicable memories branded on my flesh and my mind of what happened to men.

How different the place was now compared to my arrival seventeen years before when the hostility and violence were ubiquitous and unrelenting. Not only had we chipped away at their system and extracted penal reform but we had changed attitudes and I know views will differ on this, but I believe we gradually created a cultural change where republican POWs (and hopefully all prisoners) are treated with dignity and respect. I'm not suggesting all screws bought into this but the bigots, who would have loved a return to a brutal regime where they had a free rein, appeared to be in a minority and were restrained by the changing culture.

The change was a two-way process. We treated them with respect and dignity and no longer tarred them with the one brush. I was a latecomer to that change because I used to burn up on seeing lads engaging in friendly conversations with screws. Communication made better relations and broke down the stereotypes we had of each other. After release I would come across some screws on my travels. Most put their heads down and hurried on, but one or two, realising that I was acknowledging them in a friendly way, did stop and speak.

I was guest of honour at the going-away concert. I was filled with pride at the effort put into the event and the things my comrades said. I made a speech of my own, thanking them and, choking with emotion, I told them I was really going to miss the comradeship because I knew I would never, ever experience anything like it again. They presented me with a harp and Celtic painting which I hold dearly in my home to this day. In the morning I would go around the other wings in the block and say my farewells before my final walk through those grilles to the cheers of the lads.

Looking around at the faces gathered in the canteen, others haunted me. I was leaving the 'ten men' and Seany Bateson behind. They would forever be in the H-Blocks and would never experience freedom. It was an honour and privilege to have known them, shared experiences and served time with them and have them as comrades. What had kept me and my comrades going was succinctly summed up by Bobby Sands in his poem *The Rhythm of Time*:

> It lights the dark of this prison cell,
> It thunders forth its might,
> It is 'the undauntable thought', my friend,
> That thought that says, "I'm right!"

As I lay in my cell that night for the last time, I had a sense of accomplishment. I felt I had acquitted myself well, as a republican should. My principles were intact; my commitment was, if anything, stronger; there was no sense of bitterness or regret; and I was eagerly looking forward to the challenges ahead and leading a purposeful, fulfilling life. I was on a high, filled with pride and buzzing with excitement.

Yet it didn't last.

Thoughts of Joe came flooding into my mind and changing my mood. It was as if he was calling me up to the window, but I didn't want to go there as I preferred to bask in the warmth of triumphalism and vanity. But Joe didn't take 'no' for an answer. There was still a connection as the walls of the H-Blocks resonated with his presence. Would that connection end with my departure? Would I soon forget my friend and comrade? My conscience was pricking, and not for the first time, but never as acutely.

Over the years, thoughts of Joe involuntarily came at times. But that night, anxious to assure myself that I'd never forget, I willed myself to recall his heroic qualities in particular throughout the heavy days in the lead up to and during the hunger strike.

Reminiscing intensified my mood as the pride swelled in me, feeling an enormous sense of privilege and honour that I had shared time with him. He never faltered, never wavered, and his selflessness and dedication to a cause he would never allow to be criminalised would instil national pride and admiration for this giant of a man.

I knew he would live forever not only in my mind but as a republican icon in the history books. Conscience eased, I drifted to sleep contented.

ACKNOWLEDGEMENTS

I owe an enormous debt of gratitude to my family who during my years of imprisonment stood by me and suffered in silence, only to discover I could be a bigger headache released.

I would like to thank Kieron Magee who first mooted the idea to record my jail experiences and even put pen to paper. I am so lucky and grateful that my wife Marian kept badgering me to do it myself and then gave me the space and time to write, a licence which I must admit I unashamedly exploited.

To Danny Morrison I extend my sincere thanks. With pen in one hand and my script in the other, fingers crossed, he saved me blushes over grammatical errors. His advice, the confidence he instilled and the long hours he freely gave editing were invaluable and without which, to this day, I would still be at a loss what to do with an unpolished script. I'd also like to thank my publisher Thomas Pago of Elsinor Verlag. To Tina Neylon for her work on the manuscript and her suggestions. And to Christina Herdman, Mitchell-Kane, for her work and production on the final typesetting.

I must acknowledge the great Tony Bell for his brilliant art work on the cover of *6000 Days*. Initially, my brother Eamonn was to do the design but tragically and heartbreakingly for us his family Eamonn died from cancer before the book was completed. He is forever in our thoughts.

Finally, I would like to acknowledge my children, Naoise, Christine and James, who unbeknownst to them, inspired me to write this period of my life of which they knew little or nothing. I leave them this, my story.

Jim McCann
Belfast, 2021